Arthur Naylor Wollaston, Colonel Sir Lewis Pelly

The Miracle Play of Hasan and Husain

Vol. 1

Arthur Naylor Wollaston, Colonel Sir Lewis Pelly

The Miracle Play of Hasan and Husain
Vol. 1

ISBN/EAN: 9783743370623

Manufactured in Europe, USA, Canada, Australia, Japa

Cover: Foto ©ninafisch / pixelio.de

Manufactured and distributed by brebook publishing software (www.brebook.com)

Arthur Naylor Wollaston, Colonel Sir Lewis Pelly

The Miracle Play of Hasan and Husain

THE MIRACLE PLAY

OF

HASAN AND HUSAIN,

COLLECTED FROM ORAL TRADITION

BY

COLONEL SIR LEWIS PELLY, K.C.B., K.C.S.I.,
FORMERLY SERVING IN PERSIA AS SECRETARY OF LEGATION,
AND POLITICAL RESIDENT IN THE PERSIAN GULF.

REVISED WITH EXPLANATORY NOTES BY

ARTHUR N. WOLLASTON,
H.M. INDIAN (HOME) SERVICE, TRANSLATOR OF THE "ANWAR-I-SUHAILI," ETC.

VOL. I.

LONDON:
WM. H. ALLEN AND CO., 13 WATERLOO PLACE.
PUBLISHERS TO THE INDIA OFFICE.

1879.

LONDON:
PRINTED BY W. H. ALLEN AND CO., 13 WATERLOO PLACE.

PREFACE.

IF the success of a drama is to be measured by the effects which it produces upon the people for whom it is composed, or upon the audiences before whom it is represented, no play has ever surpassed the tragedy known in the Mussulman world as that of Hasan and Husain. Mr. Mathew Arnold, in his "Essays on Criticism," elegantly sketches the story and effects of this "Persian Passion Play," while Macaulay's Essay on Lord Clive has encircled the "Mystery" with a halo of immortality.

In common with all my countrymen who have long resided in India, I was annually impressed by the scenes which had place in the native theatres while the recital of the woes of Hasan and Husain went on from night to night during the month of Mohurrum. On joining H.M.'s Legation in Persia in 1859 I was yet more struck by the effect produced upon all classes of society at the capital as they listened, day after day, to this unprecedentedly long tragedy. From the palace to the bazaar there was wailing and beating of breasts, and bursts of impassioned grief from scores of houses wheresoever a noble, or the merchants, or others were giving a *tazia*.

On proceeding in 1862 to the Persian Gulf as Political Resident, my attention was again attracted to the recitations of this tragedy, as also to those of favourite episodes from the Shah Nameh of Ferdousi. As I watched some public story-teller, seated in the bazaar on a rude dais, intoning the story of Sohrab and Rustum, and gradually raising his voice until, towards the close of the hexameter, it seemed to pause and then fall into the following line, while the miscellaneous street assembly listened with rapt attention, I fancied I had there before me a counterpart of the early recitations of the Iliad. And, in respect to the tragedy, it recurred to me that in the West we possessed no complete translation of this singular drama.

It so happened that I was acquainted with a Persian who had long been engaged as a teacher and prompter of actors. I arranged with this man that, assisted by some of his dramatic friends, he should gradually collect and dictate all the scenes of the Hasan and Husain tragedy. This he did, and during the course of several years they were carefully written out and corrected in English by two of my assistants, Mr. James Edwards and Mr. George Lucas, to both of whom I shall always feel most sincerely grateful for their kind and efficient aid upon this and every other occasion on which they were associated with me during a period of eleven years passed on the Arabian and Persian shores of the Gulf.

On quitting the Residency in 1873 the Government of India employed me successively on the East Coast of Africa, in Rajpootana, at Baroda, and on the Afghan Frontier; and thus any projects I might have entertained of literary work were necessarily postponed. At length, in 1878, I disinterred my voluminous MS., and communicated with Mr. Wollaston of the India Office, and with the enterprising publishers, Messrs. Allen and Co., concerning the advisability, or otherwise, of publishing this Mystery. Mr. Wollaston at once accepted the onerous task of revising and annotating the text, and I am indebted to that accomplished scholar for having performed this portion of the work with a degree of learning to which I can make no pretension. I trust he will permit me to avail myself of this opportunity of tendering him my warmest acknowledgments for his invaluable labours, in the absence of which it would have been impracticable for me to issue the translation at the present moment.

The scenes of this play as collected were fifty-two in number, from among which thirty-seven are now presented to the public. For even in harrowing the feelings, one must draw the line somewhere; and it has been said that a sad tale saddens doubly when it's long.

I observed above that this drama is singular. It is so in many respects. It is singular in its intolerable length; in the fact of the representation of it extending over many days; in its marvellous effects upon a Mussulman audience, both male and female; in the curious mixture of hyperbole and archaic simplicity of language; and in the circumstance that the so-called unities of time and space are not only ignored, but abolished. The Prophet Mohammed and his family are at once the central figures and moving spirits of the whole, whether the scene may be that of Joseph and his brethren on earth, or of the Patriarchal Family at the Judgment Day. Mohammed appears on the scene at will; and with him, as with the Creator, it seems to be a universal Here and a universal Now.

A Persian artist at Shiraz painted for me, in oils, six pictures, eight feet by four, illustrative of incidents described in the play. These paintings are full of quaint interest.

For the better understanding of this "Miracle Play" I will now add a sketch of the origin of the Shiah schism, and of the manner of the performance of the play of Hasan and Husain in the East. This account has been obligingly furnished by my friend Dr. Birdwood, C.S.I.

'*The Shiah Sect.*—Leaving out of consideration the false prophets "Moseilmah the Liar," al Aswad, Toleiha, and the prophetess Sejaj, who all set up their pretensions in the year that Mohammed died; the terrible al Makanna, "the veiled prophet of Khorassan," who appeared in the reign of al Mohdi, the third of the Abbasside Caliphs of Baghdad; and the fanatical Karmathians, or Ismalians, better known under the name of "Assassins," Mohammedans may be divided into the two great sects of Sunnis and Shiahs.

'The Sunnis, or "Traditionists," are so called because they acknowledge the authority of the Sunna, a body of moral traditions of the sayings and doings of Mohammed, which the Shiahs utterly reject; and uphold the succession of Abu Beker, Omar, and Othman, whom the Shiahs denounce as usurpers of the Caliphate.

'The Shiahs, or "Dissenters," who sprung up soon after the death of Othman, declare that Ali, his two sons Hasan and Husain, and the descendants of the latter, are the only true Imams or Sovereign Pontiffs, and that a belief in their inalienable right to the Caliphate comprises the most important article of the faith of Islam.

'The Coreish were the most renowned of the children of Ishmael, and during the fifth century became the head of all the Arab tribes whose centre of worship and of tribal sovereignty was Mecca; and the sanctity of the Caaba at Mecca above all other Sabæan shrines had always been recognised by the tribes of peninsular Arabia. In the sixth century Abd Manaf was the Chief of the Coreish and Prince of Mecca, and the second of his family on whom the sacerdotal charge of the Caaba had devolved in direct descent. It was in his time that the Abyssinians sent an army against Mecca, which was signally defeated by one of his sons, named Hashim, the great-grandfather of Mohammed; and it was in consequence of this victory that Hashim and his descendants obtained the ascendancy in the tribe of the Coreish, and the custody of the Caaba, which would otherwise have passed to Abd Shams, the eldest son of Abd Manaf, and the father of Ommiyah, the progenitor of the Ommiyah Caliphs of Damascus (A.D. 661–750), and Cordova (A.D. 755–1031); and thus originated the family feud between the Hashimites, as the descendants of Hashim are called, and the house of Ommiyah

(Ommiades), which for centuries influenced the whole history of Islam. Abdal Motalleb, the son of Hashim, had three sons, Abdallah, the father of Mohammed, and Abbas and Abu Talib. Abbas was the progenitor of the Abbaside Caliphs, who, after driving the last of the Ommiades to Spain, set up their own rule at Baghdad, A.D. 750, where they reigned until the Eastern Caliphate was subverted, A.D. 1258, by the Turks and Mongols under Hulaku Khan, a grandson of Chinghiz Khan. Ali, the son of Abu Talib, married Mohammed's daughter Fatima, and it was Ayesha's jealousy of the children of Mohammed's first wife, Cadijah, and her special antipathy to Ali personally, which at last hastened the family quarrel between the Hashimites and house of Ommiyah to the tragical catastrophe which is the subject of the Persian Passion Play of Hasan and Husain. The domestic feuds of the Hashimites and the house of Ommiyah thus foreshadowed the complete outline of the history of Islam under the Arabs, while the Shiah heresy still divides Islam under the Persians from Islam under the Turks and Mongols. The heterodox Fatimites or Aliades of Egypt were pretenders to a descent from Ali and Fatima. Their colour was green, which only the true lineage of the Prophet are to wear; that of the Abbasides black, and of the Ommiades white.

'When Mohammed died, his religion might have perished with him, and the unruly tribes of Arabia, to whom, through his immense personal influence, he, for the first time in their history, had given political unity and a national organisation, have fallen back into their ancient anarchy, but for the astuteness and energy of Omar, who, so long as he lived, was the ruling spirit of Islam. There were four claimants to the Caliphate—Ali, the first cousin of the Prophet and the husband of Fatima his youngest daughter and only surviving child; Abu Beker, "the Father of the Virgin," that is, of Ayesha, the favorite wife of Mohammed; Omar, the father of Hafsa, another of his wives; and Othman, the only member of the house of Ommiyah who had voluntarily embraced the religion of the Prophet, and who had married two of his daughters, both of whom were now dead, as also their children. Beyond doubt the succession lay with Ali, but Ayesha, who had never forgiven Ali for inclining his ear to the celebrated charge of incontinence against her, successfully used her influence to prevent his election. All the Coreish also of the house of Ommiyah were opposed to Ali. The disruption of Islam seemed imminent. It was actually proposed to elect two chiefs, when Omar vehemently forbade it, exclaiming, "Two blades cannot go into one scabbard." Then Abu Beker proposed Omar as worthy of the succession, on which Omar suddenly rising up hailed Abu Beker as Caliph, and, stepping forward, bowed down and kissed his hand in token of allegiance, and swore to obey him as his sovereign. The example of Omar was followed by all present, whereupon he at once ascended the pulpit and publicly proclaimed Abu Beker. He went so far, it is said, as to surround the house of Fatima, and threaten to burn it down, and put all within to death unless they acknowledged the newly chosen Caliph. Ali accepted the election in words, but spurned it in his heart, and retired from Mecca into the desert of Arabia, with his two sons Hasan and Husain, the only surviving grandchildren of Mohammed; their descendants to this day are considered noble in every country of Islam, and wear the green turban as the outward sign of their almost sacred lineage. On the death of Abu Beker, Ayesha secured the election of Omar, in which Ali, seeing that opposition was useless, acquiesced. When Omar died the Caliphate was offered to Ali, on the condition that he would govern according to the Coran, and the Traditions of Mohammed established by Abu Beker and his successor. Ali replied that he would govern according to the Coran, but in other respects he would act on his own judgment, without reference to "the traditions of the elders." This reply not being satisfactory, the election devolved on Othman. He at once advanced different members of the house of Ommiyah to the highest and most responsible offices in the empire, and Moawiyah, the son of Abu Sofyan, the deadliest enemy of the descendants of Hashim, he appointed Governor of Syria. Othman was assassinated A.H. 35 (A.D. 655), and on Ali being at last elected, on his own terms, and in spite of the opposition of Ayesha, to the Caliphate, one of his first acts was to recall Moawiyah from Syria. Moawiyah refused to obey, and claimed the Caliphate for himself, a pretension in which he was supported by Ayesha. In the battle of the Camel, so called because the virago herself was present mounted on a camel, Ali was victorious, and Talha and Zobair, the commanders of the rebels, were both killed, and Ayesha was taken prisoner. The contest was renewed at Siffen, on which occasion, notwithstanding that the Syrian army was led by Moawiyah in person, Ali had almost won, when a device of Amrou, the conqueror of Egypt, suddenly paralysed the onset of the Caliph's army in the very moment of victory. That arch intriguer ordered his soldiers to raise copies of the Coran on their spears, and to shout as they advanced, "Let the blood of the Faithful cease to flow; if the Syrian army be destroyed who will defend the frontier against the Greeks? If the army of Irak be destroyed who will defend it against the Persians and Turks? Let the word of God decide between us!" "God is great," shouted back the army of Ali, "we must all submit to the arbitrament of the Book."

'It was in vain that Ali protested against the false and hollow pretence of Amrou, and the two armies arranged that the claims of Ali and Moawiyah should be adjudicated by two arbitrators, one chosen by each side. Immediately a controversy broke out among Ali's troops as to the lawfulness of this mode of settling the dispute; and on his arriving at Cufa, twelve thousand of them, who had been the most clamorous to abide by the decision of the Coran, deserted from him. These men were the original Kharegites or "Separatists," an heretical sect of Mohammedans, who reject the lawful government established by public consent. Ali never recovered this defection. While he was gathering together a fresh army against his enemies, three of these Kharegites met by accident, as pilgrims, in the mosque at Mecca, and joining at first in lamentations over the dissensions of the Faithful, ended in planning a sort of Nihilist conspiracy to assassinate on one and the same day Moawiyah, Amrou, and Ali, to whose rivalry they attributed all the troubles of Islam. The names of the conspirators were Barak, Amrou, and Abdalrahman.

'Barak repaired to Damascus, and on Friday, the 17th Ramadan, while Moawiyah was officiating in the mosque, struck at him what the assassin hoped was a fatal blow. But though the wound was desperate, Moawiyah recovered. Amrou, the second of the assassins, at the same hour entered the mosque in Cairo, and at one blow killed Karijah who happened to be officiating, imagining him to be Amrou. Being led to execution the murderer calmly exclaimed, "I intended Amrou, but God intended Karijah." The third conspirator, Abdalrahman, repaired to Cufa, where, as Ali entered the mosque, he was felled to the ground by a fatal blow on the head, A.H. 40 (A.D. 660). His body was buried five miles from Cufa; and in after times a magnificent tomb was erected over his grave, which became the site of a city, called Meshed Ali, or "the Sepulchre of Ali." On his death his eldest son Hasan (*i.e.* "the Handsome") was elected to the Caliphate without opposition, but he resigned it in favour of Moawiyah, on condition that he should resume it on the death of the latter, who had the less scruple in assenting to the arrangement, owing to his secret determination that his son Yezid should be his successor. At the instigation of Moawiyah Hasan was poisoned by his wife, A.H. 49 (A.D. 668). In his last agonies his brother Husain asked him to name whom it was he supposed to be his murderer, but Hasan refused, saying, " This world is only for a night, leave him alone until he and I shall meet at the Judgment Day before the presence of the Most High God."

'Hasan had several wives, and one of them was the beautiful Shahrbanu, daughter of Yezdegird, the last of the Sassanian Kings of Persia. He left altogether fifteen sons and five daughters. It was his wish to be buried by the sepulchre of Ali, but the implacable Ayesha refused her consent, and his body was laid in the common burial-ground beyond the city. A.H. 56 (A.D. 676), Ayesha herself died. The story is told of how she was trapped by Moawiyah down a well, covered all over with green branches, through which, as, in response to his warm welcome into his garden, she sat thereon, the irrepressible dowager sank softly into everlasting night. Moawiyah died A.H. 60 (A.D. 679). The latter was succeeded by his son Yezid, " the Polluted," without election; and thus was established the dynasty of the Ommiades, which held the Caliphate at Damascus for one hundred years. But the family feud between the descendants of Hashim and Abd Shams, the sons of Abd Manaf, continued without abatement, and Islam was for ever rent in twain by the great Shiah schism.

'*The Legend of the Plain of Kerbela.*—Shortly after the accession of Yezid, Husain received at Mecca secret messages from the people of Cufa, entreating him to place himself at the head of the Faithful in Babylonia. Yezid, however, had full intimation of the intended revolt, and long before Husain could reach Cufa, the too easy governor of that city had been replaced by Obaidallah, the resolute ruler of Bussorah, who, by his rapid measures, disconcerted the plans of the conspirators, and drove them to a premature outbreak, and the surrender of their leader Muslim. The latter foresaw the ruin which he had brought on Husain, and shed bitter tears on that account when captured. His head was struck off and sent to Yezid. On Husain arriving at the confines of Babylonia he was met by Harro, who had been sent out by Obaidallah, with a body of horsemen, to intercept his approach. Husain, addressing them, asserted his title to the Caliphate, and invited them to submit to him. Harro replied, " We are commanded as soon as we meet you to bring you directly to Cufa into the presence of Obaidallah the son of Ziyad." Husain answered, " I would sooner die than submit to that," and gave the word to his men to ride on; but Harro wheeled about and intercepted them. At the same time Harro said, "I have no commission to fight with you, but I am commanded not to part with you until I have conducted you into Cufa:" but he bade Husain to choose any road into that city "that did not go directly back to Mecca," and "do you," said he, "write to Yezid or Obaidallah, and I will write to Obaidallah, and perhaps it may please God I may meet with something that may bring me off without my being forced to an extremity on your account." Then he retreated his force a little to allow Husain to lead the way towards Cufa: and Husain took the road that leads by Adib and Cadisia. This was on Thursday the 1st of Mohurrum, A.H. 61 (A.D. 680). When night came on he still continued his march all through the night. As he rode on he nodded a little, and waking again, said, "Men travel by night, and the destinies travel toward them; this I know to be a message of death."

'In the morning, after prayers were over, he mended his pace, and as he rode on there came up a horseman who took no notice of him, but saluted Harro, and delivered to him a letter, giving orders from Obaidallah to lead Husain and his men into a place where was neither town nor fortification, and there leave them till the Syrian forces should surround them. This was on Friday the 2nd of Mohurrum. The day after, Amer the son of Saed came upon them with four thousand men, who were on their march to Dailam. They had been encamped without the walls of Cufa, and when Obaidallah heard of Husain's coming, he commanded Amer to defer his march to Dailam and go against Husain. But one and all dissuaded him:—" Beware that you go not against Husain, and rebel against your Lord, and cut off mercy from you; for you had better be deprived of the dominion of the whole world than meet your Lord with the blood of Husain upon you." Amer was fain to acquiesce, but upon Obaidallah renewing his command with threats, he marched against Husain, and came up with him as aforesaid, on Saturday, the 3rd of Mohurrum.

'On Amer sending to inquire of Husain what brought him thither, the latter replied, "The Cufans wrote to me, but since they reject me I am willing to return to Mecca." Amer was glad when he heard it, and said, " I hope to God I may be excused from fighting against him." Then he wrote to this purpose to Obaidallah, but Obaidallah sternly replied, "Get between him and the river," and Amer did so ; and the name of the place where he cut Husain off from the Euphrates was called Kerbela:—" Kerb (anguish) and Bala (vexation), Trouble and Affliction," said Husain when he heard it.

' Then Husain sought a conference with Amer, in which he proposed either to go to Yezid, to return to Mecca, or, as some add, but others deny, to fight against the Turks. Obaidallah was at first inclined to accede to these conditions, until Shamer stood up and swore that no terms should be made with Husain, adding significantly that he had been informed of a long conference between Husain and Amer. Then Obaidallah sent Shamer with orders to Amer that if Husain would surrender unconditionally he would be received ; if not, Amer was to fall upon him and his men, and trample them under his feet. Should he refuse to do so, Shamer was to strike off Amer's head, and himself command the attack against Husain. Thus passed Sunday, Monday, Tuesday, Wednesday, Thursday, and Friday, the 4th, 5th, 6th, 7th, 8th, and 9th of Mohurrum. On the evening of the 9th, Amer drew up his forces close to Husain's camp, and himself rode up to Husain as he was sitting in the door of his tent just after the evening prayer, and told him of the conditions offered by Obaidallah. Husain desired Amer to give him time until the next morning, when he would make his answer.

' In the night his sister came weeping to his bed-side, and awaking him, exclaimed, " Alas for the desolation of my family ! my mother Fatima is dead, and my father Ali, and my brother Hasan. Alas for the destruction that is past! and alas for the destruction that is to come!" " Sister,"

Husain replied, "put your trust in God, and know that man is born to die, and that the heavens shall not remain; everything shall pass away but the presence of God, who created all things by His power, and shall make them by His power to pass away, and they shall return to Him alone. My father was better than me, and my mother was better than me, and my brother was better than me; and they and we, and all Moslems, have an example in the 'Apostle of God.'" Then he told his men that Obaidallah wanted nobody but him, and that they should go away to their homes. But they said, "God forbid that we should ever see the day wherein we survive you!" Then he commanded them to cord their tents close together, and make a line of them so as to keep out the enemy's horse. And he digged a trench behind his camp, which he filled with wood, to be set on fire, so that he could only be attacked in front. The rest of the night he spent in prayer and supplication, while the enemy's guard patrolled all night long round and round his camp.

'The next morning both sides prepared for the slaughter. Husain first washed and anointed himself with musk, and several of his chief men did the like; and one asking them what it meant, Husain replied, pleasantly, "Alas! there is nothing between us and the black-eyed girls of Paradise but that these troopers come down upon us and slay us!" Then he mounted his horse, and set the Coran before him, crying, "O God, Thou art my confidence in every trouble, and my hope in every adversity," and submitted himself to the judgment of his companions before the opened pages of the sacred volume. At this his sisters and daughters began to weep, when he cried out in bitter anguish, self-reproachfully, "God reward the son of Abbas," in allusion to advice which his cousin, Abdullah ibn Abbas, had given him to leave the women behind in Mecca. At this moment a party of the enemy's horse wheeled about and came up to Husain, who expected to be attacked by them. But it was Harro, who had quitted the ranks of the Syrian army, and had now come to die with Husain, and testify his repentance before men and God. As Harro rode into the doomed camp he shouted back to Amer, "Alas for you!" Whereupon Amer commanded his men to "bring up the colours." As soon as they were set in front of the troops, Shamer shot an arrow into the camp, saying, "Bear witness that I shot the first arrow;" and so the fight began on both sides. It raged, chiefly in a series of single combats, until noonday, when both sides retired to prayer, Husain adding to the usual office the "prayer of fear," never used but in cases of extremity. When shortly afterward the fight was renewed Husain was struck on the head by a sword. Faint with the loss of blood, he sat down by his tent, and took up on his lap his little son Abdullah, who was at once killed by a flying arrow. He placed the little corpse upon the ground, crying out "We come from God, and we return to Him. O God, give me strength to bear these misfortunes." Growing thirsty, he ran toward the Euphrates, where, as he stooped to drink, an arrow struck him in the mouth. Raising his hands, all besmeared and dripping with blood, to heaven, he stood for awhile and prayed earnestly. His little nephew, a beautiful child, who went up to kiss him, had his hand cut off with a sword, on which Husain again wept, saying, "Thy reward, dear child, is with thy forefathers in the realms of bliss."

'Hounded on by Shamer, the Syrian troops now surrounded him, but Husain, nothing daunted, charged them right and left. In the midst of the fighting his sister came between him and his slayers, crying out to Amer, how he could stand by and see Husain slain. Whereupon, with tears trickling down his beard, Amer turned his face away; but Shamer, with threats and curses, set on his soldiers again, and at last one wounded Husain upon the hand, and a second gashed him on the neck, and a third thrust him through the body with a spear. No sooner had he fallen to the ground than Shamer rode a troop of horsemen over his corpse, backwards and forwards, over and over again, until it was trampled into the very ground, a scarcely-recognisable mass of mangled flesh and mud.

'Thus, twelve years after the death of his brother Hasan, Husain, the second son of Ali, met his own death on the bloody plain of Kerbela on Saturday the 10th day of Mohurrum, A.H. 61 (A.D. 680). This is the "Martyrdom of Husain," celebrated every year during the first ten days of Mohurrum by the Shiahs all over India and Persia, with an intensity of feeling which ever keeps open, between the Sunni and Shiah Mahommedans, the wound first inflicted more than a thousand years ago; and lends to the performance of the "Miracle Play," in which all the scenes and incidents of the last days of the Imaum Husain are enacted, the character of absolute reality.

'*The Persian revolt.*—Though the personal history of Ali and his sons was the exciting cause of the Shiah schism, its predisposing cause lies far deeper in the impassable ethnological gulf which separates the Aryan and Semitic races. Owing to their strongly centralised form of Government the empire of the Sassanides succumbed at once before the onslaught of the Saracens; still Persia was never really converted to Islam, and when Mohammed, the son of Ali, the son of Abdullah, the son of Abbas, the uncle of the Prophet Mohammed, proclaimed the Imamate as inherent of divine right, in the descendants of the Caliph Ali, the vanquished Persians rose as one man against their Arab conquerors. The sons of Abbas had all espoused the cause of their cousin Ali against Moawiyah, and when Yezid succeeded to the Caliphate Abdullah refused to acknowledge him and retired to Mecca. It was he who tried to dissuade Husain from going to Cufa. His son was Ali, who by order of the Caliph Walid was flogged and paraded through the streets of Damascus, mounted on a camel with his face to its tail; and it was to avenge this insult on his father that Mohammed resolved to overthrow the dynasty of the Ommiades.

'The Persians, in their hatred of the Arabs, had from the first accepted the rights of the sons of Ali and Fatima to the Imamate; and Mohammed cunningly represented to them that the Imamate had been transmitted to him by Abou Hashim, the son of Mohammed, another son of the Caliph Ali, whose mother was a daughter of the tribe of Hanifa. This was a gross fraud on the descendants of Fatima, but the Persians cared not, so long as they threw off the Arab yoke. When Mohammed died, A.H. 124 (A.D. 742), they at once acknowledged his son Ibrahim as Imaum, and on the latter being taken prisoner by the Caliph Merwan, he transmitted the Imamate to his brother Abdullah, who overthrew his Ommiade antagonist in the battle of Zab, and was proclaimed Caliph at Cufa A.H. 132 (A.D. 749). Thus fell the last eastern Caliph of the house of Ommiyah, on the ruins of which was established the dynasty of the house of Abbas, which reigned at Baghdad until A.D. 1258.

'The Persians were oppressed by the Abbasides as intolerably as they had been by the Ommiades, but as the vigour of the Caliphate began to abate they again rose in rebellion. In 808 Yakoob, the son of a brazier (saffar), of Siestan, subdued Cabool, Balk, and Fars, and threatened Baghdad itself. His brother, who succeeded him, was overthrown by Ismail Samany, the founder of the Samanian dynasty of Khorassan and Bokhara. At the same time the Dailamy or Bouyide dynasty, so called after Abu'l Bouya, a-fisherman, of Dailam, on the Caspian, established themselves in Fars and Irak. In the contentions which began to distract and undermine the Caliphate at Baghdad during the tenth century the Sunnis all ranged themselves under the Turks, while the Shiahs adopted the cause of the Bouides. It was Asadud Daulah (reigned A.D. 977–982), the grandson of the fisherman of Dailam, who restored the sacred buildings at Kerbela. The native Sufawi dynasty of Persia which succeeded to the Mongol dynasties, and immediately preceded the present Kajar dynasty, derived its descent direct from the Caliph Ali through Ismael Safi, the son of Sultan Haidar, the founder of the Haidari sect of Shiahs.

'*The Mohurrum in India.*—The Martyrdom of Hasan and Husain is celebrated by the Shiahs all over India during the

b

first ten days of the month of Mohurrum, which begins when the new moon which ushers in the month is first seen. Attached to every great Shiah's house is an Imambarrah—a hall or enclosure—built expressly for the celebration of the anniversary of the death of Husain. The enclosure is generally arcaded along its sides, and in most instances it is covered in with a domed roof. Against the side of the Imambarrah directed toward Mecca is set the *tabut*—also called *tazia*—or model of the tombs at Kerbela. In the houses of the wealthier Shiahs these *tabuts* are fixtures, and are beautifully fashioned of silver and gold, or of ivory and ebony, embellished all over with inlaid work. The poorer Shiahs provide themselves with a *tabut* made for the occasion, of lath and plaster, tricked out in mica and tinsel. A week before the new moon of the Mohurrum they enclose a space called the *tabut khana*, in which the *tabut* is prepared; and the very moment the new moon is seen a spade is struck into the ground before "the enclosure of the Tombs," where a pit is afterwards dug, in which a bonfire is lighted and kept burning through all the ten days of the Mohurrum solemnities. Those who cannot afford to erect a *tabut khana*, or even to put up a little *tabut* or *tazia* in their dwelling-house, always have a Mohurrum fire lighted, if it consist only of a night-light floating at the bottom of an earthen pot or basin sunk in the ground. It is doubtful whether this custom refers to the trench of fire Husain set blazing behind his camp, or is a survival from the older *Ashura* ("ten days") festival which is said to have been instituted in commemoration of the deliverance of the Hebrew Arabs from Pharaoh and his host at the Red Sea; or from the yet more ancient Bael fire; but, in India, these Mohurrum fires, especially among the more ignorant populace, Hindus as well as Mohammedans, are regarded with the most superstitious reverence, and have a greater hold on them even than the *tabuts*. All day long the passers by stop before the fires and make their vows over them, and all night long the crowds dance round them, and leap through the flames and scatter about the burning brands snatched from them. The *tabut* is lighted up, like an altar, with innumerable green wax candles, and nothing can be more brilliant than the appearance of an Imambarrah of white stone, or polished white stucco, picked out in green, lighted up with glass chandeliers, sconces, and oil lamps arranged along the leading architectural lines of the building, with its *tabut* on one side, dazzling to blindness. Before the *tabut* are placed the " properties " to be used by the celebrants in the " Passion Play," the bows and arrows, the sword and spear, and the banners of Husain, &c.; and in front of it is set a movable pulpit, also made of the richest materials, and covered with rich brocades in green and gold. Such is the theatre in which, twice daily during the first ten days of the month of Mohurrum, the deaths of the first martyrs of Islam are yearly commemorated in India. Each day has its special solemnity, corresponding with the succession of events during the ten days that Husain was encamped on the fatal plain of Kerbela, but the prescribed order of the services in the daily development of the great Shiah function of the Mohurrum would appear not to be always strictly observed in Bombay.

'During the four days after the *tabuts* have been carried to the houses of those who do not possess permanent representations of the tombs of Kerbela, there is little unusual excitement to be observed among the Shiahs in any Indian city, and the time is usually devoted to paying visits to the various *tabut khanas* and Imambarrahs. Women and children, as well as men, are allowed to enter them, and Hindus and Christians, if they please, may join the company. Only the Sunni Mohammedans are denied, and, under the English rule, prevented admission.

'The thronging visitors at first cover the whole area of the enclosure, laughing and talking like a crowd at a fair. But in the midst of the hubbub a signal is given, it may be by the muffled beating of a drum, in slow time, the measured beats becoming fainter and more faint, until step by step the people fall back into their places, and are at length hushed in a silence which is most expressive in its dramatic effect. Then a *moullah* enters the pulpit, and intones a sort of "argument" or prelude to the play. He begins in some such form as this: "O ye Faithful, give ear! and open your hearts to the wrongs and sufferings of His Highness the Imaum Ali, the vicegerent of the Prophet, and let your eyes flow with tears, as a river, for the woes that befell their Highnesses the beloved Imaums Hasan and Husain, the foremost of the bright youths of Paradise."

'For a while he proceeds amid the deep silence of the eager audience, but as he goes on, they will be observed to be swaying to and fro, and all together; at first almost imperceptibly, but gradually with a motion that becomes more and more marked. Suddenly a stifled sob is heard, or a cry, followed by more and more sobbing and crying, and rapidly the swaying to and fro becomes a violent agitation of the whole assembly, which rises in a mass, every one smiting his breast with open hand, and raising the wild rhythmical wail of "*Ya Ali! Ai Hasan, Ai Husain, Ai Hasan, Ai Husain, Husain Shah!* As the wailing gathers force, and threatens to become ungovernable, a chorus of mourners, which has formed almost without observation on the arena, begins chanting, in regular Gregorian music, a metrical version of the story, which calls back the audience from themselves, and imperceptibly at last soothes and quiets them again. At the same time the celebrants come forward, and take up the "properties" before the *tabut*, and one represents Husain, another al Abbas, his brother and standard bearer, another Harro, and another Shamer, all going through their parts (which it seems to be the duty of the chorus every now and then more fully to explain), not after the manner of actors, but of earnest men, absorbed in some high sacrament, without consciousness of themselves or their audience.

'The first day's performance should represent the departure of Husain, against the moving entreaties of his family, from Mecca, and the subsequent murder of his cousin Muslim and his children; and so day after day each succeeding act of the events at Kerbela should be represented. It is open to question whether this is ever actually done in India: but always on the fifth day the banners of Husain are taken in procession through the streets, and his horse is paraded, attended by men bearing *murchals* [peacock tails] and *chauries* [whisps made of yak tails, or shreds of ivory or sandalwood], and *aftabis* [banners embroidered in gold with the figure of the sun], which are recognised everywhere in the East as the most imposing insignia of royalty and empire; on the seventh day the marriage of Cossim with Fatimah is represented by a wedding procession through the streets by torchlight, a quire of young men chanting funeral dirges, in place of the usual troop of dancing girls, going before the bridegroom, who is distinguished by a gold or silver umbrella held over his head; and on the tenth, in commemoration of the death of Husain on that day of the month, the *tabuts* are carried to the Mohammedan cemetery, as representing "the plain of Kerbela," and at magnificent Bombay —which Sir Bartle Frere has built—into the sea, which there does not simply stand mystically for the Euphrates, but is regarded as the River itself, seeing that in a sense it may be said to flow down the coast of Western India. When Husain's horse is brought into the arena of the Imambarrah, and his little sons, and daughters and nephews appear on the scene, raised on thrones carried on men's shoulders, the rage and agony of the people become perfectly uncontrollable; for which reason no representations of the dead Husain, or of his children, or horse, are allowed to be taken through the streets of Bombay, for fear of exciting outrages against the Sunnis.

'On the 10th of Mohurrum every house in which a *tabut* is kept, or in which one has been put up for the occasion, sends forth its separate cavalcade or company to join the general funeral procession, which in the native Mohammedan States sometimes assumes the character of a solemn military pomp. First go the musicians, with pipes and cymbals, high horns, and deafening drums, followed by the arms and banners of

Hasan and Husain, and the ensigns and crests, in gold and silver, or other metals, of Ali and Fatima, and these by a chorus of men chanting a funeral dirge, followed in turn by Husain's horse. Next come men bearing censers of burning myrrh and frankincense, and aloes wood and gum benjamin before the *tabut* or model of the tombs of Hasan and Husain, which is raised aloft on poles, or borne on an elephant. Models of the sepulchre of Ali also, and of Mohammed at Medina, and representations of the Seraph-Beast *Burak*, on which Mohammed is said to have performed his journey from Jerusalem to Heaven, are also carried along with the *tabut*. There may be one or two hundred of these separate funeral companies or cavalcades in the general procession, which is further swollen by crowds of faquirs, and clowns, or "Mohurrum faquirs," got up for the occasion in marvellously fantastic masquerade, figuring, one, "Jack Priest," another "King Tatterdamalion," and others "King Clout," "King Ragamuffin," "King Double Dumb," and a hundred others of the following of the "Lord of Misrule," or "Abbot of Unreason," of our Catholic forefathers. An immense concourse of people, representatives of every country and costume of Central and Southern Asia, runs along with the procession. In Bombay, after gathering its contingent from every Shiah household as it winds its way through the tortuous streets of the native town, the living stream at length emerges on the Esplanade on the side opposite Back Bay—the whole Esplanade—"the plain of Kerbela" for the day—from Bombay Harbour to Back Bay lying almost flush with the sea. The confused uproar of its advance can be heard a mile away, and long before the procession takes definite shape through the clouds of dust and incense which move before it. It moves headlong onward in an endless line of flashing swords, blasoned suns (*aftabis*) and waving banners, State umbrellas, thrones, and canopies, and towering above all the *tabuts*, framed of the most elegant shapes of Saracenic architecture, glittering in silver and green and gold, and rocking backwards and forwards in high air, like great ships upon a rolling sea, with the rapid movement of the hurrying crowd, beating drums, chanting hymns, and shrieking, " *Ya Ali, Ai Hasan, Ai Husain, Husain Shah!* drowned, drowned, in blood, in blood; all three, fallen prostrate, dead! *Ya Ali! Ai Hasan, Ai Husain, Husain Shah!*" until the whole welkin seems to ring and pulsate with the terrific wail. Ever and anon a band of naked men, drunk with opium or hemp, and painted like tigers or leopards, makes a rush through the ranks of the procession, leaping furiously, and brandishing their swords and spears and clubs in the air. The route, however, is strictly defined by a line of native policemen, and before these representatives of British law and order, the infuriated zealots will suddenly bring themselves in full charge to a halt, wheel round, and retreat back into the body of the procession, howling and shrieking like a flight of baffled fiends.

'So, for a mile in length, the rout advances, against the rays of the now declining sun, until the sea is reached, where it spreads out along the beach in a line at right angles to the "sacred way" by which it has come across the Esplanade. Nothing can be more picturesque than the arrival and break up of the procession in Back Bay. The temporary *tabuts* are taken out into the bay as far as they can be carried, and abandoned to the waves, into which all the temporary adornments of the permanent *tabuts* are also thrown. This operation has a wonderfully cooling effect on the mob. Their frantic clamours suddenly cease. In fact, the mourners of Hasan and Husain, having buried their *tabuts* in the sea, seize the opportunity to have a good bath; and a little after the sun has finally dropped below the western horizon, the whole of the vast multitude is seen in the vivid moonlight to be slowly and peacefully regathering itself across the wide Esplanade into its homes again, and the Saturnalia into which the last act of the Mystery of Hasan and Husain has degenerated in India is closed for another year.

'Up country, where the *tabuts* are carried to the Mohammedan cemeteries, and Sunnis and Shiahs meet face to face before the open graves of Hasan and Husain, the feuds between them, which have been pent up all the year, are often fought out to a bloody end. The custom of carrying the *tabuts* into the sea at Bombay no doubt contributes to the peace with which the Mohurrum is observed by the Mohammedans of that city.

'The 11th and 12th of Mohurrum should be spent in meditation by the graves in which the *tabuts* have been laid, and in Bombay by the sea; but as a spectacle the Mohurrum celebration is over with the wild masquerade of the 10th day.'

LEWIS PELLY.

Athenæum Club,
    1st June 1879.

EDITORIAL NOTE.

The MS. of the accompanying work was some time since placed in my hands by Sir Lewis Pelly, who desired to lay before the public a play which, whatever may be its defects, is certainly a literary curiosity, and, as the embodiment of sentiments which powerfully appeal to the passions of many millions of the human race, must command a certain amount of interest, so long as it holds true that "the proper study of mankind is man."

A very cursory glance at once showed that, to render the text intelligible to an ordinary reader, notes would be required explanatory of the many allusions which are scattered throughout the scenes; without them the spirit of the play would be lost to all but the comparatively limited number of scholars to whom the subject might happen to be familiar.

In nearly every instance where explanation has been afforded authorities have been cited. The adoption of this course will, I think, be more satisfactory to the reader than would have been dogmatic assertions by a writer who can claim no personal authority.

The introductory remarks which precede the various scenes are intended to convey concisely the substance of what follows, and by way of imparting an additional interest to them they are, as far as possible, given in the words of some author who may happen to have described similar incidents.

Faults will doubtless be detected both in the body of the work and also in the explanatory notes. While in no way wishing to plead any extenuation for such errors as may be due to ignorance or carelessness, I may perhaps be permitted to urge that, in the absence of the Persian text, it has been difficult to avoid mistakes which might not otherwise have occurred. This remark particularly applies to the spelling of Oriental names, since the transliteration adopted, though possibly correct in itself, may not in all instances accurately represent the idea of the writer of the play. Again, in a lengthy work in which the family connection between the numerous characters is intricate, while the allusions to tradition are frequent, the desultory mode of work which circumstances made unavoidable, rendered more than usually difficult a task which, under the most favourable conditions, must, to a certain degree, have been perplexing.

It only remains to express my obligations for the valuable assistance which I have received from the Rev. Dr. Badger, who has been good enough to afford me information on obscure points which would otherwise have remained unintelligible. Nor must I omit to record my acknowledgments to Dr Rost, the courteous Librarian of the India Office, whose wide acquaintance with Oriental literature has enabled me to consult some comparatively unknown works of reference, without which I could not have completed my task in a way which would have been even moderately worthy of the subject, or of the distinguished diplomatist to whom the public are indebted for the accompanying unique collection of scenes.

ARTHUR N. WOLLASTON.

Glen Hill, Walmer,
    May, 1879.

CONTENTS.

	PAGE
PREFACE	iii
EDITORIAL NOTE	xxv
DRAMATIS PERSONÆ	xxix
Scene I.—Joseph and his Brethren	1
Scene II.—Death of Ibráhím the Son of Muhammad	19
Scene III.—The Disobedient Son	33
Scene IV.—Magnanimous offer of 'Alí to sacrifice his Life for a Fellow-creature	51
Scene V.—Death of the Prophet Muhammad	71
Scene VI.—The Seizure of the Khalífat by Abú Bakr	92
Scene VII.—Death of Fátimah the Daughter of the Prophet Muhammad	110
Scene VIII.—The Martyrdom of 'Alí the Son of Abú Tálib	133
Scene IX.—The Martyrdom of Hasan the Son of 'Alí	154
Scene X.—The Martyrdom of Muslim the Envoy of Husain	171
Scene XI.—Murder of the Sons of Muslim	190

		PAGE
Scene XII.—The Departure of Husain from Madínah on his way to Kúfah		207
Scene XIII.—Withdrawal of Husain from the road to Kúfah		224
Scene XIV.—The Martyrdom of Húr		236
Scene XV.—The Martyrdom of 'Abís and Shauzab in defence of Husain		250
Scene XVI.—A Night Assault on Husain's Camp		270
Scene XVII.—Death of 'Alí Akbar		287

DRAMATIS PERSONÆ.
(VOL. I.)

'Abbás, uncle of the Prophet Muhammad.
'Abbás, brother of Husain.
'Abís, son of Shíb, and a martyr in defence of Husain.
Abú Bakr, a companion of the Prophet Muhammad, and subsequently the usurper of the Khalífat.
'Alí, husband of Fátimah the daughter of the Prophet Muhammad.
'Alí Akbar, eldest son of Husain.
Almighty, the.
'A'yishah, wife of the Prophet Muhammad.

Benjamin, son of Jacob.
Bilál, crier for prayer.
Blind man.

Dinah, sister of Joseph.
Disobedient child.
—— Mother of.

Fátimah, daughter of Muhammad, and wife of 'Alí.

Fátimah's maid.
Fátimah, daughter of Husain, and wife of Kásim.

Gabriel, Angel.

Hání, a principal person in Kúfah.
Háris, soldier in the Syrian army.
—— Wife of.
—— —— Maid of.
Hasan, son of 'Alí and Fátimah.
—— Younger son of.
Húr, martyr in defence of Husain.
—— Son of.
Husain, son of 'Alí and Fátimah.

Ibn Muljam, murderer of 'Alí.
Ibn Sa'd or *'Umar,* commander of Syrian troops.
Ibn Ziyád or *'Ubaidullah,* Governor of Busrah.
Ibráhím, son of the Prophet Muhammad.
—— Schoolmaster of.
Ibráhím, son of Muslim the martyr.
'Izráíl, Angel of Death.

Jacob, Patriarch.
Ja'dah, the wife and murderess of Hasan.
Joseph, son of Jacob.
Judah, son of Jacob.

Kásim, son of Hasan, and husband of Fátimah.
—— Brother of.
—— Mother of.
Katámah, mistress of Ibn Muljam.
Kulsúm, daughter of 'Alí, and sister of Hasan and Husain.

Marwán, Governor of Madínah.
Mashkúr, a gaoler.
Michael, Angel.

Muhammad, the Prophet.
—— Spirit of.
Muhammad, son of Muslim the Martyr.
Muhammad Hanífah, son of 'Alí, and half-brother of Hasan and Husain.
Muhammad-i-A'shúftah, soldier in Syrian army.
Músab, brother of Húr the martyr.
Muslim, cousin of Husain, and a martyr in defence of the latter.

Na'mán Surgeon.

Procuress.

Reuben, son of Jacob.

Salmán the Persian, companion of the Prophet Muhammad.
Shári', a principal person in Kúfah.
Shauzab, slave of 'Abís.
Shimar, murderer of Husain.
Simeon, son of Jacob.
Simeon, the Jew.
Sukainah, daughter of Husain.

Táwah, pious old woman.
—— Son of.

'Ubaidullah or *Ibn Ziyád*, Governor of Busrah.
'Umar, companion of the Prophet Muhammad.
'Umar or *Ibn Sa'd*, commander of Syrian troops.
Umm Lailah, mother of 'Alí Akbar.

Youth in love.
—— Uncle of.

Zahír, Arab chief.
Zainab, daughter of 'Alí, and sister of Hasan and Husain.
—— Camel-driver of.

Angels in Paradise.
Companions of the Prophet Muhammad.
Executioner.
Household of 'Alí.
Inhabitants of Kúfah.
Inhabitants of Madínah.
Marwán's servant.
Messenger from Kúfah.
Messenger of Mu'áwiyah, Governor of Syria.
Nymphs in Paradise.
Patrol.
Servant of 'Alí.
Voice from the Sepulchre of the Prophet Muhammad.

SCENE I.

JOSEPH AND HIS BRETHREN.

This Scene, which is a paraphrase of the Biblical story of Joseph and his brethren, is doubtless founded on the 12th chapter in the Kur'án (Sale's edition). "The confidence," says Muir, "with which Mahomet refers to the testimony of the Jews and of their Scriptures, is very remarkable. It leaves us no room to doubt that some amongst the Jews, possessed probably of an imperfect and superficial acquaintance with their own books and traditions, encouraged Mahomet in the idea that he might be, or positively affirmed that he was, *that Prophet whom the Lord their God should raise up unto them of their brethren.* . . . . But whoever his Jewish friends may have been, it is evident that they had a knowledge—rude and imperfect, perhaps, but comprehensive—of the outline of Jewish history and tradition. These, distorted by rabbinical fable, and embellished or parodied by the Prophet's fancy, supplied the material for the Scriptural stories, which begin to form a chief portion of the Coran."—(Muir's "Life of Mahomet," vol. ii. p. 183, ed. 1858.) The source whence Muhammad derived many of the traditions in the Kur'án was indeed an ill-concealed secret in the earlier portion of his career; later on, when the religion of the Prophet became firmly established, no one ventured, says Mr. Rodwell, "to doubt the divine origin of the entire book."

The object of introducing into the present Scene events which occurred so many years antecedent to the rise of Islám, is apparently to institute a comparison between the sufferings of Joseph and those of the martyrs at Karbalá, and thereby to raise feelings of pity for the family, whose "sad voices shall reach the very throne of the Majesty on high."

Jacob (eulogising God).—O Cause of the existence of all things, Thou Who art omnipotent to save and help all Thy servants, Whose door of mercy is open for all! Thou art the sole Creator of all things, worship is due to Thee alone. Thou, being the First and the Last, mayest with propriety be called the Eternal and Everlasting God! Thou alone art able to produce day and night; Thou alone knowest the secret recesses of every heart.

Joseph (awaking from his sleep).—Oh! what sort of dream is this that I have just dreamt, which has made my body tremble like a sea of quicksilver? Oh! what vision is this that I, a poor creature, saw just now, a little before I awoke? The sight is so fresh to my memory.

Jacob (to Joseph).—O light of my two eyes, thou the dearest to me of all my children! thou whose dreams are better than the waking thoughts of others, tell me, why dost thou look so thoughtful and sad?

Joseph.—I saw, O honoured father, in a dream, that I was wearing a crown of pearls and gems on my head, and was seated on a high and lofty throne, studded like the heavens with kingly diadems and other precious stones; that the sun descended from his heavenly station accompanied by the moon and all the planets and fixed stars, and came and stood respectfully before me on my right hand and on my left, and that the sun, moon, and eleven[*] stars fell down and worshipped me in a most submissive manner.

Jacob.—Be not troubled, O dear child, for the things about which thou hast dreamed. Be gentle in thine answers and questions, and try to fall asleep in my lap for a while. But as to the interpretation of thy dream, O my happy son, know that thou shalt be raised in time to the honour of being a king, and that these thy brothers shall become thy humble servants. But thou must not tell thy dream to anybody, for it is a secret of God's mystery, and ought to be kept as such.

Joseph.—Thanks be to God the great Creator in thus making me superior to my brothers; and I heartily thank Thee, O beneficent Lover of all Thy creatures, for the honour I have in being called the least of Thy servants.

---

[*] This is probably an allusion to the eleven Imáms who, according to the Shí'ah tradition, succeeded 'Alí.

Simeon (Joseph's brother).—Come, my brethren, come, let us untie the knot of one another's affairs. Come, let me tell you the feelings of my heart. Help me, dear brothers, for a while, for a fire has kindled in my soul and body, which will consume me unless you, as kind brothers of mine, help me to have it quenched.

Judah.—Tell us thy circumstances, O Simeon, let us know why tears of blood run down thy cheeks. Why dost thou groan so sadly? Let us know what is the matter with thee.

Simeon.—Let it be known unto you, O shrubs of the garden of Paradise, that Joseph our brother has dreamt that the sun and the moon and eleven stars have worshipped him in this plain. Our father, interpreting the dream according to his fancy, has told him that he will be as high as the heaven, and we as the dust of the earth beneath him. You must now help yourselves in the best possible way you can, before you be publicly put to shame by both the father and the son.

Judah.—What is your advice in this important piece of business, O friends? You well know that our father does not care about any of us as he does for Joseph. What reason has he to be unkind to us, and give the best of his caressing indulgences to Joseph? Are we not all of us his children called Jacob's sons? Why should our father prefer him to any of us, thinking highly of him and meanly of us? Are we not all plants of one and the same meadow, expecting our father's kind approval of us alike? We must therefore contrive some plan to remove away Joseph from the presence of our father.

Simeon.—Yes, dearly beloved, it is just and proper that we should turn him out from the presence of our father. I think we must all go most respectfully to our sire, and ask his permission to take Joseph out with us into some field for a walk. When once away from our parent's sight we will all endeavour to put our brother to death, and remove this sharp thorn from our father's path. You must know that, as soon as Joseph is gone or hidden from our parent's sight, we shall at once become dear, and find favour in his eyes. When Joseph is no longer seen by him, he of course will begin to love us more than he now does.

Judah.—I do not by any means think it advisable to put Joseph to death. You must abandon this intention, and seek another better plan. Is he not after all our dear brother? Why should we be so malicious as to wish to kill him?

Simeon.—Well, tell us what we must do in order to get rid of our brother, and be delivered from the grievous pain and trouble he causes us. For, so long as he is alive it is impossible that our father should have any kind or affectionate regard for us.

Judah.—O my dear brothers! hearken to the thing which has just occurred to me, and do not deviate from the advice tendered to you. There is a well in this wilderness so deep and dark that even a dragon cannot bear to dwell in it. You should strip Joseph of his coat, and cast him at once into that pit.

Simeon.—What a wonderful contrivance is this, O brother! nothing can surpass it in excellence. Since we intend simply that our father shall no longer see him, let us then cast him into that dismal pit, where perpetual night will be his companion, and pricking thorns his cushion and pillow; where he will have no bread but the cake of the sun about which he has dreamed, nor any water but the tears of despair. He will die there most miserably after he shall have remained there for some time. Come along, then, O assembly of brethren, let us go to our father and persuade him to send Joseph with us, that we may turn to dark evening the bright morning of his life.

Judah (to Jacob).—Peace be unto thee, O honourable father, may the shadow of thy kindness never be removed from our head! We have a certain request from thy honour, which we hope thou wilt be kind enough to grant us.

Jacob.—On you be peace, my beloved children, from

whose dear faces my spirits receive refreshment. Let me know what your request is, that I may with pleasure grant it you accordingly.

Judah.—May I be a sacrifice for thee, O father! this is our humble request: we feel very dull here now that the autumn and winter are passed away to make room for the vernal season, the tulips having already encamped at the foot of the mountains, and the notes of the nightingales being distinctly heard everywhere because of the abundance of violets, wild roses, tulips, and hyacinths. As the gazelles, the partridges, and other game are all running to and fro in the plains and valleys, and also all birds and beasts are at this time moving about, let it please thee to permit us to set out one day for a pleasure-trip in these plains.

Jacob.—My dear sons, I have with pleasure given you leave to walk out when and where you like. Go and amuse yourselves in some of the orchards or gardens in the country, and refresh your nostrils with the scent of the hyacinth and the rose.

Judah.—May I be a sacrifice for thee, O chief of this our family! May the soul of all thy children be an offering for thy dear name! Allow Joseph also to go out with his brothers into the fields and amuse himself with the wild rose, that his mind may be relieved from dulness, and enjoy the brightness of the scene.

Jacob.—Oh, I adjure you not to talk to me on this subject any more, for Joseph shall not be separated from me even for an hour. Do not call him Joseph, term him rather the nourishment of my being; he is not Joseph, but my very soul and body.

Judah.—O father! we adjure thee, by the Lord, the sole Creator of all things, not to refuse us this request, nor to be so very concerned about Joseph as to mistrust us, for he is our brother, and dear to us as the souls in our bodies. Consider, how is it possible for us without the rose of his sweet face to look at blossoms and flowers?

Or how can we go without him into the field to amuse ourselves?

Jacob.—Although all of you are dear to me as my inmost soul, yet you should know that I love Joseph best. I would rather suffer my breath to depart from my body than allow Joseph to go from my sight.

Judah.—Do not trouble thyself as to his inability to walk far, nor be thus sighing and groaning to show thy anxiety for him. We shall carry him like a cup, from hand to hand, or like a great bottle, from shoulder to shoulder. Since he is so dearly loved by thee, we will all try as slaves to serve him.

Jacob.—I dread lest some one should molest him, or maliciously shed his blood. The intention is cruel. You had better abandon this your request, and make no mention of the subject any more.

Judah.—Benjamin, thou light of our two eyes, go thou this very minute to Joseph our dear brother himself, and tell him beseechingly that we must now start hunting, and we fervently desire him to accompany us in this excursion. We hope, dear Benjamin, thou mayest be able to persuade him to come with us.

Benjamin (to Joseph).—Darling brother, seeing that it is the time of cheerfulness, the season of sport and amusement, all old leaves having fallen off from the trees, and the whole land being beautifully decorated with verdure and flowers, we request thee to walk out with us, for the air everywhere is pregnant with sweet odours, and the birds are singing their lovely notes. We all are prepared to set out to visit for a while a certain garden; but where thou likest best to be, there we must seek our pleasure.

Joseph.—I fear you will separate me from my father, and this being done, will begin to ill-treat me and ill-use me. I dread lest you should make me acquainted with grief, pain, and trouble, as soon as you have removed me from my dear father's presence. I therefore beg you to forbear asking me to go with you; for why should you become the occasion of my destined fate?

Benjamin.—Arise, O unique of the age, and have not the least suspicion, for how can we be so cruel as to seek our own brother's hurt. Oh! may it never happen that we should live without thee. Never believe we can derive any pleasure from this our trip unless thou be with us. Up, let us be going out to some field, and then see what love and affection we will show thee.

Joseph.—Dear brother, thou brightness of my tearful eyes, may my soul be a ransom for thee! I will just accompany thee whithersoever thou goest, let happen what may.

Benjamin (to Jacob).—Know, O father, that Joseph has assented to accompany us in our excursion; be thou also so kind as to give him leave, and oblige thereby thy humble servants.

Jacob (to Benjamin).—May I be a ransom for thee, O thou light of my eyes, joy of my heart, and peace of my disquieted soul! I cannot feel sure that if Joseph go with thee he will return free from injury, hurt, or damage. I fear, if I send him out with his brothers, some plot or stratagem will be laid against him by cruel fate, and in this way I shall lose sight of my dear son for ever and ever.

Judah.—Fear not, dear father, my dear brother Joseph is esteemed by me as equal to my own soul. I shall take great care of him, and keep him like the apple of mine eye. Go home, beloved father, and rest assured.

Jacob.—Oh, may my soul be a ransom for thy beautiful face, O my poor sorrowful Joseph! Wait a minute, that I may prepare thee some food, O thou moon-faced* youth! Take these loaves of bread and this jug of water with thee, lest thou faint on the way from hunger and thirst.

Judah.—We will carefully bring him home to-night, and deliver him safe into thy hands. As for his food, we have provided everything for him to make matters pleasant.

---

* To have a round face, like a moon, is considered in Persia the highest type of beauty.

Jacob.—I submit to the decrees of my beneficent Lord, though my heart is adverse to this deed. Be it easy or hard, I must not deviate from the path of my duty as a servant.

Judah.—Be not at all anxious about Joseph, kind father, we shall carry him on our shoulders, as it were our souls in our bosoms. Should a jasmin leaf touch the sole of his delicate foot against his will, we shall root up all the jasmin plants from the meadow.

Jacob (to Joseph).—Oh, my poor oppressed Joseph, may my soul be a ransom for thee! come, let me caress thee as a token of my best love to thee! Oh, how can I permit thee to go from my presence, thou light of my eyes? or allow thee to journey with thy brethren? Tell me what to do after thou art gone, or how to bear the grievous burden of separation from thee; I would rend to pieces the garment of patience.

Joseph.—Do not be so sad, dear father, I shall soon return to thee. How can I leave thee all alone? If I be removed from thy dear presence but for one night, I doubt if I should live to see the succeeding morning.

Jacob (to Judah).—Come, Judah, take from me this packet of bread, take also this vase of milk, and this skin of fresh water. Whenever my dear Joseph gets thirsty, instead of water give him milk sweetened with sugar. Thou must take care he shall never suffer thirst when fatigued on the road; for the very hearing of such a thing is enough to make me yield up the ghost.

Joseph (to Jacob).—Come, father, let me respectfully kiss thy sacred feet; forgive me my faults, O lord of my bosom. Take care not to weep for the absence of thy son, nor ever beat thy head and breast. Dost thou not know that Husain's beloved son, 'Alí Akbar,* shall be separated from his father

---

* 'Alí Akbar, the son of Husain the Martyr, was slain, A.D. 680, on the plain of Karbalá, a town in Turkish Arabia (N. lat. 32° 32′, E. long. 44° 5′), and one of the sacred cities in the East.

with wailing, lamentation, and weeping, to go to the field of battle and fight with the inhabitants of Kúfah,* where by means of spears and arrows his body shall be cut to pieces, and he shall fall on the ground rolling in his own blood? In spite of all this, his father will neither weep or cause his voice to be heard, nor ever complain to God for such a great loss. Why, then, shouldst thou mourn and groan, or weep and lament, because I am going to some rose-garden to amuse myself, dear father?

Jacob.—Oh, what shall I do? I am unable to bear thy separation; thy absence is very grievous to me to contemplate. Behold how my back is bent from the weight of this burden! Oh, how can I live without thee? Although thy departure will make me miserable, still go thou in peace; but remember, thou art ever in my memory.

---

* Kúfah is situate about twenty-five miles south of the ruins of Babylon, in the pashalik of Baghdád, lat. 32° 5′ north, long. 44° 30′ east. Though now a decayed place, it was formerly a "hot-bed of Muhammadan bigotry, the favourite home of Koran readers, doctors of the law, disputants, and talkers of all kinds. The interpretation of the Koran, the rights of succession to the Imamate, all the multitudinous and bewildering refinements of Muhammadan theology, are in great measure due to the endless controversies of which Koufa was the theatre. The people breathed an atmosphere charged with religious fanaticism. Fierce gusts of theological controversy drove them this way and that, like a shifting gale which carries before it the sands of a desert. Eager, fierce, and impetuous, the people of Koufa were utterly wanting in perseverance and steadiness. They knew not their own minds from day to day. One moment ardent as fire for some cause or person, the next they were as cold as ice and indifferent as the dead. The fiercest conflicts that shook the Muhammadan world during these, the earliest, years of its history raged round Koufa. The annals of that city are a series of narratives of causes taken up without calculation of consequences, and abandoned with the same thoughtless precipitation; of aspirants after power lured on by specious promises, and then basely abandoned to their doom; of the people themselves rushing madly into excesses to be savagely slaughtered back into a state of quiescence."— Osborn's "Islam under the Arabs," chap. iv. p. 121, ed. 1876.

Joseph.—God be with thee, father; I am now going. It is the beginning of separation; father, adieu!

Jacob.—May I be a sacrifice for thy good feelings! Joseph, thou beloved of the Lord, do not make pomegranate tears flow down my cheeks. Come back and sit by me a little longer; talk not of separation for a while, but be still.

Joseph.—Thy lost Joseph will come back to Canaan; be not grieved, the house of mourning will be turned one day into a pleasure-garden; be not sad! Have patience, dear father, night and day after my separation or departure; thou shalt at last rejoice in my company and smile; be not distressed!

Dinah (Joseph's sister).—How is it I do not behold Joseph? Is it because he is not here? Wherever I look I see no sign of my brother. Oh, may the soul of thy sister be a ransom for thee! Where art thou, my poor, dear brother? come and see how I pour down tears for thee!

Joseph.—I am here, my distressed, impatient sister. Come, thou solace of my ardent soul! Come, let me look at thee, my luminous sun, for I am afraid I shall not be able to see thy face any more.

Dinah.—Wait for some minutes, dear brother, that I may see thy sweet face, which shines like a bright moon. Do not go until I be satiated with the sight of thy lovely cheeks, and gather a few roses from this beautiful rose-garden.

Joseph (to Dinah).—Come, sister, it is time to bid adieu! Heaven seems to have been maliciously set against us. Separation is undermining the foundation of our lives. May God protect us!

Dinah (to Joseph).—I do not feel easy at heart that thou shouldst go away with thy brethren, and that thou shouldst march towards the plain like a walking cypress tree.* I forbode some evil in this thy journey, thy path

---

* The Persians are very fond of comparing any one they esteem to a cypress tree, an ideal type of beauty.

to the rose-garden appears to me to be spread with thorns.

Joseph.—Why shouldst thou entertain any fears about my departure, sister? and why shouldst thou attempt to prevent me from such a pleasant journey? Are not my brothers kind to me in the extreme? There is no occasion at all for any suspicion or doubt. Do they intend to take me out to hurt or ill-treat me? God forbid! Such cruelty will never be perpetrated by my good brothers.

Joseph's sister.—May I be a ransom for thee! The reason of my anxiety and fear about thy going is, that I have distinctly seen in a dream that some ravenous wolves fell upon thee, and tore thee to pieces. It is this dream that has inspired doubts concerning thee, and now compels me to deter thee from thy present journey.

Joseph.—Be not anxious about me, my comely sister, the Creator of spirits and men keeps all from danger. But thou must be kind enough not to forget me before God, for intercession is necessary for those under trials. Pray, therefore, that the Almighty make thee not brotherless, nor suffer ashes to be scattered on thy head at any time.*

Dinah.—O Lord God! I adjure Thee by my father, who is Thy prophet; by that great messenger of Thine, whose name is Muhammad, the Arabian; by the blood of the throat of 'Alí Akbar, poor Husain's youth; and by the merit of 'Alí Asghar's† life-stream shed lamentably; bring back my dear Joseph from this his journey, and let Thy humble maiden see him again.

Joseph.—O gracious and beneficent Lord! let me find grace in the sight of my brethren; small and great, let them show me tokens of love and affection, that I may come back with cheerfulness to see again my dear father's face.

---

* An Eastern mode of evincing grief and distress.

† A son of Husain; together with his father and brothers he was murdered at Karbalá in A.D. 680.

Joseph's sister.—O beloved brother! thou hast at last gone from my side; grief for thee has gathered the dust of the world, and cast it on my head. May I die for thee; have pity on my tearful eyes.

Joseph.—Adieu, my moon-faced sister, adieu! thou light of my tearful eyes. I am going from thy presence with a bleeding heart, with an anguished soul, and moist eyes!

Joseph's sister.—Separation, O light of my eyes, separation! Alas! O strength of my soul, alas! thou art gone, leaving me alone to suffer grief. O my bright moon! Alas! separation.

Judah (addressing Joseph).—Come on my shoulders, thou light of both mine eyes, thou joy of my heart, and beloved of the father! Let us go to the field with a cheerful heart, let us for a while forget the sorrows of this world.

Simeon (to Joseph).—Go on, O sweet-looking child, walk on before me that I may see what thou doest. Stay nowhere on the road, but make speed, for thou art indeed the beloved of thy father.

Reuben (to Judah).—Cast down Joseph from thy shoulders. Let his soul be taken out from his body. Let me give some good blows on the head of this beloved of our father. Let his soul taste the violence of my fury before we proceed further.

Joseph.—Are you so tired of me as to treat me as your enemy? What has made you forget your love to me, so that you talk of nothing else but hatred and enmity? Why are you striking my moon-like face? And with all your pretended affection, why experience I nothing on your part but spite and malice?

Simeon.—Know well that we all are seeking thy life to destroy it. We are thinking how to put an end to thy prating. We mean to shed thy blood on the ground, and to fell this thy delicate cypress-like stature.

Reuben.—I intend to take away the soul from thy body, and to consign thy elegant frame afterwards to the earth. I am thinking what to do, that thou mayest never see thy father's face again, but mayest carry his desire with thee to the grave.

Joseph.—Oh, why do you not pity my diminutive frame? What necessity is there at this time to put me in bonds? O dear brothers, my heart is burning within me through thirst! Oh! I am quite undone for want of a little water to drink. Give me, for God's sake, a drop of liquid, for my soul is consumed through the heat.

Judah.—Thou shalt see no water except the tears of thy eyes. Thou shalt behold no liquid save the blood of thy heart. If all the surface of this land be covered with fresh springs, we shall not let a drop pass down thy throat.

Reuben.—Do not think of water, thou good-principled boy, for in this land none shall give thee to drink. In this desert thou mayest quaff water from the edges of the swords. Now I shall cut thy body to pieces with my scymetar.

Joseph.—Am I not thy brother, thou treacherous wretch? I am a poor oppressed soul, a helpless little child. Behold how thirst is killing me; why should I die parched? Nay, dear brother, bethink thee about some water for me, and thereby prove thy fraternal affection.

Simeon.—Never imagine that thou shalt see water again. Thou mayest see limpid streams in thy dreams if thou choosest. Order the sun that worshipped thee to bring thee a draught, or let the bright moon fetch thee liquid from the sky. Command the brilliant stars to fill their cups with dew, and hasten to slake thy thirst. Wash thy hands of life, and prepare thyself for death. Think how thou must receive the strokes of swords and daggers before thou givest up the ghost.

Joseph (addressing Reuben).—O Lord, who has ever seen a family acting thus towards their own brother? See the injury and the cruelty they do to this poor child! May I be sacrificed for thee, dear brother, thou being the eldest, and therefore a father to all, especially to me. I beg thee to give me some water to drink, for I am like a fish in agonies of thirst rolling on the surface of a dry hot ground.

Simeon (spilling the water).—Oh, I am abashed before thee now; may I be a sacrifice for thee and thy pretty face! Although thirst has quite undone thee, I advise thee to have patience in all things, for it is not lawful at this time to give thee water. Thou mayest instead take poison; that is better!

Joseph.—O God! my soul is going to perish from thirst, and they inconsiderately spill the water on the ground. I am thirsty, hungry, and weeping; pity my miserable condition, O Lord God of all creatures! May I be a ransom for thee, O Husain, thou thirsty-lipped * king, for, alas! when parched thou shalt be slain by the edge of a sharp dagger. My own brethren being so cruel to me, and oppressing me in such a manner, I wonder what will the inhabitants of Kúfah, being altogether strangers, do to thee, O my Lord, in that burning land of Karbalá! How great must be thy sufferings from thirst at that hottest part of the year.

Simeon.—O despairing creature! bewail no longer, nor make any ado, for thou shalt never see cold water again. Strip thy feet at once, and walk barefoot in this plain.

Joseph.—Where art thou, O my kind father? Come and save me, for I am helpless among my brethren. Come and see the boils on my feet, father! Behold my sad condition!

Simeon.—Do not cry, and make so much noise. I will at once cut thy throat in the most cruel way possible. Get me a rope and a sharp knife, that I may put an end to this boy's screams by cutting his throat forthwith.

---

* So called because, at the moment he was transfixed with an arrow on the plain of Karbalá, he was hastening towards the Euphrates to drink.

Joseph.—O brother Judah, come, let me kiss thy hands. O Reuben, may I be a ransom for thee! let me kiss thy feet.

Judah.—It is not advisable for us to kill our brother. Have patience with him, and torment him not. For my soul's sake cease troubling him. You may cast him in this pit if you like.

Simeon.—Be stripped of thy garments, for we will contrive to cast thee in this well, poor thing! (*Addressing his brethren.*) Cast Joseph into this pit, and throw a stone also on his well-shaped head. Thanks be unto God, we are now at ease in our minds. We can all return to our father with cheerful hearts.

Jacob (mourning).—O God! my Joseph is gone and not come back. What must have happened to my dear son Joseph? How I long to see his face, and kiss his hair another time.

Joseph (in the well).—O father! behold my wretched state; see how miserable I am. O Zephyr! go to sorrowful Jacob, and tell him Joseph his son is put into a pit.

Gabriel.*—O heavenly moon! why shouldst thou be in a well? O reviver of the soul! who has put [thee in this place? Lift up thine head (may I be a ransom for thy bright moon-like face!), and talk to me (may I be a sacrifice for thy beautiful head!).

Joseph.—Where wast thou, father? May my soul be a ransom for thee! Come, come, let me be a sacrifice for thy faithfulness. Thou dost not know what has happened to me; how my brothers have cruelly treated me.

Gabriel (to Joseph).—Be not sorry; I am an angel of

---

* Gabriel, called by the Persians "the Angel of Revelations," was, according to tradition, frequently sent from heaven on errands of this kind. "The existence of angels and their purity," says Sale, "are absolutely required to be believed in the Korán. . . . . They hold that some of them are employed in writing down the actions of men, others in carrying the throne of God and other services."—Koran, Prel. Disc., sec. iv. p. 71, ed. 1734.

the great Lord, sent to thee by Him to comfort thee. I am ordered to be day and night with thee to strengthen thy mind, and to console thee for thy past sufferings.

Jacob.—Night has arrived, and my Joseph has not returned. Oh, I do not know what has become of my darling son! If it be evening, why do not I see my moon? Why should my full moon be among valleys and mountains up to this time?

Judah.—Dearly beloved brethren, let us arise and go to our father, carrying with us Joseph's coat dipped in blood, and tell that chosen of the Lord, our parent, lamentingly, that a ravenous wolf, or some other wild beast, must have devoured Joseph, and say, "the upper flower of thy basket has withered."

Joseph's sister (to Jacob).—May I be a ransom for thee, dear father, the brethren are coming, but I see no Joseph with them!

The brethren of Joseph.—O dear brother! O our beloved brother! brother! how didst thou roll in blood and dust, poor thing!

Jacob.—What has happened to you that you are crying so sadly? Where is my Joseph, who is not with his brethren? What has separated Joseph from you? or why is he hidden from my view?

Simeon.—O father! do not ask us about our dear Joseph, for that blessed of the Lord was devoured by a wolf. Here is his coat, take it and kiss it, for thou wilt not smell the perfume of Joseph save from his coat.

Jacob.—May thy father be a sacrifice for thy coat, my son! May he bleed at heart in sorrow for thee, my son! O Lord God, although I know that no wolf has eaten my Joseph, still I am extremely moved at the sight of his foully stained coat. I wonder what will be the feelings of Fátimah,* the mother of Husain, when she sees her son's

---

* Fátimah was the daughter of the Prophet Muhammad, the wife of 'Alí, and the mother of Hasan and Husain the martyrs.

blood-stained torn coat or shirt after he shall have been put to death in a most cruel manner? O Lord God! for the merit of the blood of Husain's son, 'Alí Akbar, for the righteousness of his own brother 'Abbás,* enable me to see my Joseph another time, and let not my anguished heart be scarred by perpetual separation from him.

Gabriel (to Jacob).—Peace be unto thee, thou wise prophet; the incomparable God, sending thee salutation, says: "What thinkest thou, O afflicted one? Is thy Joseph more precious than Muhammad's dear grandson, before whose eyes all his companions were first slain, and his own body being riddled by arrows, he was afterwards most cruelly put to death, and his corpse thrown on the ground?"

Jacob.—Oh, may a thousand ones like me and my Joseph be a ransom for Husain! May a thousand Josephs be the dust of his feet! May the curse of God rest on Yazíd † and his party, who cruelly murdered that Imám. Come, O Gabriel! show me the plain of Karbalá, for God's sake!

Gabriel.—O Jacob, may Gabriel be a ransom for thee! May I perish for thy name, thou manifest messenger of God! Come and peep through my finger. Behold thence the land of Karbalá.

Jacob.—Declare unto me, O messenger of the glorious

---

* 'Abbás, the brother of Husain, was slain at Karbalá, A.D. 680.

† Khalíf, A.D. 679. His animosity against Husain and his family was most uncompromising, and he used every endeavour to exterminate the whole race. The name of him or any of his descendants is never repeated "without an attestation of scorn and execration."—Price's "Chronological Retrospect of Mahommedan History," vol. i. p. 419, ed. 1811.

"The Shafei school allows its disciples to curse El Yezid, the son of Muawiyah, whose cruelties to the descendants of the Prophet, and crimes and vices, have made him the Judas Iscariot of El Islam. I have heard Hanafi Moslems, especially Sayyids, revile him; but this is not, strictly speaking, correct. The Shiahs, of course, place no limits to their abuse of him. You first call a man 'Omar,' then 'Shimr' (the slayer of El Husayn), and, lastly, 'Yezid,' beyond which insult does not extend."—Burton's "El Medinah and Meccah," vol. ii. p. 37, ed. 1857.

Lord, part of the sad transaction of Karbalá, for thy speech has greatly grieved me; it has rendered my eyes like the river Jaihún.*

Gabriel.—Alas! the tyranny of the cruel spheres! who can hear the sad things done in Karbalá! Injustice and oppression, hatred and enmity, shall attain to their perfection in that plain of trial as regards the descendants of God's Prophet. One shall hear no cry from that holy family but for bread and water. Their sad voices shall reach the very throne of the Majesty on high. Their tears shall saturate all that field of battle. The children of that king of religion shall subsist on the tears alone of their own eyes.

---

* Oxus.

SCENE II.

DEATH OF IBRAHIM THE SON OF MUHAMMAD.

IBRAHIM was the son of Muhammad by Máriyah, a Coptic girl sent as a present to the Prophet by the Governor of Alexandria. His father was much attached to the child, and "with his own hand piled earth upon the grave and sprinkled it with water—a ceremony then first performed—disposed small stones upon it, and pronounced the final salutation." (Burton's "El Medinah and Meccah," chap. xxii. vol. ii. p. 38, ed. 1857.) The infant's death, which occurred about A.D. 631, is thus pathetically described by Sir William Muir:—
"When aged but fifteen or sixteen months, Ibrahím fell sick, and it was soon apparent that he would not survive. The child lay in a palm-grove near the house of his nurse. There his mother Mary, with her sister Shirín, tended his dying-bed. And there, too, was Mahomet in deep and bitter grief. Seeing that the child was soon to breathe his last, he took him up in his arms and sobbed aloud. The bystanders tried to comfort him. They reminded him of his exhortations to others that they should not wail. 'Nay,' said Mahomet, calming himself by an effort as he hung over the expiring infant, ' it is not this that I forbade, but loud wailing and false laudation of the dead. This that ye see in me is but the working of pity in the heart: he that showeth no pity, unto him shall no pity be shown. We grieve for the child, the eye runneth down with tears, and the heart swelleth inwardly; yet we say not aught that would offend our Lord. Ibrahím, O Ibrahím! if it were not that the promise is faithful, and the hope of resurrection sure,—if it were not that this is the way to be trodden by all, and the last of us shall join the first, I would grieve for thee with a grief deeper even than this.' But the spirit had already passed away, and the last fond words of Mahomet fell on ears that could no longer hear them. So he laid down the infant's body, saying; 'The remainder of the days of his nursing shall be fulfilled in Paradise.' "—Muir's "Life of Mahomet," vol. iv. p. 164, ed. 1861.

The Prophet (speaking of God's Providence).—O Lord, Thou art the cherisher of all. Thou exaltest one, putting him in affluent circumstances like Korah,* and reducest another to the lowest degree [of poverty, mingling his food with blood and ashes. ' Thou raisest up one, and givest him the throne of the kingdom, and sendest down another to the deep to be food for the fish of the sea. Thou art the sole Creator of good and evil. Grant, O Lord, to Thy peculiar people the blessings of eternity.

Husain (the Prophet's grandson).—Peace be unto thee, O Messenger of God. Peace be unto thee, O my grandfather the chosen. May my heart and soul be offered as a ransom unto thee, and may both of them have the honour to be trampled under thy feet! The army of sleep, Sir, has sore attacked me, so that no part of my body and soul is left unconquered. Be mindful of me, who am altogether weary, quite overcome by drowsiness, without any apparent cause.

The Prophet.—O thou, the brightness of my penetrating eyes, my highly valued and beloved child! Thy dreams are better to me than the waking imaginations of my many companions; better sleep on in the sacred lap of thy beloved grandfather. We are one another's soul and body. We are each other's reputation and glory. He who strives with thee, or advances toward thee with cruel intentions, is not contending with thee, but with me; he does not spill thy blood, but mine. If any one lift up his sword against

---

* Korah, or Kárún, is alluded to in the Kur'án as being possessed of much wealth. "For we had given him such treasure that its keys would have burdened a company of men of strength." . . . "And Korah went forth to his people in his pomp. Those who were greedy for this present life said, 'Oh that we had the like of that which hath been bestowed on Korah! Truly he is possessed of great good fortune.'"—Rodwell's Koran, Súra xxviii., lines 76 and 79, p. 312, ed. 1861.

thee, or touch thy dear neck with his poignard, he unsheathes his weapon against me, he cuts my throat with a dagger.

Ibráhím (the Prophet's son).—Peace be on thee, thou chief elect of God! peace be on thee, O my reverenced father! O Messenger of God, the gracious Lord of all, may the soul of Ibráhím be offered a ransom for thee! I do not say I am the light of thine eyes; enough if I be the dust of thy feet, and of those of Husain. Receive me as him in thy sacred lap. Let an insignificant atom be attracted by a glorious sun.*

The Prophet.—On thee be peace, O my love! On thee be peace, O my dear child! Be gentle in thy conversation, for Husain is sleeping in my lap. Raise not thy voice when speaking to me. I fear my dear Husain should awake.

Ibráhím.—With all my heart, O highly exalted one, I will, as much as possible, be gentle in my conversation. Dear father, last night when I slept I dreamed a most wonderful dream. I saw that Máriyah, my mother, appeared to me with her usual love and tenderness, and said to me, " O Ibráhím, most respectfully bid adieu to thy father, for to-morrow evening thou shalt be with me in Paradise." What is the interpretation of my dream, O father? Be so kind as to declare it to me.

The Prophet.—O beloved of the father! thou needest not be troubled in thy mind for what thou hast seen in thy dreams. Be not sorry for having lost a mother, since thou hast the kind protection of an affectionate father. Place thy feet gently on the ground, my child, that the faithful spirit (Gabriel) may not be disturbed.

Gabriel† (*addressing the Prophet*).—O chief of the

---

* Though in this scene Ibráhím is made to carry on a conversation with the Prophet, yet he is generally supposed to have died when only about fifteen or sixteen months old.

† See note, p. 15.

virtuous, peace be on thee! O lord of the elect, peace be on thee! Of these two bouquets of thy flower-beds, yea, of these two nightingales of thy rose-garden, be pleased to tell me which one is dearer to thee? though both of them are thy flesh and thy bones.

The Prophet.—O faithful Gabriel, on thee be peace! O bearer of the manifest truth, blessings be thine! Thou askest me, O trustee of the merciful Lord, whether Husain is dearer to me, or Ibráhím. I speak the truth, I cannot see the difference. Please tell me the reason why thou makest this inquiry?

Gabriel.—The reason of this inquiry, O asylum of the world, is as follows:—thus saith the Lord—"Since We have found in thy heart too much love and affection for Husain and Ibráhím, and seeing it is not proper there should be two loves in one heart, for no end is obtained thereby, it seemeth therefore good in Our sight to share with thee thy burdens, and divide Husain and Ibráhím between thee and Us. Take, therefore, which one of the two thou likest for thyself, and deliver the other unto Us."

The Prophet.—O brother! since such is the will of the merciful Lord, I yield most submissively to His orders. But I am greatly perplexed as to my choice between these two dear ones. For if I suffer Husain to depart, I fear Zahrah,* my daughter, will be overwhelmed with grief for her darling. Granting I allow her to be thus sorry, what shall I do with 'Alí, the child's father, and Hasan, its brother? For I cannot see 'Alí distressed on account of his son. Wherefore, if it please the living and eternal God, I shall choose that Ibráhím be sacrificed in preference to Husain.

---

* An epithet applied to Fátimah, the daughter of Muhammad; it is rendered by Burckhardt "bright, blooming Fátimah."—Burton's "El Medinah and Meccah," chap. xvi. vol. i. p. 315, ed. 1857.

Gabriel.—Because thou hast chosen, O Messenger of the Gracious God, that Ibráhím should be a ransom for Husain, consider the sinful state of thy poor people, and make the latter a propitiation for their sins, that the Lord of all beings may, in the Day of Judgment, have mercy on all of them for Husain's sake.

The Prophet.—Alas, O Gabriel! for the misery of my people. Alas! for the tears they will have to shed in that day. Though Husain is my wisest child, being a light to my eyes, and most dearly loved, still, God knows that my beloved people, being my true family, my poor broken-winged birds, ought to be more pitied. I will, therefore, in order to save my people from the wrath to come, make Husain a propitiation for their sins.

Gabriel.—Well done, well done, for this generosity. Bravo! bravo! for such magnanimity, since thou makest Husain a man of sorrow, and acquainted with grief, on behalf of thy people, no doubt God will forgive all of them in that day, for the Imám's meritorious blood's sake.

The Prophet.—O how admirable is Husain! how great is his merit! Blessed is he who mourns for Husain, and happy he who weeps for him!

'Izráíl* (*saluting the Prophet*).—O judge of both terrestrial and heavenly affairs, peace be on thee! O

---

* The tradition respecting 'Izráíl is as follows:—When the Almighty was about to create Adam it is said that "the angels Gabriel, Michael, and Israfil were sent by God one after another, to fetch for that purpose seven handfuls of earth from different depths and of different colours (whence some account for the various complexions of mankind); but the earth, being apprehensive of the consequence, and desiring them to represent her fear to God, that the creature He designed to form would rebel against Him, and draw down His curse upon her, they returned without performing God's command; whereupon He sent Azráíl on the same errand, who executed His commission without remorse, for which reason God appointed that angel to separate the soul from the bodies, being therefore called '*the angel of death.*'"—Sale's "Koran," chap. ii. p. 4, ed. 1734.

lord of men and jinns,* peace be on thee! I am thy servant, nay, thy most humble and despicable slave, 'Izráíl. I am sent by the gracious God unto thee to perform thy orders.

The Prophet.—O messenger of the Lord of the Universe, on thee be peace! O ravisher of the souls of men and jinns, on thee be peace! Let the Lord's order be performed, and His will be done as concerns me, who am encompassed about with His grace on every side. Being the submissive servant of the Gracious One, my duty is but to fulfil His will. But I beg that the child should be respited until to-morrow, that I may enjoy his presence one day more, before I lose sight of him for ever.

'Izráíl.—Oh, what grace! Oh, what goodness! I willingly comply with this thy request, Sir. How could I dare to take any creature's son without thy permission?

Ibráhím (in school reading the Kur'án).—"I fly unto God for refuge from Satan the reprobate. In the name of God, the gracious, the merciful, O thou soul which art at rest, return unto thy Lord well pleased, and well pleasing; enter among my servants, and enjoy my paradise."

The Prophet.—How pleasant it is to listen to the Kur'án from thee, O thou loveliest child! to look on thy beautiful face, and hear from thy mouth the word of the living God!

Ibráhím.—"O Prophet, verily we have sent thee to be a witness, a bearer of good tidings, a denouncer of threats, an inviter unto God (through His permission), and a

---

"* Besides angels and devils the *Mohammedans* are taught by the *Korán* to believe an intermediate order of creatures, which they call *Jin* or *Genii*, created also of fire, but of a grosser fabric than angels, since they eat and drink . . . and are subject to death. Some of these are supposed to be good and others bad, and capable of future salvation or damnation as men are, whence *Mohammed* pretended to be sent for the conversion of *Genii* as well as men."—Sale's "Koran," Prel. Dis. sec. iv. p. 72, ed. 1734.

shining light. Bear glad news, therefore, unto the true believers, that they shall receive great abundance from God."

The Prophet.—Oh how delightful is thy voice, child, when you read the Kur'án! and how handsomely does thy face shine!

Ibráhím.—Alas! alas! whence that voice? Methinks it was the voice of the Messenger of God. O thou by whose message the earth is turned into heaven, and by the light of whose direction minds are enlightened! wherefore hast thou put thy head against the wall, and weepest so sadly, O thou illustrious Messenger?

The Prophet.—O dearly beloved son, know that a certain visitor asks for thee. Go to thy master, and request his permission to come home without delay.

Ibráhím.—Master, my father, the universal Apostle of God, giving thee his greeting, asks thee to send me home, intending to despatch me on a journey. It is a journey whence, most probably, I shall not return. Wherefore I beg thy pardon for my past faults and neglected duties.

The Schoolmaster.—O Ibráhím, thou light of virtue, and the shining candle of piety, it is not mid-day, nor is it time for going home. Tell me why thou askest leave in this way, and at such an improper time?

Ibráhím.—My father did not tell me why he called me away from school. He only said I had to prepare myself for a journey. But as I saw the Apostle of God weeping, and much agitated in mind, I am led to suppose that the journey is one after which none shall hear anything concerning me.

The Schoolmaster.—Thy saying is kindling a fire in my body such as to burn the very marrow of my bones. If death, God forbid, should succeed in separating thee from me, my school will be ruined together with myself.

Ibráhím.—O my school-fellows, alas! we are to be

separated. But how unbearable such trials are. Dear companions! I beg you to remember me while you read the Holy Book of God together. Alas! my comrades, death may take me away, ere you see my nuptials with delight. (*Turning to the Prophet.*) O father, the asylum of God's creatures, say what is thy order. Please let me know why thou art so sad, and walkest before me, while I follow thee? (*Frightened by the sight of the Angel of Death.*) Ah! father, rest is at once removed from me; my heart begins to palpitate. Oh! who is that strange, dreadful being opposite to me? How awful his sight! how frightful his looks! Father! father! shelter me from him.

The Prophet.—Have patience, O thou brightness of mine eyes, and fear not this venerable person at all. He is the companion of thy way, my child. He will accompany thee on this thy journey.

Ibráhím.—The frightful sight of this companion has made my heart throb within my breast. Father, my hand is shivering, my lips are quivering, my legs are tottering, and my whole body is ready to fall! Whither shall I flee, who am a motherless child? The time of my departure draws near. Where is my sister to sympathise with me? Oh, where shall I hide myself from this dreadful being's presence? Pity me, pity me, O my friends!

The Prophet.—Let not thy heart be troubled, my dear child. Thy companion will be very kind to thee on the way. He is more compassionate to thee than thy father, more affectionate than thy mother. He sympathises with thee in all thy sorrows.

Ibráhím.—Dear father! the bright world is turned into the utmost darkness to me; I see death with my own eyes. The day of life is changed into black night. Fear and grief have brought fever on me. Alas! I have no mother on whose knees I can lay my head, to comb my hair with caressing love, and shed for me tears of affection. Let my sister Fátimah come and mourn for me, and dress me for the grave.*

Fátimah, the daughter of Muhammad, comes to visit her brother Ibráhím.—O Lord God! I am much grieved at heart, I can no longer bear myself. For three days my heart has been bursting within me. I long to see the pretty face of my dear brother Ibráhím. Oh! let me go and look at the light of thy bleeding eyes, ere my precious gem lose its natural brightness. Dearly beloved brother, why art thou thus rolling in the dust, and groaning with pain?

Ibráhím.—Welcome! welcome! dear sympathising sister. May ill be far from thee! I suffer grievously from a burning fever!

Fátimah.—What has rendered thy pretty face so pale?

Ibráhím.—Oh! feel not my pulse, dear worthy sister.

Fátimah.—Why should I not, seeing my joy is turned into sorrow?

Ibráhím.—I fear, dear sister, lest the fire of my fever burn thee.

Fátimah.—Tell me, dear brother, what are the things thou mostly desirest?

Ibráhím.—Three things chiefly do I desire, kind sister.

Fátimah.—What may they be, O crown of my head?

Ibráhím.—First (alas! it cannot be), I wish to see my mother.

Fátimah.—Why do you wish to see thy mother, matchless youth?

Ibráhím.—That she should hold my head in her bosom for awhile.

Fátimah.—What is the second request, brother? Tell me.

---

* Dressing a corpse for the grave is an invariable ceremony, immediately on the death of a Muhammadan.

Ibráhím.—That thou shouldest close mine eyes when I die.

Fátimah.—And the third, O apple of my eye?

Ibráhím.—That thou shouldest beg Husain to honour me with his presence.

Fátimah.—What dost thou expect him to do for thee?

Ibráhím.—That he should sit by my death-bed when I die.

Fátimah.—Hast thou any dread of death, my soul?

Ibráhím.—I rather fear the angel of death.

Fátimah.—Fear not, O pupil of mine eye!

Ibráhím.—For God's sake, bring me Husain quickly!

Fátimah.—Be pleased, O Husain, to come for a minute; and make haste, for my beloved brother Ibráhím wants thee.

Husain.—Yes, yes; I am coming to thee. What is thine object in calling me? May I request the pleasure of knowing it?

Ibráhím.—Oh! how pleasant is thy savour, O Husain! May I be offered a sacrifice for thee and thy throat! Thanks be to God! I am dying for thee. Nay, I am become as one of thy holy pilgrims. Though my sorrow is very great in being separated from thee, yet I comfort myself in this, that I suffer death for thy sake.

Husain.—Come, come; let me wipe off the tears from thy lovely face. Oh! how much it grieves me that thou leavest this world. But what can one do, since such is God's command? Who can resist His will?

Ibráhím.—How deep is thy compassion, O Husain! How great are thy love and humility! Thou art sad for me because I die in the prime of life. Thou needest not be so much grieved for me. Am I more in thy sight than 'Alí Akbar,* thy future son, who shall be deprived so cruelly of his youthful pleasures? May hundreds of youths like me be a ransom for 'Abbás,† thy young brave

---

* See note, p. 8.   † See note *, p. 17.

brother! The time of death draws near. Sit still, that I may cast my soul at thy feet. Behold! 'Izráíl, the angel of death, awaits me! Lay mercifully my head on thy sacred knees, O Husain.

Husain.—Lay thy head on my knees, dear Ibráhím. Be not overwhelmed with sorrow, for I am tending thee most affectionately.

'Izráíl, the angel of death (addressing the Prophet).—O heavenly-throned, but earthly habitationed king! O thou who art entitled by God "The bearer of good tidings and the denouncer of threats," since yesterday it pleased thy majesty to defer the matter till the morrow, behold! here am I, and here is the day.

The Prophet.—Thou art permitted to take the soul of my beloved son Ibráhím, but thou must do it in the gentlest way possible; he is a poor, helpless, broken-hearted, sick child. See how my eyes shed red tears at his departure.

'Izráíl.—O thou under whose protection angels of God seek their refuge, I swear by Him who has given thee this great authority, that, be it easy or be it hard, as thou commandest so I obey. But first of all let me know, O Messenger of the gracious Lord, who is that youth with Ibráhím.

The Prophet.—It is Husain, 'Alí's most beloved son, the ornament of the throne of the Majesty on high.

'Izráíl.—O Muhammad! there is a positive saying which I remember to have read in the preserved table of God's fore-knowledge, that "He who loves Husain and mourns for him, has passed from death to life." I am, therefore, ashamed, in Husain's own presence, to turn his joy into sorrow. How can I grieve for one whom the beneficent Creator Himself has ever wished joy and happiness? I beg thee, therefore, O Messenger of the glorious God, to send Husain away for a moment.

The Prophet.—Thus saith the Lord, thy Creator, unto thee, O Husain! depart from Ibráhím for awhile.

Ibráhím.—O Husain! O Husain! where art thou going? Why dost thou leave me alone? O Husain! be not far from me. Let mine eyes be enlightened by thy presence. For God's sake, O Husain! for the merit of my father, leave me not alone when I am dying.

The Prophet.—Dear child, let Husain go, and obey thou the positive ordinance of thy loving Lord.

Ibráhím.—No father, why should I be troubled so long? I shall never let Husain go. Let my body be as the earth of Husain's tomb; let my head be as the dust of his feet. O Husain! let me be offered as a ransom for thy handsome throat, which thy sister* is about to see cut with a dagger. Oh, that I were as one of the pilgrims who shall visit thy sacred sepulchre! one of those who shall offer themselves unto thee.

The Prophet.— Darling child, do not so cling to Husain.

Ibráhím.—Nay, father, let him be with me now.

The Prophet.—Why, O delight of my soul and spirit?

Ibráhím.—Because he is the physician of those that suffer pain.

The Prophet.—Why art thou so fearful, my dear child?

Ibráhím.—I am afraid, father, of the angel of death.

The Prophet.—There is no occasion to fear him so.

Ibráhím.—His looks, father, have turned my day into night.

The Prophet.—Have no dread of him, thou pupil of mine eye.

Ibráhím.—O Husain! make intercession with him for me.

Husain.—O 'Izráíl! though thou art sent by the glorious God to execute His Divine pleasure, yet I beg of thee

---

* Zainab, the sister of Husain, was present at his martyrdom in the plain of Karbalá.

the favour that thou wilt take this child's life as gently as possible.

'Izráíl.—Oh! weep not, weep not so much, Husain. May I be sacrificed for thee, O pupil of mine eye! Know this, that whenever any one is thy real friend, I will, at any rate, take his soul in a gentle mode. Especially when he observes the ceremonies of mourning, or weeps for thee. (*Turning to Ibráhím.*) Sit with thy face pointing to Makkah,* O poor sufferer!

Ibráhím.—Who art thou, O man? leave me to myself.

'Izráíl.—I am 'Izráíl, the angel of death, O little boy!

Ibráhím.—I beg thee to take my soul gently.

'Izráíl.—Cry not so much, O flower of the age!

Ibráhím.—Why, my veins and arteries are all cut into pieces.

'Izráíl.—Thy groanings have kindled a fire in my body.

Ibráhím.—Why should I not mourn? seeing I have no mother to alleviate my sorrows.

'Izráíl.—These are the pangs of death, child; dost thou not know it?

Ibráhím.—Woe unto me! Woe unto me! for it is bitterness.

'Izráíl.—Poor frail creature, weep not so much.

Ibráhím.—Pity me, young man. I am quite helpless.

'Izráíl.—O thou fragrant flower of the prophetical garden! in what state art thou? how farest thou? Now is the time to go to God, the Friend of all; take, then, this apple and smell it, and see how nice is the perfume.

Ibráhím (*giving up the ghost*).—Alas! O Lord God, what is this burning sensation I feel within myself? It has rendered my soul quite restless. I am altogether

---

* Muhammadans when about to die deem it right to turn their face towards Makkah, the sacred city of their prayers.

undone! Behold, I am going the way of all the earth, "I, therefore, bear witness, that there is no other god but God."*

---

* This phrase is usually put into the mouth of all Muhammadans when dying.

SCENE III.

THE DISOBEDIENT SON.

THIS Scene opens with a description of the various sects who will be consigned to everlasting perdition. The account of the persons who will inhabit the seven stories of which, according to the Muhammadans, the abode of torture is composed, differs in some respects from the generally received traditions on the subject; but the Muslims are by no means agreed amongst themselves as to the denizens of the infernal regions, and each sect has, to some extent, its own opinion in the matter.

The Prophet, finding that his own people are not exempt in all cases from the pains of future torment, retires to his chamber in a pensive mood, reflecting on the sins and punishment of his people. While thus sad in mind and distressed in soul, he hears a pitiful voice, which on inquiry turns out to be that of an unfortunate youth, who, in consequence of disobedience to his parents, has been consigned to perdition. Moved by compassion, Muhammad sends for the lad's mother, and intercedes on the boy's behalf. But she is inexorable. 'Alí, Fátimah, and Hasan are equally unsuccessful. Husain then joins his endeavours, and backed by an angel, who utters terrible denunciations against the woman in the event of her continuing obdurate, and refusing to listen to the petition of the Imám of the Lord, she at last relents, and her son is delivered from his torments. In gratitude he is proud to acknowledge himself as " a dog of Husain's threshold," and begs to be allowed to become " a sacrifice for the Imám's Shí'ahs."

The Prophet Muhammad.—O almighty and self-sufficient God, whose door of mercy is open to all, Thou art the Creator, and Thine is the worship of all creatures. Thou art the eternal King whose kingdom remains for ever; Thou art the Maker of day and night, who knowest all thoughts. Seeing thou art the Sole Doer of all things, grant, therefore, Paradise to those who believe in Thy saints.

Gabriel.—Thou of generous disposition, who art good in all thine actions, thou Prophet of all mankind, and intercessor for all nations, peace be unto thee! Oh! what attributes shall I ascribe to thee, thou universal Prophet? Thou art the most beloved of God, the best of all His creatures; thou art the cause of the creation of all possible things. Thou being the messenger general of the glorious God, I, Gabriel the archangel, am the humblest servant of thy supreme court.

The Prophet.—On thee be peace, O my brother Gabriel! Where hast thou been? O heavenly messenger of the glorious Lord! why has the colour of thy face gone? Why have thy handsome cheeks turned pale?

Gabriel.—Know, O Prophet of the beneficent God, that to-day I passed by the abode of the accursed. How shall I say what I felt when I looked at the flames? No eye is able to see it, no mind can conceive it. It consists of seven stories one above the other, each appropriated to a particular nation; and I am sent now to inform thee, O messenger of mankind in general, about each and every one of them.

The Prophet.—Alas! this thy speech has brought my soul to the tip of my lip; my heart has begun to palpitate within me at these thy words. What terrifying message is this thou hast brought me, which has made blood gush out of my eyes? Well; tell me after all, O happy Gabriel, whose abode shall the seventh story be—the lowest part of the dwelling of the lost?

Gabriel.—Know, O Prophet of God, that the seventh shall be the abode of the people of Moses,* or the Jews.

---

* The company in the mansions of the lost is somewhat differently given in Sale's Koran, Preliminary Discourse, sect. iv. p. 92; ed. 1734. Speaking of the apartments, he says:—" The first, which they call *Jehennam,* they say, will be the receptacle of those who acknowledged one God, that is the wicked *Mohammedans,* who, after having there been punished according to their demerits, will at length be released. The second, named *Ladhá,* they assign to the *Jews*; the third, named *Al*

The Prophet.—O faithful minister of God, the glorious Lord of all, tell me, whose abode is the sixth?

Gabriel.—The sixth, which bites the soul with its tortures, belongeth to the people of Shís,* poor things!

The Prophet.—O bearer of God's revelations, tell me, whose abode shall be the fifth?

Gabriel.—The fifth, O good Prophet, is an abode for the followers of Abraham.

The Prophet.—Whose is the fourth story, O brother Gabriel? Tell me, for God's sake.

Gabriel.—There is a prophet named Jirjís; † this part of the fire of the infernal regions belongeth to his people.

The Prophet.—Tell me, who shall have to abide in the third story?

Gabriel.—The third, O intercessor at the Day of Judgment, is for the people of Jonas the prophet.

The Prophet.—Tell me, O brother, whose will be the second? for I have lost all control and patience.

Hotama, to the *Christians*; the fourth, named *Al Säir*, to the *Sabians*; the fifth, named *Sakar*, to the *Magians*; the sixth, named *Al Jahím*, to the idolaters; and the seventh, which is the lowest and worst of all, and is called *Al Háwiyat*, to the hypocrites, or those who outwardly professed some religion, but in their hearts were of none. Over each of these apartments they believe there will be set a guard of angels, nineteen in number, to whom the damned will confess the just judgment of God, and beg them to intercede with Him for some alleviation of their pain, or that they may be delivered by being annihilated." D'Herbelot, however, gives a different version (see "Gehennem").

* Shís or Shais is the name given by the Persians to Seth, the son of Adam. When he was born the light of the future prophet "shone in his forehead," and subsequently he was honoured by being the recipient at the hands of the Most High of the "Book of Adam," concerning what the Almighty "has created, and what He has decreed in heaven and earth, respecting things temporal and eternal."—Merrick's "Life of Mohammed, pp. 10 and 315, ed 1850.

† Probably St. George, whom the Muhammadans confound with the Prophet Elias.

Gabriel.—The second, O my lord, is the abode of Christian sinners.

The Prophet.—Tell me, for what miserable nation is the first or the uppermost story prepared? (*Gabriel not answering the Prophet, he repeats the question.*) Why hast thou hung down thy head? Deliver my mind from confusion.

Gabriel.—I am ashamed before thee to make such a thing known to thy honour. Although the declaration is unpleasant, still I must say it belongs to sinners of thy people.*

The Prophet.—Ah me! this news consumes my life; it burns the very marrow of my bones. Thy speech, O Gabriel, doth kindle a fire in my soul; it consumes the very bones of my body. Alas! O Gabriel, for the trouble of my people; woe unto me for the tearfulness of their eyes. O God! my people are as it were my own family; they are my broken-winged birds. I am so sorry for my dear followers' sake that I will now get me into my chamber, and shut the door upon myself, not meaning ever again to come forth. Oh! the sorrow of my people has broken my back. O merciful God! have pity on my poor miserable servants.

Bilál,† having proclaimed for prayer, Salmán addresses the companions.—O small and great of this assembly! tell

---

* It may be inferred that in all the above cases only those are consigned to everlasting perdition who disobey the precepts of their religion, inasmuch as in the case of Christians and Muhammadans, who are included in the list, specific reference is made to "sinners"; in the case of the followers of Muhammad, punishment is but temporary.

† "Of the slaves ransomed by Abu Bakr from persecution, for their adherence to the new doctrine, the foremost is Bilál, the son of an Abyssinian slave-girl. He was tall, dark, and gaunt, with negro features and bushy hair. Mahomet honoured and distinguished him as "*the first-fruits of Abyssinia*;" and to this day he is renowned throughout the Moslem world as the first Müadzzin, or crier to prayer." (Muir's "Life of Mahomet," vol. ii. p. 107, ed. 1858.) He was noted for his voice.

Salmán the Persian, one of the Prophet's companions, "is said to have

out if you know anything touching Ahmad * the elect of God. It being three days since the Prophet of the Lord of all creatures has attended public worship, let us repair to 'Alí, his cousin, and ask him the reason of this absence. He may be able to cheer our sorrowful hearts, by assigning some good reason for this sad event.

Salmán (to 'Alí).—May we be a ransom for thy soul, O Imám of all men! Tell us, what has become of God's Prophet that he does not come out?

'Alí, the son of Abú Tálib † (to Salmán).—O poor afflicted Salmán, thou chief of the faithful companions, I am like thyself in respect to his melancholy absence. O Fátimah! thou my laudable companion, thou peace of my disquieted heart, tell me where is thy sad father, the strength of thy scarred heart?

Fátimah.—It is now three days since my father shut himself up in his closet, lamenting there the miserable state of his sorrowful people, and praying to God for their deliverance from everlasting death.

'Alí (knocking at the door of the Prophet's closet).—O incomparable Messenger of God! thou Prophet of the Lord! why dost thou not come out from thy closet and sit in the pulpit, that we may see thy moon-like‡ face, and hear thy sweet discourse?

The Prophet.—I am much troubled for the sake of my people, because they are doomed to destruction. O God! look upon the sad condition of my servants. O gracious Lord! for the merit of 'Alí's soul, forgive all those who love him dearly.

'Alí.—O Lord! I cannot tell why the Prophet weeps so

---

been a Christian captive of Mesopotamia, bought by a Jew from the Bani Kalb, and ransomed on his profession of Islam."—Muir's "Life of Mahomet," vol. iii. p. 256, ed. 1861.

* Ahmad is the name by which the Prophet Muhammad is supposed to have been predicted in Scripture.—See Rodwell's Koran, p. 522, ed. 1861.

† Abú Tálib was uncle of Muhammad and father of 'Alí, which latter married the Prophet's daughter Fátimah.

‡ See note, page 7.

bitterly. None knows the secret of this matter besides Thee, O powerful and gracious Creator! Ah, Salmán! the Prophet of both worlds, having shut the door of his chamber on himself, is weeping there with a loud voice. Thou well knowest that without his permission we cannot enter his chamber. Go, therefore, to his daughter Zahrah;* she may be able to solve this difficulty for us.

Salmán (to Fátimah).—O offspring of Ahmad's body! mercy! have compassion on me, a destitute soul brought very low. Thy father has hidden his face from us, leaving us to suffer pain at his separation. Seeing we have no chief or leader, and no prophet besides him, we beg thee to kindly represent to him our sad case; it may be thou shalt prevail upon him, and bring him out.

Fátimah (standing at the door).—O father, thou intercessor at the Day of Judgment! behold Salmán and other companions are standing without waiting for thee to come forth and honour them with thy presence. They are mourning grievously for thy disappearance, believing it is a prelude to the Day of Resurrection.

The Prophet.—Know thou, O Fátimah! thou light of my eye, joy of my heart, and peace of my troubled soul, I am shedding tears for my sinful people, imploring God to have mercy on them, and forgive them. O Lord! have compassion on my followers, and mercifully pardon their sins.

Fátimah.—O God! what can I do to relieve my father? O my dear child Hasan! help me. Come, let me send thee to thy honoured grandfather to persuade him to come out from his closet.

Hasan (going to the door).—O my noble and majestic grandfather, thou great chief of all believers! why dost thou appear thus stupified, and sittest there all alone? Be pleased to come out and rejoice somewhat the heart of the people who are waiting anxiously for thee.

---

* See note, p. 22.

The Prophet.—O Hasan; I am sore distressed in heart on behalf of my people. It is for them that I am thus shedding tears. Know thou that God intends to consign my people to everlasting perdition in the next world. O God! for the merit of the dignity of Hasan, forgive my followers through me.

Hasan.—O my poor broken-hearted mother! have pity on thy own condition. Grandfather is writhing on the ground and moaning. He pours showers of tears from his eyes. He is restless and impatient, and does not kindly receive my petition.

Fátimah.—O Salmán! what shall I do to relieve my father, and make the Prophet of the universe leave his chamber, and come out? But I can show thee, Salmán, what thou mayest do. Go at once to Husain, and leave him not, for he is the remedy for every diseased and grieved heart; he is a key to the lock of sorrows, when they torment the hearts of friends and companions.

Salmán.—O ye friends! begin to mourn with lamentable sighs. It is time for intercession, go and tell Husain. Place your turbans now on the ground, and walk off bare-headed to the hospital of faith. O Husain! thou light of the eye of Haidar [*] the warrior, O Husain! thou salve for the heart of poor Fátimah, God forbid we should leave thy skirt, until thou make thy noble grandfather come out from his chamber.

Husain (to Salmán).—On my eye! on my eye! do not cry so sadly, O Salmán! Why shouldst thou shed tears

---

[*] Haidar means "Lion," and may not impossibly have been given to 'Alí in consequence of his dauntless valour. It is stated, however, in Price's "Chronological Retrospect of Mahommedan History," vol. i. p. 364, ed. 1811, that it was the name which he originally received from his mother Fátimah, very possibly in honour of his grandsire Asad, with whose name that of "Haidar" is synonymous; and that the name of 'Alí was only at a later period bestowed upon him by his cousin, the Prophet of Arabia.

so copiously? I am a key for the lock of thy sorrow; I am the sum and substance of every hope. (*Turning to the Prophet.*) O thou glory of men and jinns!* have a gracious regard for me. I am Husain, here behind the door; wilt thou be kind enough to open it for me? O intercessor at the Day of Judgment! O ornament of God's throne! I am thy beloved Husain; open the door, open it for my sake. Behold thy darling Husain sitting down among ashes and flinging earth † on his head, and be pleased to open the door for him.

Gabriel (coming to Muhammad).—O Muhammad, Muhammad, arise! A great tumult has taken place in the whole universe. Behold, Husain has fallen on the ground moaning, and shedding tears. Thus says the Lord, the Lover of all: "Lift up Husain's head from the ground, and that very soon; for the holy ones in heaven are all weeping for him, and being distressed on his behalf have left off their particular duties."

The Prophet, coming forth, says to Husain.—May thy grandfather and thy parents be offered as a ransom for thee! Why hast thou laid thy head on ashes? O Husain, may I be a sacrifice for this thy head, which thy sister shall see severed from the body! Grant the request of thy grandfather, and hold up thy neck from the dust of the road.

Husain.—Peace be upon thee, O seal of the prophet! ‡

---

* See note, p. 24.

† See note *, p. 11.

‡ "*The Seal of Prophecy on the back of Mahomet.* This, says one, was a protuberance on the Prophet's back of the size and appearance of a pigeon's egg. Abdallah ibn Sarjas describes it as having been as large as his closed fist, with moles round about it. Abu Ramtha, whose family were skilled in surgery, offered to remove it, but Mahomet refused, saying: '*The Physician thereof is He who placed it where it is!*' According to another tradition, Mahomet said to Abu Ramtha, '*Come hither and touch my back,*' which he did, drawing his fingers over the

peace be upon thee, thou leader of men and jinns! Tell me, O glory of the age, why hast thou shut the door on thyself?

The Prophet.—Dear grandchild, Gabriel told me that the glorious Creator had said, "The sinners of my poor people shall, on the Day of Judgment, be cast into everlasting flames." It is for the sake of my people that I am so sorry, O Husain; for this reason I pour down tears from my eyes.

Gabriel.—O King, who in dignity art like the throne of God Himself, and whose dominion extends over the whole earth! thou who art entitled by God "a bearer of good tidings and a warner," O thou whose protection is an asylum for angels! by that God who gave thee this authority, pray thou for the sinners of thy people, that God may forgive them all for thy sake.

The Prophet.—Know thou, O Gabriel, that I am always weeping sadly on behalf of my people. Yet come to me, O my afflicted girl Fátimah, and dishevel thy locks for the followers of thy father; and O 'Alí, thou emperor of the two worlds, thou strength of Muhammad's spirit! I conjure thee, by the name of the Prophet and by his soul, to come also to me; and ye, the light of the eye of the

---

prophetical seal; and behold there was a collection of hairs upon the spot.

"I have not noticed this 'seal' in the body of the work, because it has been so surrounded by tradition with supernatural tales that it is extremely difficult to determine what it really was. It is said to have been the *divine* seal which, according to the predictions of the Scriptures, marked Mahomet as the last of the prophets. How far Mahomet himself encouraged this idea it is impossible to say. From the traditions quoted above it would seem to have been nothing more that a mole of unusual size; and his saying that 'God had placed it there' was probably the germ of the supernatural assertions which grew up concerning it. Had Mahomet really attributed any divine virtue to it, he would have spoken very differently to one who offered to lance or remove it."—Muir's "Life of Mahomet," vol. iv. p. 331, ed. 1861.

chief of men and jinns, ye plants of the flower-garden of the best* among women, Hasan and Husain, take off your turbans from your heads, and begin to pour tears of grief on your moon-like faces. In short, pray all of you to God to have mercy on my people; for besides us, they have none to save them, poor souls.

'Ali.—Lord, I adjure thee by the body and soul of thy Prophet; by thy messenger Muhammad, the Arabian, to forgive the sins of the Shí'ahs† in the Day of Judgment, to have mercy on the people of God's Prophet.

Fátimah.—O great God, I adjure thee by the honour of my father, by the merit of my sorrowful husband, by my own moistened eyes, and by these my children—the very soul of God's Messenger—to pardon in the Day of Resurrection the sins of the Gentiles who believe on Muhammad.

Hasan.—O God, for the honour, dignity, and glory of the chosen Prophet, Muhammad; for the sake of the anguish of his household and family; on my account also, who am Hasan, Thy imploring servant, forgive the sins of the followers of my grandfather.

---

* That is Fátimah, who was declared by the Prophet himself as one of the four best of women.

† Respecting the "great schism at this day subsisting between the Sunnís and the Shí'ahs, or partisans of 'Alí, and maintained on either side with implacable hatred and zeal," Sale remarks: "The chief points wherein they differ are—(1) That the *Shiites* reject *Abu Becr, Omar,* and *Othmán,* the three first *Khalifs,* as usurpers and intruders, whereas the *Sonnites* acknowledge and respect them as rightful *Imáms.* (2) The *Shiites* prefer *Ali* to *Mohammed,* or at least, esteem them both equal; but the *Sonnites* admit neither *Ali,* nor any of the prophets, to be equal to *Mohammed.* (3) The *Sonnites* charge the *Shiites* with corrupting the *Korán* and neglecting its precepts; and the *Shiites* retort the same charge on the *Sonnites.* (4) The *Sonnites* receive the '*Sonna,*' or book of traditions of their Prophet, as of canonical authority; whereas the *Shiites* reject it as apocryphal and unworthy of credit. And to these disputes, and some others of less moment, is principally owing the antipathy which has long reigned between the *Turks,* who are *Sonnites,* and the *Persians,* who are of the sect of *Ali.*"—Sale's Koran, Prel. Discourse, sec. viii. p. 178, ed. 1734.

Husain.—O great God, I adjure Thee by the verity of my maternal grandfather Muhammad, and my father 'Alí, and by that moment when Shimar* shall draw his dagger over my face, do not, O Lord, grieve my distressed heart, but graciously overlook the faults of Thy servants, Muhammad's followers.

Gabriel (to Muhammad).—O corporeal and spiritual judge of all! peace be upon thee! O chief of men and jinns! hail to thee! O thou by whose mission the world is turned into a flower-garden, and by whose directing-light hearts are illuminated, God, sending thee greeting, says, "Be not sorry, O distressed one for the sake of thy poor people, for on the Day of Judgment, in the presence of all My prophets, I will have mercy on so many of thy people, that thou, O loving Prophet, shall be well pleased in the abundance of My mercy."

Muhammad.—O faithful bearer of God's revelation, on thee be peace! O rejoicer of hearts afflicted with painful sorrow, hail to thee! Thou art welcome, O comely Gabriel! By our Lord Creator, thou hast made me quite cheerful by bringing me such good tidings from the Lord.

Gabriel.—I have received, O Muhammad, another command from the Living and Eternal God to tell thee. If thou wishest to be fully acquainted with the state of thy people, whether good or bad, walk out to the grave-yard of thy people, and behold their miserable condition.

The Prophet (to his companions).—O my sorrowful companions, be ye all gathered together around me in perfect sincerity and fidelity, for thus hath the Lord of the whole world said, that we must go out for a while to the grave-yard to behold there the unhappy state of our

---

* Shimar was one of the Khalíf Yazíd's generals, and slew Husain in the plain of Karbalá, A.D. 680.

poor people; peradventure we may be able, by some suitable means, to remedy their sad condition.

One who had been disobedient to his parents cries out in the grave, while flames come out from the tomb.—O God's Messenger, save me from the anguish of torment, I beseech thee! I am burning. Mercy! mercy! mercy! O Muhammad, I am scorching in fire, and am unable to deliver my soul from the flames. Behold me consuming away in this abode of the lost, and pity me!

Muhammad.—Why am I again distressed in my mind, O Lord? What is this pitiful cry that reaches my ears? Why should this miserable youth be thus tormented? Let it be revealed to me, O merciful God, who is this young man that is thus in torture.

Gabriel.—Peace be on thee! O glory of earth and heaven, thus has the Creator of the two worlds said:—"The young man who is thus tormented in the flames is one of thy people. When alive, he was disobedient to his parents. Send for his mother and ask her about him, she will tell thee the truth of his sad case."

The Prophet.—Kindly, O Salmán, go to the town for my sake, and summon quickly to me the mother of this young man.

Salmán (to the mother).—O good woman, come with me to the Prophet of the worlds. For the glory of heaven and earth, the intercessor of the Day of Judgment, the spiritual guide of the whole universe, wants thee.

The Woman.—I do not know, O manifest God, what has happened, or why Thy faithful Messenger calls me. May I be a ransom for the dust of thy feet! for what service has thy holiness summoned me?

The Prophet.—Why dost not thou care for this wretched child of thine, who is suffering punishment in the flames? What has hardened thy heart so as to become cruel to the son of thy womb? Come, O woman, I adjure thee by the Lord, forgive the faults of this youth for my sake, before thou goest from this world.

The Woman.—May my soul be a ransom for thine, O mediator of both small as well as great! all thy words, O bearer of good tidings and denouncer of threats, are quite true. But thou dost not know what this youth has done to me, how he has unjustly treated me; otherwise thou wouldst not have asked me to forgive him. He used to vex me to please his wife; this very youth has cast me alive into a flaming fire. How can I forget and forgive his wicked actions? I would rather ask God to increase his torments. (*Fire comes forth from the grave.*)

The Disobedient Boy.—Ah me! my heart has lost its patience, O Muhammad, I am grievously tormented. The fire hath dried up all my strength; save me, I beseech thee, save!

Muhammad.—O 'Alí, the apostle of God, thou remover of the gate of Khaibar,* go thou and ask this woman to forgive her child, and to sincerely pray for her own flesh and bone.

'Alí (to the Woman).—O mournful woman! dost thou not know that my name is 'Alí, the 'Amrúnite? † It is I that

---

* Khaibar, a town about one hundred miles to the north of Madínah, was one of the strongholds of the Jews. In A.D. 628 it was attacked by Muhammad, into whose hands it fell; the chief was beheaded, and his wife enrolled amongst the Prophet's wives.

† Various reasons may be assigned why 'Alí is called the "'Amrúnite." In A.D. 627, when Muhammad was attacked in Madínah by the Karaish tribe, "Amr, son of Abd Wudd, an aged chief . . . challenged his adversaries to single combat. Ali forthwith accepted the challenge, and the two stood alone in the open plain. Amr, dismounting, maimed his horse, in token of his resolve to conquer or to die. They closed, and for a short time were hidden in a cloud of dust. But it was not long before the well-known Takbír 'Great is the Lord' from the lips of Ali, made known that he was the victor."—Muir's "Life of Mahomet," vol. iii. p. 262, ed. 1861.

But two years previous to the above event, when Muhammad was attacked and discomfited at Ohod, the famous "'Amrú," or more pro-

help and succour all strangers wherever they be, I am the friend of all widows and orphans. Come, for my sake,

---

perly 'Amr ibn Aás, one of the leaders of the Karaishite horse, was attacked and discomfited at Madínah. The Arab custom of battle was to commence with single combats. The "Meccan ranks might be seen to quiver," says Muir, in his graphic account of that fatal day, as "Abu Dujána, distinguished by the red kerchief wound round his helmet, swept along, and, with a sword given him by Mahomet, dealt death on every side. Hamza, conspicuous from his waving ostrich feather; 'Alí, marked by his long white plume; and Zobeir, known by his bright yellow turban—like heroes in the battles of the Iliad—carried confusion wherever they appeared." (Muir's "Life of Mahomet," vol. iii. p. 169, ed. 1861). Well may 'Alí have exclaimed after the battle, when giving his blood-stained sword to his wife to be washed, "Take this sword, for it is not a despicable one."

Nor was this the only occasion on which 'Amrú fought in the ranks of 'Alí's enemies, since many years afterwards (A.D. 657) he joined Mu'áwiyah, the son of the Governor of Syria, and took up arms against the Prophet's son-in-law. They met at Siffin, a broad plain extending along the banks of the Euphrates. After months had been passed in skirmishing, a general engagement occurred. The following graphic account of this battle is from Major R. D. Osborn's "Islam under the Arabs," p. 116, ed. 1876:—"The action rapidly became general. The press was so close that the bows were flung away as useless, and men fought sabre to sabre. The sun gradually mounted to the zenith, and then gradually disappeared in the west, and still the conflict raged unceasingly. The clear stars of an Oriental sky shone all the night through upon the same stormy scene. The battle-songs of the Arabs mingled with the crash of breaking lances and the noises of the battle. The morning sun rising, pierced the clouds of dust, and revealed the battle-field strewn thickly with the wounded and the dead. The times of prayer passed unheeded. Ali was to be seen wherever the battle was hottest. Every time he struck a blow he shouted 'God is great!' and every blow he struck sent an infidel to hell. Five hundred men are said to have fallen beneath his single sabre. 'Never,' said Muawia, as he watched the havoc he wrought in the ranks of his army, 'was there a man who crossed swords with Ali and returned alive from the encounter.'" No mention is, however, made of a personal encounter between 'Alí and 'Amrú, on the occasion either of this battle, or the encounter at Ohod. But a few months later (658) the rivals again met, when 'Alí, making a well-intended lunge, the point of his lance passed through the skirt of 'Amrú's coat of mail, which brought him

forgive the sins of thy son, and pity thine own child for the sake of God's Prophet.

The Woman.—May my soul be a ransom for the dust of thy feet! Would to God my head were to become an offering for thee. I know thou art the lion of the glorious Lord, the beloved of the Eternal One; but I beg thee not to be offended when I tell thee I cannot comply with thy request. I shall never be pleased with my son, never, but wish that he should continue in his tortures.

The Disobedient Son.—Alas! I am surrounded with flames, my body is quite consumed with fire. O Muhammad, come to my assistance and deliver me.

The Prophet (to Fátimah).—Come to me, O Zahrah, thou my lovely daughter, the joy of my sorrowful heart. Being very sorry for this youth, whose bones are melted in this fire, I pray thee go to this woman his mother, and ask her to forgive the poor youth.

Fátimah.—Hear, O woman, I am going to tell thee somewhat. There will come a time when I shall sigh sadly even from the bottom of my heart, yea, my groans shall set even the stack of heaven on fire, my body being bruised by a door struck against it. I shall lie down in bed complaining of pain, now in my sides, now in my back. And when I become an orphan, and behold that 'Alí is desolate, I shall lay one hand on my heart and with the other begin to strike my head. Now bewailing with Hasan, now lamenting with Husain; at one time I shall heave a sigh from the heart, at another time draw a deep

---

head foremost to the earth," with "his heels in the air." "In this situation 'Alí scorned to do him any further injury, and suffered him to escape, with the contemptuous remark that he 'was never to forget the circumstance to which he was indebted for life and safety.'" (Price's "Chronological Retrospect of Mahommedan History," vol. i. p. 288, ed. 1811.

breath from my inmost soul. Be kind, therefore, and forgive the sins of thy son for the merit of my sufferings, that I may on the Day of Judgment set up my flag of intercession for thee.

The Woman.—Thou queen of the palace of the matchless royal youth 'Alí! thou model of chastity and modesty! O orbit of a couple of suns, mine of two precious gems, mother of two great chiefs, thou consort of 'Alí, the heart-strings of the Prophet, mistress of all creatures, and beloved of God, I beg thee to give up this request of thine, for I can in no wise forgive my son, nor can I be pleased with him. O great God, I adjure Thee, by Zahrah's dignity, to increase the torments of my son!

The Disobedient Son crying out.—O Musulmáns, run to save me! I am burning in the flames! relieve me even for one moment! O thou that intercedest for sinners in the Day of Judgment, for God's sake have compassion on me!

The Prophet (to Hasan).—Come to me, thou light of my two tearful eyes, let me send thee to this inexorable woman, to entreat her to do thy grandfather the favour of forgiving her own sinful son; peradventure thou mayest be able to persuade her to do it.

Hasan.—Hearken to me, O thou benevolent lady, listen to my sad tale with sympathetic affection. Thou hast already heard, I think, that I have one day to drink poison,[*] that parts of my body have to be thrown up in a basin, and that when my ruby-like lips turn bluish-green from the mortal effect of the poison, I shall have no father or mother to mourn for me, even my grandfather, Muhammad, shall not be present at that time at my bed-side, to condole with my poor afflicted sister over my remains; come now, for the sake of my sad state at that time, forgive the sins

---

[*] Alluding to his mode of death.

of thy poor son, that he may come out from this place of torment. Yea, O woman, do not grieve the spirit of the Prophet of God, but, with a willing heart, comply with this my request.

The Woman.—I know that every slave of thy court is a great Cæsar, and that all of you here present are healing balms for hearts affected with cankering sin : but, alas ! I am sorry thou knowest nothing about what my son has done to me, for thou hast not seen him doing it. O great Lord, this is 'Alí's son, Hasan, who, with tearful eyes, entreats me to forgive my sinful child; be Thou a witness that I have not granted his request, seeing my son has greatly injured me. O God, for the sake of my injured heart, fill Thou the tomb of this my child with the flames of the fire of Thy fury.

The Disobedient Son.—Alas ! O Lord God, what fire is this which is kindled in my soul, and which has deprived me of all strength and patience to endure ? What flame is this that consumes my body and soul ? It is hell-fire wherein I am so burning. Could none by intercession prevail on my mother to forgive me. Is not Husain here to try ?

The Prophet (to Husain).—Where art thou, dear Husain, where art thou ? Why art thou at such a season separated from me ? It is the time for thee to weep, the day for thee to assist, a fitting opportunity for thee to make intercession. Go thou from me to this woman, and beseech her in a most humble manner to forgive her child for thy sake.

Husain.—Come, O woman, let me tell thee plainly the story of my cruel sufferings in Karbalá. Hast thou heard that a certain one named Husain will in future go to Karbalá? Hast thou been told that some wicked party will cruelly sever his head from his body ?. Hast thou read that his praise-worthy sister Zainab will put on black garments after his death ? I am that Husain, the pacifier of the mind of the chosen Prophet ; I am that Husain, the joy of the heart of Fátimah, the best among women. All rational creatures, men and jinns, who inhabit the present and future worlds, are sunk in sin, and have but one Husain to save them. Come, O woman, for God's sake do not break my heart, but forgive thy son for me.

An Angel (to the Woman).—O woman, take care, and forgive thy son for Husain's sake, for if, God forbid, the latter, the king of men and jinns, be offended with thee for refusing to comply with his request, be sure we will give thee such blows on thy head with these fiery maces in our hands, that thou shalt immediately find thyself in the lowest part of the bottomless pit.

The Woman (to Husain).—O dear Husain, may I be a ransom for thy handsome face, and a sacrifice for thy throat and hair! Weep not, weep not, sweet Husain, thou light of my eyes, I adjure thee! O God of the East and West, be Thou a witness that I have forgiven my son for Husain's sake.

The Disobedient Son in torment coming out of the grave.—Praise be unto thee, O God of the whole world, in that Thou hast delivered me from the fires of destruction. O Husain, O Husain, thou son of 'Alí, may I be a ransom for thee! may I be a sacrifice for the dust of thy feet! I subscribe myself a dog of thy threshold. May I be a sacrifice for thy Shí'ahs!

The Prophet.—O great God, I adjure thee by myself, named Thy Prophet, and by 'Alí my cousin, the conqueror and destroyer of Khaibar, that Thou, O Guardian of men and jinns, be gracious towards my sinful followers, for the merit of the blood of Husain! Grant, O Lord, the requests of all my people, and of Thy grace remove their difficulties.

SCENE IV.

MAGNANIMOUS OFFER OF ALI TO SACRIFICE HIS LIFE FOR A FELLOW CREATURE.

THIS Scene opens with invocations to the Almighty on the part successively of Muhammad, 'Alí, Fátimah, Hasan, and Husain, on behalf of the Shí'ahs. The Prophet then proceeds to predict the death of the martyrs on the plain of Karbalá. The distress of the family, however, is not altogether due to future troubles, since they are represented as in want of the very necessaries of life, being even compelled to sell the shirts on their backs to procure food, and being kept from starvation solely by the interposition of some nymphs of Paradise, who bring down trays of fresh dates from the regions of bliss. In the quaint Eastern phraseology of the text, the Prophet's family "feed at the table of grace."

In anguish of mind 'Alí goes out for a ride on his mule, partly with the view of seeking employment, and partly with the idea of driving care from his mind. On his way he meets with a young man anxious to slay him, and thereby obtain as wife a certain lady, whose father desired the head of 'Alí as a dowry for his daughter. "Sever my head from the body, thou foolish young man, and return to thy country rejoicing," was the ready rejoinder of the Bayard of Islám, who made no scruple to sacrifice his own life in order to benefit a fellow creature. The eyes of the youth, however, were suddenly enlightened, and he begged forgiveness. "Declare that there is no God but God, that Muhammad is His Prophet, and 'Alí His vice-regent" (the key-note of the Shí'ah doctrine) was the only condition imposed upon the offender, who at once repeated the formula, and was saved!

The Prophet (to God).—O Lord! I adjure thee by Thine own essential nature (for Thou art the Sole, the Self-sufficient, and Thy being is far removed from all imperfection of others; without Thy wisdom Adam could not be called Adam, for Thou causedst him to appear out of earth and water); I adjure Thee, Lord, by Thine own great Name, to shorten for my people the horror of the long commotion in the Day of Judgment.

'Alí (to God).—O Lord! I adjure Thee by the flame-scattering sigh of Thy chosen Prophet, and by the merit of his blood-pouring eyes, to raise to life, with the holy family of the Prophet himself, every Shí'ah who assists us in our sorrows.

Fátimah.—O Lord! may the soul of Fátimah be a sacrifice for Thy mercy! May her heart ever rejoice in remembrance of Thee! I beseech Thee, Lord, to shelter Fátimah's maidens by Thine own grace from the scorching heat of the Day of Resurrection, and especially to guard her who weeps in the spring of life over the drought of the field of Fátimah's children.

Hasan.—O Lord! how can Hasan's heart be relieved? When shall his sorrowful mind rejoice? But, as Thou hast said that Thou wilt forgive Ahmad's [*] people on the Day of Resurrection through the merit of Hasan's soul destroyed by poison, if he be so fortunate as to find such favour in Thy sight, no doubt his wandering mind will soon be settled.

Husain.—O Lord! for the merit of Husain's father, mother, and grandfather,[†] deliver Husain's pearl-producing eyes from the trouble of long expectation. Thou hast promised to invest me with the robe of martyrdom, to exalt my crown of glory on high with this Thy peculiar gift; and Husain's throat longs to meet the cutting dagger of the inhabitants of Kúfah. How glad am I to become a sacrifice for mankind! I do not know when Husain's full moon will rise from her eastern horizon.

The Prophet.—O. Lord! for the honour of the Lion of

---

[*] See note *, p. 37.
[†] *i.e.* 'Alí, Fátimah, and the Prophet Muhammad.

God, Haidar,* the foremost in the kingdom of valour, make the account of the Day of Resurrection easy to my destitute people at that time.

'Alí (to the Prophet).—O chief of all the prophets, peace be on thee! Thou who art a soul to my body, hail to thee! May 'Alí, O monarch of the kingdom of creation, be a sacrifice for thee! May my eye never see the light without thy presence! If, God forbid, I be removed from thy side, I shall be made, like my fortune, blind of both eyes.

The Prophet.—O leader of all God's creatures, on thee be peace! O helper and reliever of this poor one, hail! Though I am thy soul, thou art also my soul; thou art the strength, not of the body only, but of my very bones.

'Alí.—Who am I, O Prophet of God, that I should abide in the place where thou sittest? Although thy grace is sought by all creatures, yet if 'Alí be counted a servant of thee, it is good for him. Thou art he for whom God did create all things; do not put me to shame any more. May I be a sacrifice for thee!

The Prophet.—Sit down before Muhammad. May thy father be a ransom for thee! Thou art for me, as I am for thee†; let us not be separated the one from the other. Thou, O 'Alí, standest alone in the age as regards thy faith; thou shalt be a martyr through oppression and cruelty. None, O 'Alí, has been created equal to thee; none has ever existed thy match in the world.

'Alí.—May God make me a ransom for thy head! thy caresses to me are paternal. I have told thee a thousand times that I, 'Alí, am thy slave. I am one of thy servants, bought by thee with money.

The Prophet.—Thou, O God of the whole world, well knowest 'Alí's temper; forgive Thou my people for 'Alí's merit. O 'Alí! none can equal thee in rank and dignity.

---

* See note, p. 39.

† Muhammad is reported to have said of his son-in-law, "'Alí is for me, and I am for him."

Why, thy moon-like* face is bedewed with perspiration! Oh! it is time I should rend my heart to pieces through my sorrow for thee. Come near; let me wipe off the drops from thy beautiful face. O great God! I adjure Thee, by 'Alí's might and honour, to forgive his Shí'ahs in the Day of Judgment.

'Alí.—May 'Alí's head be an offering for thee and thy people! Where shall I go, or what shall I do? Shame has rendered me blind. Though I am sure of thy loving regard for me, still I wonder why thy noble mind is so sad. Thou art, it is true, extremely loving and compassionate, but why shouldst thou weep, rubbing continually thy hand over my face, and wondering?

The Prophet.—O 'Alí! my tears are not for the present state of things, but for what shall happen hereafter. A certain man shall cleave thy hand with his sword in the manner thou didst split the pate of 'Amrú,† O leader of the just! Oh that I were present to behold thy body in blood, to rub my face on thine and make it rose-coloured!

'Alí.—Be not grieved. May I be a sacrifice for thy sighing and weeping! for the fervour of thy condolence has made me devoid of patience. If I were able to possess a thousand souls in this life I would willingly offer all as a sacrifice for thy people's sake, especially to one that weeps for Hasan and Husain, and spends his pearly tears for the latter.

Husain.—Dear brother, thou light of the eye of the people of the age, thou art going to be made a martyr by means of poison. O Hasan! thy brother Husain is suffering severely from hunger. I am about to be destroyed craving after food and drink. Come, let us go home to our mother, for the light of my eyes is turned dim with hunger.

---

* See note, p. 7. † See note †, p. 45.

Hasan.—Dear Husain, may I be a ransom for thee! Do not be so restless on account of thy hunger, for I am in the same state of misery. I am so famished as to be distracted in my mind; but being anxious regarding my mother, I cannot come home with thee, but shall remain here.

Husain (to his mother).—May I be a ransom for thy soul, O afflicted mother! May the souls of Husain and Hasan be sacrificed for thee! We are hungry and in great trouble. Oh that thou wouldst accept our supplications! None among the Arabs is in our sad condition. How is it we have not a slice of bread in our house?

Fátimah.—Ah me! O thirsty-lipped * martyr of Karbalá, my dear Husain! O stranger of the valley of affliction and trials, my dear son, woe be to me! I know no other diet but life-blood, which, sorrowing, I drink continually, owing to my misfortune. The vicissitudes of time have left me nothing, dry or moist. I am sorry to say, dear child, I have no food † for thee.

---

* See note, p. 14.

† *Narrowness of his means at Medína.*—A long chapter is devoted to this subject, containing many such traditions as the following. " Fátima once brought Mahomed a piece of bread; it was the first that had passed his lips for three days. Ayesha tells us that for months together Mahomet did not get a full meal. 'Months used to pass,' she says again, 'and no fire would be lighted in Mahomet's house, either for baking bread or cooking meat. *How then did he live?* By the "two black things" (dates and water), and by what the citizens used to send unto us. The Lord requite them! Such of them as had milch cattle would send us a little milk. The Prophet never enjoyed the luxury of two kinds of food the same day; if he had flesh, there was nothing else; and so if he had dates; so likewise if he had bread. We possessed no sieves, but used to bruise the grain and blow off the husks.' One night Abu-Bakr sent Mahomet the leg of a kid. Ayesha held it while the Prophet cut off a piece for himself in the dark; and in his turn the Prophet held it while Ayesha cut off a piece for herself. ' *What!*' exclaimed the listeners, '*and ye ate without a lamp!*' 'Yea,' replied Ayesha; ' had we possessed oil for a lamp, think ye not that we should have used it for our food?' "—Muir's " Life of Mahomet," vol. iv. p. 329, ed. 1861.

Husain.—I adjure thee, O mother! by the dignity of thine own father, the Prophet of God, tell me whether, since thou hast put on the crown of existence, thou hast seen any in Madínah as poor as we are. Every one has in his house food, clothes, and furniture; why should we be deprived of these necessaries in our house?

Fátimah.—Thou speakest truth, O my darling child! I have neither seen nor heard of any in such wretched plight, for in every house there can be found some clothing, whether new or old. And every table has some bread thereon, it may chance be wheat or barley; but in our house there is no furniture save a common reed matting. Poor ourselves, we are sometimes full, but oftener hungry.

Husain.—Do not call us poor, mother, we are kings; we are all the family of 'Alí the 'Amrúnite.* We may seem humble and mean in the sight of the infidels, but we are the descendants of the faithful and chosen Messenger of God. Take us two oppressed ones to the Prophet, to whom we will state our case, hoping to find favour with him.

Fátimah.—O God! look upon Fátimah's condition; how her anxiety is ever increasing. What can I do? What are these two children saying? How long must I continue sorrowful? I will go to the faithful Prophet, and tell him what Hasan and Husain have spoken; but I am ashamed to complain to my father respecting 'Alí my husband.

Gabriel (to Muhammad).—O sphere of faith, peace be on thee! thou elected Prophet of God, hail to thee! The holy God has commanded thee, O cause of the creation of heaven and earth, to do a certain thing, and thou must be diligent in the performance of it, with befitting respect.

Muhammad.—On thee be peace, O Gabriel! welcome, thou messenger of the glorious Maker! What may be the order of the Creator of the two worlds? Let Muhammad

---

* See note †, p. 45.

be offered a sacrifice for it! I am ready, with all my soul, to obey the commands of the glorious Maker.

Gabriel.—Open thine eyes to see thy servant, to behold a resurrection exhibited, in that this woman calls out "Hasan! Husain!" Hunger has consumed her heart, and destroyed the habitation of her patience. She is coming to thee distracted with pain, anxious to get a morsel of bread. Be thou a cure for her suffering heart by becoming the friend of her who is in such a state, that the grace of God may be manifested to all, believers or unbelievers.

The Prophet.—O Lord, the Bestower of favours, the Eternal; Thou who art ever glorious and beneficent! for the honour of 'Alí, Thy elect, and Fátimah the virgin,*- accept this my prayer, which is that Thou wilt rejoice my soul by Thy grace, and graciously forgive my people.

Fátimah (to Muhammad).—O Prophet of all mankind, peace be on thee! My father, the chosen of God, peace be on thee! Husain and Hasan have left me no rest, and I hardly know what to do with them. They ask me for bread to sustain their hungry souls, and keep them from starvation; but I am sorry to say I cannot afford it. Oh, pity me, dear father, I am holding thy skirt entreatingly.

The Prophet.—Be not sorry, O brilliant star of the constellation of virtue! thou light of the eye of God's elect! all good servants of God suffer tribulation and hardship, notwithstanding the abundance of grace they have found in God's sight. Thou being in God's sight the Mary of this people, the Creator will grant thee patience. Come to me, Hasan and Husain, and apply some ointment to my wounded heart. Tell me, O Hasan, why thy face has become void of colour.

---

* "The perpetual virginity of Fátimah, even after the motherhood, is a point of orthodoxy in El Islám."—Burton's "El Medinah and Meccah," vol. i. p. 315, ed. 1857.

Hasan.—O glory of the world, it is now three days since a bit of bread has passed my mouth. My legs have become so weak that they can hardly support my body. If thou approvest that I be thus troubled, have mercy on my poor brother's impatient soul!

The Prophet.—Alas! my child, that I should see thee slain with deadly poison! Why should I behold thee rolling in dust, and see thy body cut to pieces? O Husain, may thy grandfather be a sacrifice for thy head! tell me what is the state of thy sorrowful heart, even thou?

Husain.—O Messenger of the glorious Lord, why shouldst thou ask how fares this poor wretch? O king of all goodness and generosity, give me bread; I am dead, grant me a new life. O my noble grandfather, my eyes are turned dim, hunger has rendered them blind.

The Prophet.—O Husain, thou strength of my soul, be not grieved; O foremost verse of the Kur'án, be not desolate. There will come a day that thou shalt be killed by the enemy, when thou art in a hungry and thirsty condition; be not dejected. These lips which have to-day turned blue, shall become besmeared with blood; destroy not thyself. This throat which I am now continually kissing shall be cut with a sharp sword; be not sad. And this body which I am pressing to my bosom shall be trodden under the hoofs of horses; be not distracted.*

Fátimah.—Dear father, I have to tell thee a story, to narrate something about thy Hasan and Husain. If thou givest me permission I will declare it, in order to allay the sorrows of my heart.

The Prophet.—Thou tattered page in sorrow's volume, thou foremost of all on the Day of Salvation, thou art certainly permitted to say what thou likest, without ever faltering, or having the least occasion for reserve.

---

* "Mohammed foretold the martyrdom of Imám Husayn and his family, with the attending circumstances."—Merrick's "Life of Mohammed," p. 181, ed. 1850.

Fátimah.—O Messenger of the whole universe, when my Hasan and Husain came home hungry and weeping, they took hold of my skirt and asked me the following question:—"Good and worthy mother, is there any throughout the city of Madínah as famished as we are? Does any family suffer like Muhammad's family?" From the time I heard them speak thus I have not been able to restrain my tears.

The Prophet.—Let not this saying grieve thee, O Zahrah,* but think over the transaction of Karbalá for comfort! Thou art in grace, dignity, and position, like Mary. Make ready for me, for I have to dine with thee; prepare some good meal for us, for 'Alí and I will soon return with Hasan and Husain.

Fátimah.—Behold the condition of me, the broken-hearted, O God! the thread of my patience is snapped, O Lord.

Gabriel.—Behold the state of the disconsolate Zahrah, O God! how she suffers great anguish of heart, O Lord!

Fátimah.—O God, put me not to shame before Muhammad, nor let me blush before that eternal king. Let me not be lightly esteemed by my father, O God! Supply my wants for the merits of my father, the asylum of all God's creatures.

Gabriel.—The connecting tie of the nine spheres is broken up by Fátimah's groans and sighs, by the restlessness of mind of the daughter of God's Prophet. Angels are lamenting for her, they are beating on their breasts and crying.

Michael.—O assembly of angels, begin ye to shed tears, cast dust on your heads all of you, for Fátimah, the mother of Husain, has fallen down, fainting from exhaustion and grief. O holy ones of God, advertise this in all the

---

* See note, p. 22.

heavens! Let all angels lift up their hands toward the Court of the Great Judge to entreat Him to pity Fátimah's condition. Zahrah is in trouble because the Prophet is become her guest, while she has nothing at home to put before him. Pray, therefore, to God not to disappoint her.

Gabriel.—O Lord the Saviour, have mercy on Fátimah, with whose cries and groans the heavens are echoing. Thy beloved Muhammad is become Fátimah's guest, for which reason her complaints are tinged with bitter grief.

The Supreme Being (to the Nymphs of Paradise).—O nymphs, nymphs, behold the daughter of the Prophet complaining sadly of poverty, and falling on the ground like a fading flower! Carry these trays of fresh dates from Paradise for the Prince of Arabia, Ahmad, the asylum of the prophets.

Fátimah.—O Searcher of the heart and Judge of religion, see Zahrah's condition, how I am sorrowfully sitting in ashes! My father has become my guest while I have no other food at hand but my own heart's blood. Oh, earth be sprinkled on my head! how am I brought low!

The Nymphs.—How long wilt thou continue sad, O daughter of the holy Prophet? Cry and lament no more, thy prayer is accepted by thy Creator.

The Prophet (to 'Alí).—O 'Alí, thou vicegerent of God, thou full moon of the firmament of perfection, be not distracted in thy mind, let us return home; and ye Hasan and Husain, stars of the constellation of hope, walk on before your father and grandfather, for we all have to dine with Fátimah, and, by God's command, <u>feed at the table</u> of grace.

Hasan and Husain.—We have no strength to walk on foot, O Messenger of God! you two may go home before us. We shall come slowly behind you like shadows, till we reach the house.

The Prophet.—O Husain and Hasan, ye lights of the eye of God's elect, ye two ornaments of the shoulders of

Muhammad the chosen of God, come and ride both of you on my back, that I may take you to your mother.

'Alí.—O God's Messenger, this is not kind! Is not 'Alí one of the least of thy servants? give Hasan to me, that I also may be benefited, and, by God's holy orders, may perform a righteous act.

The Prophet.—O 'Alí, since I always bear the burden of sorrow for my people, carrying it day and night, that I may be able to make intercession for them, allow me to lift Hasan and Husain. O God, I adjure Thee by the merit of my cousin, the Lion of God, and by these two dear things I am supporting on my shoulders, freely have mercy on 'Alí's followers in the Day of Resurrection, as I voluntarily suffer ignominy in this world for their sake.

Fátimah.—O God, Muhammad is coming, what shall I do? how can I have patience when my heart is in anguish? Oh, I am altogether ashamed to look at him! Oh, with what face shall I see him!

'Alí.—Dear Fátimah, thy father is just coming, hasten to receive him most respectfully. Thy dear visitor is arriving; if thou hast got anything befitting the dignity of thy father, be quick and offer it to him.

Fátimah.—O God's Lion, I possess nothing at home but a soul in my body; there is not either gold, silver, or property in this house. Dear cousin, better take this shirt of mine and sell it, and buy with the proceeds some barley from Simeon the Jew,* that I may not suffer so much shame, but bake some barley-cakes for my father; peradventure my present sorrow will be turned into joy.

The Prophet.—Dear Fátimah, thou nightingale of my orchard, my soul, my heart, my very flesh and bones! trouble not thyself so much, nor suffer thy father to be ashamed, but sit down by my side that I may console thy tearful eyes.

---

* The expression "Simeon the Jew" is probably intended to convey rather that the trader was a "Jew," than that his name was Simeon.

Gabriel.—O cause of the creation of all, thou mirror of God's perspicuous light! I have brought thee a compliment from thy Creator, and in addition to the compliment a message. God says, "What dost thou like best of the fruits of Paradise, apples, pomegranates, dates, quinces, or grapes? What thou preferest I will send thee to-day, as an entertainment from Zahrah."

The Prophet (to his family).—O ye, who sit in the pavilion of Divine glory, there came the message of the Mighty, the glorious Lord, saying:—" Choose what thou likest best, that I, instead of Fátimah, may bring it to thee."

Husain (to the Prophet).—May I be offered as a sacrifice for thy soul! seeing I am the humblest of the family, it is but right that thou shouldst consult my wishes, and be favourable to me, who am the youngest, for the prayer of the sore-hearted, they say, is sooner heard. If thou wilt grant me permission to speak, I will tell thee what I desire most.

The Prophet.—Yes, Husain, thou art right in calling thyself the youngest, but why dost thou not make thy wishes known? Tell me what thou likest best, we will all yield to thy choice.

Husain.—I, who am ready to scatter my soul at thy feet—of all the fruits, I like fresh dates most. I beg thee, therefore, not to break my heart at all, but ask God to send us some dates.

The Prophet.—Enter, O Fátimah, into the inner closet, where thou shalt find some dates placed there by God's grace. Bring them out. Come, dear Husain, may my sweet soul be offered for thee! satisfy me by eating dates. Open thy mouth (may I be a sacrifice for thy throat!) that thy grandfather may feed thee with his own hands.

Michael.—O Husain, Bin 'Alí,* thou glory of men and jinns,† may this date be agreeable to thee! eat it with pleasure.

---

* That is, Husain the son of 'Alí.
† See note, p. 24.

The Prophet (to Husain).—May this fruit of the garden of Paradise be agreeable to thee! pray sincerely to thy Creator to forgive my people. O Husain, thou sorrow-seeking nightingale, open thy mouth, that thy infallible grandfather may put a fresh date therein.

Michael.—Thou cruelly poisoned one, thou keeper of the garden of Paradise, O Hasan, may the date suit thy health!

The Prophet.—May it be digested by thee, dear child Hasan! O Fátimah, thou sorrowful mother of these children, open thy mouth (may I be a sacrifice for it)!

The Nymphs.—May the date be agreeable to thee, O child of the best of the prophets! may it be pleasant to thee, thou stronghold of religion!

The Prophet.—May this fresh date, O Zahrah, be agreeable to thee! may the fruit of the garden of Paradise be pleasant to all of you! O 'Alí, open thy mouth like a rose-bud, and begin to eat fresh dates! May Muhammad be a sacrifice for thee, O royal personage who art highly honoured in the sight of God, in that He has preferred thee to all His creatures, for I have heard Him say plainly, "Be it agreeable to thee, by whose light of beauty the world is made manifest." But, alas! that I should see thee rolling in thy blood in the house of prayer, thy face cruelly turned to the colour of a tulip! Ah me! that I should then say, "Be it agreeable unto thee, O 'Alí!"

Fátimah.—May I be a sacrifice for thee, O honourable father! from the favour manifested by thee I see thou hast preferred 'Alí, who is the crown of my head, to us all, for thou continually adorest God, and sayest cheerfully to 'Alí, "Be it agreeable to thee, O 'Alí!"

The Prophet.—Know thou, O my dear Fátimah, that when I put the first date in Husain's mouth, I saw Saráfíl* and

---

* Saráfíl, or Isráfíl, is the angel who is to blow the last trumpet. He formed one of the numerous angelic host with whom Muhammad was said to hold converse. Michael, also, is supposed to have been an attendant on the Prophet to do his bidding.

Michael cheerfully wishing Husain a happy digestion. Following their example, I paid Husain the same compliment. When Hasan ate dates, Gabriel and Michael wished him an easy digestion, and I did the same thing; when you put the dates in your mouth, O Zahrah, I joined the nymphs of Paradise in congratulating thee; but when the date reached 'Alí's mouth, there came a voice from the throne of the Almighty Creator, a voice of great love accompanied by that of angels, saying, "O 'Alí, may the date be agreeable to thy taste! may the shelter of Our grace be a refuge to thy majesty!" Hearing this, by God's holy order I fell down and worshipped, letting the bridle of patience and reserve go from my hand.

Gabriel (to Muhammad).—Peace be on thee, O sphere of generosity! the gracious Creator, greeting thee, says: "''Alí, being my peculiar servant, I have made him My own vicegerent and thy successor. I swear by My own God-head, by My knowledge, long-suffering, and sovereignty, that if the Prophet had continued to put fresh dates in 'Alí's mouth until the Day of Resurrection, I would each time, with manifest grace, have said, 'May it be agreeable to thee, O 'Alí!'"

The Prophet.—Tell me, O good Gabriel, part of the dignity of Haidar the warrior in the Court of God! describe to me, O brother Gabriel, somewhat of 'Alí's great merit, so that I may, in God's name, inform the Shí'ahs.

Gabriel.—I swear, by that God who created me, and who chose me from among the angels to praise thee, that if the inhabitants of the earth knew 'Alí's position as the dwellers in heaven are aware of his excellency, and were they to love him in the same way, the Maker of heaven and earth would not have created everlasting fire at all. 'Alí is the saviour of all who die, and delivers people from the bitter pangs of death. Without his command 'Izráíl cannot snatch a soul, for 'Alí's decrees are the same as those of the glorious Lord himself. He who gives up the ghost and is a worshipper of 'Alí 'shall in the Day of Judgment find his own head in the lap of the nymphs of Paradise.

The Youth in Love.—Peace be unto thee, O my crowned uncle! I have arrived at thy Court with many hopes. I trust thou wilt lift up my head and grant my request.

The King.—What is thy request, my dear nephew? let me hear it plainly.

The Youth in Love.—I have cherished the idea in my bosom that thou wilt kindly betroth thy daughter to me, exalting me to the honour of becoming thy son-in-law, and in this way raising me to the highest degree of felicity.

The King (to the Youth).—There is no refusal to what thou sayest, but I have a request too; I demand a good dowry * for her. If thou canst get me the head of 'Alí, the chief of the true believers, as a dowry for thy cousin, thou mayest have her for a wife.

The Youth in Love.—O uncle! I have heard many say that 'Alí has a sword which in fact is a dragon. Its name is <u>Zú'l fakár,† it has two points in reference to life and death.</u> It is not an easy thing in the world to cut 'Alí's head, nor can it be performed by human agency.

The King.—There is no other way of attaining her. She cannot be had without Haidar's ‡ head.

The Youth in Love.—I go, O King! in the name of thy good fortune, hoping to bring thee 'Alí's head. I will build a whole temple with fresh ambergris, and dedi-

---

* Under the Muhammadan law a dower had to be settled upon the woman, though the omission of the settlement does not invalidate the contract.—Hughes' "Notes on Muhammadanism," p. 177, ed. 1877.

† Zú'l fakár is the name of the famous two-edged sword of 'Alí, which Muhammad reported that he had obtained from the angel Gabriel.—Johnson's Persian Dictionary, head " Zú."

‡ See note, p. 39.

cate it to idols. I will enrich all idolatrous priests with gold.

'Alí.—O Fátimah! bring me my Zú'l fakár, that I may go out for an excursion, for I feel very dull. Get me a spade also, that I may employ myself in some industry. Where is my Duldul,* that world-measuring steed, that lightning-like, wind-footed animal? Bring him to me.

Fátimah.—May I be a ransom for thee, O 'Alí Bin Abú Tálib! † thou who by generosity hast conquered the whole world. Where dost thou go, and what dost thou want to do? Thy departure kindleth a fire in my heart.

'Alí.—Be not sorry that I leave thee, for I go to procure us some sustenance. I go to the garden of the Jews, to be employed there as a waterer; peradventure I may be able to pass my time usefully.

Fátimah.—Behold, O heaven, what thou hast done to the family of the Prophet! what poverty hast thou brought on the children of Haidar the warrior! How can it be proper that the gracious "Lion of God" should go to labour in the service of the Jews merely to get wages?

'Alí.—O God! for the merit of the best of mankind, Muhammad, for the glorious situation of Makkah and the holy temple (I am glad that Thou knowest the troubles I perpetually suffer in this world), forgive the Shí'ahs in the Day of Resurrection, whether they be black or white, young or old.

The Youth in Love.—I am going to Madínah to Murtaza ‡ 'Alí to cut his head most maliciously. O death! I shall be a slave at thy gate if I hear that 'Alí is under the shadow of thy empire.

'Alí.—O Lord! 'Alí's head has never been valued by

---

* Name of 'Alí's mule.

† That is, 'Alí the son of Abú Tálib.

‡ Murtaza means "chosen, approved," and is a title given to 'Alí.

him in Thy cause. I have girded my loins day and night to serve Thee. For this reason 'Alí's back is thus bent.

The Youth (seeing the Zú'l fakár).—What precious and beautiful weapon is that? I think good luck attends me on this my journey. What have this horse and scymetar to do with a slave? Royal weapons are fit for royal persons only. O young Arab, whose are this horse and sword which cannot be equalled in all the world?

'Alí.—Know, O young man, that the heavy armour belongs to me, and the horse which thou seest is the one I ride. Tell me, why dost thou covet my things? whence comest thou, and whither art thou going?

The Youth.—O Arab! I come with a cruel intention as regards 'Alí. I have visited this country to kill God's vicegerent. If thou wishest not to be cut into two parts with my sword, kiss the horse and the weapon, and deliver them most respectfully to me.

'Alí.—O young man! do not show thy bravery to me, but talk respectfully and with decency. 'Alí is the arm of religion, the overthrower of the gate of Khaibar.* He is the champion of the faith. If thou be able to tie my arms by the strength of thy hand, I doubt not thou canst kill 'Alí too.

The Youth.—Draw thy sword and come to the field. Slay me with thy weapon if thou be able to prevail over me. I am sure, O young Arab, thou are satiated with thy life; receive, then, a blow from my sword, and learn how it tastes.

Gabriel (to the Prophet).—Peace be unto thee, O glory of heaven and earth! thus has thy Creator said, "Order all the inhabitants of Madínah, small and great, to get them

---

* "We cannot praise the modesty of romance, which represents him ('Alí) as tearing from its hinges the gate of a fortress, and wielding the ponderous buckler in his left hand."—Gibbon's "Decline and Fall of the Roman Empire" (Milman's ed. 1838), chap. iv. vol. ix. p. 300. See also note *, p. 45.

on the housetops, that they may behold how 'Alí, for our sake, will offer his head, even to an unbeliever.

The Prophet.—O people of Madínah, small and great, get you on the housetops by the command of God, the Maker, the Forgiver, the Mighty, the Conqueror, and see how 'Alí will give up his head for the sake of the Almighty.

Gabriel.—Thou prince of the two worlds, thou protector of the faithful, thou leader of men and jinns,* O chief of believers! it is engraved on the seal of the universe, "There is no youth but 'Alí, and no sword but Zú'l fakár."

Michael.—The breasts of jinns and angels are ravished with joy and delight. God and His Prophet are witness of the truth of what I say. The Creator of the world has declared that there is none like 'Alí, no youth but 'Alí, no sword but Zú'l fakár.

'Alí (putting down the Youth).—Thou unbelieving wretch, ignorant of God and his religion, bare thy neck quickly to the edge of the dagger. If thou become a Musulmán thou shalt obtain quarter; if not, thou shalt at once receive a blow from my soul-destroying sword.

The Youth in Love.—O murderer! I know no religion but that of love, which is the real object of my heart.

'Alí.—O broken-hearted youth! why dost thou sigh beneath the dagger? In whose snare art thou caught, that thou dost wane like the new moon? To whose cage dost thou belong, O melancholy bird? for thy sad notes have made me faint.

The Youth.—O young man, I have an uncle who has a daughter, with whom I am madly in love, her company being the only delight I seek. (Oh! who knows what will befall me to-day?) I came here to carry 'Alí's head to her, not knowing my own head would be borne off by thee.

'Alí.—I spare thy life, poor young man, seeing thou hast a spark of love within thee. Here is a dagger; take and

---

* See note, p. 24.

cut my head with it, and carry it to the object of thy love; then obtain her hand and live happily.

The Youth.—I did not come for thy head, noble youth, for what benefit can I derive from the head of one like thee? If thou art indeed kind to me, show me where 'Alí is, and deliver me at once from sorrow.

'Alí.—Young man, grieve no longer, I am 'Alí, the prince of the believers. I deliver up my head for the sake of God. I place my throat before the edge of the sword in His behalf. Cut off therefore my head, succeed in thy design, and set out at once for thy object.

The Youth.—I am now sure that thou art 'Alí, the prince of believers, for thy magnanimity shows that thou art he. If thou truly offerest thy head to me, tie thy hands, and make me rejoice in thy unexpected favour.

'Alí.—Come, bold man, tie my hands thyself, and lead me like a sheep to the slaughter. Sever my head from the body, thou foolish man, and return to thy country rejoicing.

The Youth.—O 'Alí, my soul rejoices in thee, my cup of pleasure is running over. Better generosity than this none has ever seen, that one should freely give his head to another man. I have already got my object through thee. If thou hast anything I can do for thee, tell me; I will hide it from thine enemies, O 'Alí!

'Alí.—There is nothing, O young man, that thou mayest do for me; all my desires are linked with God the gracious, who is merciful and favourable to me. I am willing that my Hasan should be an orphan, that my Husain should suffer grief, and my Zainab ride on camels when passing along in the streets and bázárs. There is only one petition I would make, O God, namely, that Thou shouldst forgive the sins of the Shía'hs.

Gabriel.—O holy ones! 'Alí is offering his head for the sake of the people of the Prophet's family.

Michael.—O Shí'ahs! God's lion is giving his head for

the snake of God, that in the Day of Resurrection the Shía'hs may be saved.

Hasan and Husain.—Have mercy on the sad state of the desolate, O God! for the merit of Muhammad, the asylum of all God's creatures. 'Alí is sitting in the shadow of the dagger; save him, O Lord, from the hand of this infidel.

'Alí.—Deliver me, O young man, soon. Why dost thou hesitate to slay me? I have given thee a head in behalf of God; take it, and go thy way. Take it, that the horse of thy pleasure may gallop well.

The Youth in Love.—May my hands be cut, O Imám of the age! may a thousand souls such as mine be sacrificed for thee! A peculiar light has shone in my heart from thy face. I see no other remedy for myself but to become a Musulmán. Forgive me, O 'Alí, and deliver me; enlighten me as to the fundamental parts of the Prophet's religion.

'Alí.—Blessed art thou, O young man, for thou art now saved; thou hast escaped from everlasting perdition at the hand of the Creator. Say, "I testify that there is no God but God, that Muhammad is His Prophet, and 'Alí His vice-regent."

The Youth.—Be my witness, O God, that I say, "I declare that there is no other God but God, that Muhammad is His Prophet, and 'Alí His vice-regent."

SCENE V.

DEATH OF THE PROPHET MUHAMMAD.

The death of Muhammad (or, in the language of the text, the arrival of his tossed ship "at anchor in a safe harbour") occurred at Madínah, on the 8th of June, A.D. 632. The last moments of the Prophet of Arabia were in no way unworthy either of the man, or the mission with which he claimed to have been charged. "His strength now rapidly sank. He seemed to be aware that death was drawing near. He called for a pitcher of water, and wetting his face, prayed thus: 'O Lord, I beseech Thee, assist me in the agonies of death!' Then three times he ejaculated earnestly, 'Gabriel, come close unto me!' At this time he began to blow upon himself, perhaps in the half-consciousness of delirium, repeating the while an ejaculatory form which he had been in the habit of praying over those who were very sick. When he ceased, from weakness, Ayesha took up the task, and continued to blow upon him and recite the same prayer. Then seeing that he was very low, she seized his right hand and rubbed it (another practice of the Prophet when visiting the sick), repeating all the while the earnest invocation. But Mahomet was too far gone to bear even this. He wished now to be in perfect quiet. 'Take off thy hand from me,' he said; 'that cannot benefit me now.' After a little he prayed in a whisper: 'Lord, grant me pardon, and join me to the companionship on high.' Then at intervals: 'Eternity in Paradise!' 'Pardon!' 'Yes; the blessed companionship on high!' He stretched himself gently. Then all was still. His head grew heavy on the breast of Ayesha. The Prophet of Arabia was dead. Softly removing his head from her bosom, Ayesha placed it on the pillow, and, rising up, joined the other women, who were beating their faces in bitter lamentation. The sun had but shortly passed the meridian. It was only an hour or two since Mahomet had entered the mosque, cheerful, and seemingly convalescent. He now lay cold in death."—Muir's "Life of Mahomet," vol. iv. p. 277, ed. 1861.

The Prophet.—Eternity is but a matter of time for all, to be sure. Fate's cup-bearer has in his diversified cups no draught which is everlasting. The world is a place full of commotions and perturbations, and its kingdom is a vast empire void of all order. Under the roof of this pillarless vault, no palate ever tasted the sweets of life but it must soon be embittered with death. My body is wasting rapidly from the vehemence of the fever, and my health is speedily declining. Methinks my time is finished; my moon is about to wane for ever. Come, dear daughter Fátimah! thy father is seized with fever; death, even death, will be the ultimate result, that is all!

Fátimah.—Thy words, O thou brightness of my sight, have made my poor suffering heart quite a city of confusion. Thou art men's guide in the narrow path of this uncertain life; how will they avoid straying from their road when thou art taken away from them? It is by thy blessed direction* only, that we travellers on this path can, with some tolerable degree of certainty, trace out the footsteps of the caravan of faith. Religion will, doubtless, lose its real lustre and beauty, when the author and finisher of the cause ceases any longer to support the same.

The Prophet.—Know thou, O my treasure, that some melancholy idea having got itself into my head, I seem to desire nothing else so much as death. Being weary of my sad, tiresome confinement within this limited enclosure, I have resolved to set out and betake myself into the more open and wider sphere of the heavens. My heart cannot fix its choice on any object here below, Omnipotent love having already attracted it to a different centre.

Fátimah.—May I be a ransom for thee, O thou Prophet of Madínah! Why dost thou break my heart by such sayings? Remember that thou art the nourishing flower-

---

* Verily it is our part to give direction.—Muir's "Life of Mahomet," vol. ii. p. 63, ed. 1858.

bed of my two unblown roses. Thou hast two little grandsons—the very pupils of thine eyes—Hasan and Husain. I hope thou wilt not make the former an orphan, and trust thou art not going to render the latter fatherless.

The Prophet (caressing his grandsons).—Come to me, Husain, thou flourishing rose of my prophetical garden; and come to me, Hasan, thou evergreen herb of my never fading meadow. Seeing, O Husain, that I have nourished thee, even with the fluid of my mouth; speak out, then, a few words to thy grandfather with that little tongue of thine, which is really my own.

Husain.—If thou intendest, dear grandfather, to put off the veil, to draw up the curtain, to disengage the heart from all former connections with any created being, to die, —be pleased to prophesy to me, then, what my end will be, or what will be the adventures of my life?*

The Prophet.—The Spirit of God shall take thee, after my death, dear son, to an assembly in which the curl of thy lock shall suffer some dishevelling. <u>Afterwards, thou shalt go to a country where thou shalt have none to help thee, except the spirits of the martyrs.</u> They will carry thee to a land, a dreadful land, the water of which no thirsty soul will be allowed to taste; a land wherein horses are made to tread on the bodies of the slain; a land wherein the dead do not receive any winding sheet.

Husain.—Since thou intendest to go to Heaven, the abode of peace, let me know to whose hand thou wilt commit the care of me; as I am as it were thine own soul, I beg thee to entrust me to the charge of some one whom thou lovest.

The Prophet.—Dear grandson, he whom I love above all,

---

* "One day when the Prophet was sitting with Âly, Fâtimah, Hasan, and Husayn, he said to them, 'Your graves will be scattered and separated from each other!' Husayn inquired if they should die natural deaths, or be slain. Mohammed replied, 'You and your brother and father will be slain by violence, and your children will be pursued by tyranny.'"—Merrick's "Life of Mohammed," p. 181, ed. 1850.

is 'Alí, thy father, the true successor* of myself, the elect of God, and the real friend of the Almighty Himself. Though, O 'Alí, I am extremely anxious about thyself, yet I entrust to thee these my two precious gems. Let not their truth-seeing eyes suffer from sleeplessness, or their ruby-like lips lose their freshness from thirst. But I know that Hasan shall be made to drink poisoned water when asleep, and Husain, when thirsty, shall receive a repulsive answer instead of water.

'Alí.—Thy affecting speech, O Prophet of God, hath kindled a flaming fire in my soul. Tell me, O thou full moon of direction, about what art thou anxious on my behalf?

The Prophet.—After I am gone, O 'Alí, thou shalt be altogether disregarded by this people. They will, disgracefully, put a rope round thy neck and drag thee along, notwithstanding thou art the strong cord of God's love, by which men are united to Him. Remove thy turban, O 'Alí, from off thy head, that I may reveal to thee another mystery. They shall cleave thy head with a sword, from the crown down to this part of the forehead, not regarding the repository of God's oracle. This thy beard shall they dye with the blood of thy forehead; the pulpit shall be desecrated, and the altar be brought to ruin.

'Alí.—We have received a peculiar grace from God not to complain of such trials and afflictions at all. If they are so wicked as to cast a rope round my neck, and thereby greatly disgrace me, I have a firm rock of patience to withstand against the flood of such temptations. My mind is not solicitous at all for what will happen to me in Ramazán,† all my anxiety being for the occurrences of Muharram and its victims.

---

* The Shí'ahs do not acknowledge the two first Khalífs, Abú Bakr and 'Umar.

† 'Alí was assassinated during Ramazán, and Husain was slain on the 10th of Muharram, respectively the ninth and first months of the Muhammadan year.

The Prophet.—Yes, if there be any heart at all overpowered with excessive grief, it must most certainly, O 'Alí, be with reference to the month of Muharram.

'Alí.—Let me know, O director of religion, and let my heart receive a full share of thy liberal knowledge, whether after thee, when thy people will fight with me, and obstinately distress me, must I take shelter behind the shield of patience and say nothing, or should I draw out the sword of vengeance from the sheath and defend myself?

The Prophet.—Rest quiet, O 'Alí, when that time shall come, and let the sword of thy soul remain in the sheath of silence. Be diligent to do what I am ordering thee; for thou wilt find out that the blessings of heaven consist in patience.

'Alí.—Seeing, O Prophet, that I have sold myself to do thy will, it is plain I cannot act contrary to thy orders. But, alas! how can I endure the grief of separation from thee, or where shall I find an associate thy equal?

The Prophet.—O lion of God! severity of fever has rendered me extremely weak, so that I cannot walk alone. Help me, please, and hold my arm, and take me somehow to the mosque; let all the people gather together in the same place, that I may rehearse unto them part of thy unspeakably great endowments. For fearing lest the thorn of unbelief may possibly take the place of the rose of religion, I am sorry to die while others live.

'Alí (holding the Prophet's arm).—Be it known unto you, O ye people, that the Sultán of religion is going to the mosque; the Messiah intends to ascend to heaven. Come and hear his sermons that ye may find rest for your souls, for the nightingale of God's unity* is going to pour forth his melodious notes.

---

* The unity of God is a fundamental principle in the Muhammadan religion. The "Kur'án" says, "Say God is one God: the eternal God; He begetteth not, neither is He begotten, and there is not any one like

The Prophet (in the pulpit).—Be it known unto you, O ye congregation, that I intend to tear aside and rend the curtain; I mean I am going to leave this present dangerous world. I am tired of this abode of trials, and am about to die. Being fully aware that what I announce to you will most assuredly come to pass, if you hear my voice and raise me properly from the dust, the time will arrive when I shall do the same to all of you.

The Companions.—O thou Messiah of the Lord! since thou hast set thy face steadfastly towards heaven, and art eagerly desirous to leave this world for the blessed regions of eternity, declare plainly what thy ever-remembered flock must do after thy departure.

The Prophet.—My address is to all of you who are here present, whether strangers or my own people. God's unity and His service, you must have known already, consist of two fundamental things, which I am going to repeat to you once again. First, following the incontrovertible part of the book of God, under every line of which there is a volume of mysteries; second, following the king of religion, the true successor of the Prophet, the friend of God, the moon of the garden of heaven, by name 'Alí. All creation, no less than all created beings, is in bondage; one, 'Alí, alone is free. All mankind are sunk in sleep; one, 'Alí, alone is awake and watchful.

The Companions.—The world, O highly dignified being, has but one true director at present, and that is thee. To be sure, then, there is no other right way but in obeying thee. We are quite persuaded that after the blossom of

---

unto Him." "This chapter," adds Sale, " is held in particular veneration by the Mohammedans, and declared by a tradition of their Prophet to be equal in value to a third part of the whole Korán. It is said to have been revealed in answer to the Koreish, who asked Mohammed concerning the distinguishing attributes of the God he invited them to worship."—Sale's "Koran," chap. cxii. p. 507, ed. 1734.

thy face has faded away, we can get no true rose-water having the proper scent thereof like the perspiration of 'Alí's forehead.

The Prophet.—Take me, my friends, to my own apartment, that my candle may burn out in its own proper closet; for I intend to have some private conversation with 'Alí, and mean to intrust him with the store of my mind.

'Alí.—May I be offered a sacrifice to thy dignity! Let us go home, for thou art in great trouble, thou art in much embarrassment; thy body is quite worn out with fever, and thy heart is like a grain of rue in the censor of thy breast.

The Prophet.—There is not a single breath of true life in all the kingdoms of this world. No happier abode can be found for man than the realms of eternity. The inevitable lot of both the powerful monarch and the helpless beggar is death. No indemnity is granted to either. (*Falls into a swoon.*)

'Alí.—Come, O Fátimah! see how thy father hath fallen in a swoon. The parrot of his speech is silent. Quick! let us rend the garment of patience, and see what we can do for him.

Fátimah.—My heart is turned into a boiling pot within me for the sake of the Prophet of God. What shall I do, God's Prophet has fallen in a swoon? Woe unto me! Come thou, O Husain! dishevel thy curling locks; peradventure thy perfume diffused in the air will reach his nose, and so he will recover.

Husain (*speaking to the Prophet*).—May my soul be made a sacrifice for thee! commence to speak; I am Husain, thy beloved grandson. Open once more thy all-seeing eyes, and look at me.

The Prophet.—O Husain, the light of my all-seeing eyes, may I be made an oblation for thy pleasant voice! Thou art faithful indeed, since thou hast come at such a time to visit me. If I pass away, O Husain, in this place, I thank God I shall have thee by my death-bed; but I know, dear child, thou shalt die in a place where there shall be none by thy couch except cawing birds and wild deer.

'*Alí.*—O Prophet! thou hast set fire to the soul of the whole world. Thou didst shut thine eyes, and subvert the foundations of the earth. Thou didst fall on the ground fainting, and didst roll thyself in the dust, leaving a sad scar of pain on every human breast by so doing.

The Prophet.—O 'Alí! summon my uncle 'Abbás to my presence in my private apartment, that I may converse with him a minute before I leave him for ever.

'*Alí.*—O renowned uncle! the seal* of God's Apostles has summoned thee to his presence; hasten thou to his sacred closet, since he has granted thee the privilege of becoming his privy counsellor.

'*Abbás.*—May I be a ransom for this thy body stretched on the bed! May I be made a sacrifice for this thy pallid worn-out face! May God never allow thee to see any painful trouble! May I have the happiness to know what thy uncle can do for thee?

The Prophet.—Come, uncle, see how fever has deprived me of all strength and power. Come, hold me kindly for a minute in thy arms. And thou, O 'Alí, observe how faintly I breathe, and put thy kind hands on my shoulder.

'*Alí.*—For God's sake do not close thine eyes ever upon this world, for thou art he by whose single glance this sphere came into existence.

The Prophet.—Up from thy place, O chosen 'Alí! weep not so much at the idea of separation from thy cousin. Hold me in thy arms well, O thou my beloved, and tell my uncle 'Abbás to come here to me.

'*Abbás.*—Dear nephew, I am shedding a flood of tears at thy departure. What are thy orders? Speak, that I may hasten to perform them.

The Prophet.—Since thou art the chief of this nation, O

---

* See note ‡, p. 40.

my sorrowful uncle, it is my will that thou shouldst occupy my place* after my death, inherit my patrimony, pay my debts, and kindly perform the promises I have made to men.

'Abbás.—May my body and soul be offered a sacrifice for thine! I have not strength enough for such a work, and I cannot undertake it. I possess nothing, and thy religion is worth much. This burden, therefore, is heavier than I can bear.

The Prophet (turning to 'Alí).—Neither in this nor in the next world have I a more faithful friend than.'Alí. He who is most esteemed by me, the same shall faithfully execute my will.

'Alí.—Thou mayest expect from me, O Messenger of God, nothing but fidelity and truth. Require of me, therefore, whatever thou wilt, I shall most zealously perform the same. Why shouldst thou complain of helplessness, or want of real friends, seeing thou hast one like myself ready at hand to help thee?

The Prophet.—Receive thou, O 'Alí, my heritage, pay my debts, and perform whatever promises I have made to anyone. I know thou art as sure as thy promise, and thy word as good as thyself, O 'Alí.

'Alí.—Have no suspicions at all in thy heart, for I am not faithless as others. I will most willingly do all that thou hast said.

The Prophet.—Mayest thou ever be delivered from sorrow as thou didst deliver me from the same. Come, thou, O Salmán,† my faithful Persian disciple, let me send thee to my private room or closet, to bring me thence a bundle of clothes which is in the box, my staff, and my slender whip.

Salmán.—May I be offered for thy emaciated body!

---

* This is the Shí'ah doctrine.   † See note †, p. 36.

Behold! I have brought what thou didst order me to fetch.

The Prophet.—Take from me, O 'Alí, this whip and this staff and rod. O 'Alí, this is the same rod* that was changed into a serpent in the presence of Moses. When he was feeding the flock of Jethro in the wilderness he would never be without this rod, which, O 'Alí, is a branch from the tree of Paradise.

'Alí.—May I be a sacrifice for thy miracle-working hands! O Prophet, may I be an offering for thy rod!

The Prophet.—This turban was a present to me from the bountiful Deity. In time of peace, when in society, it became a crown to me; and in time of war it may be used as a regular helmet.

'Alí.—The threshold of thy house, O Prophet, is to us the highest heaven, and the dust of thy sacred Court a sufficient crown of honour for our heads.

The Prophet.—Here, I have got a shirt; take it also from me, and know that this shirt came down from heaven on purpose for me. A day will come, O 'Alí, when this shirt shall be stained with blood. My sorrow in that day shall be more than ever.

'Alí.—Thy last saying, O Prophet, has made my soul extremely sad. Be pleased to tell me, with whose blood shall this shirt be stained?

The Prophet.—Know thou, O 'Alí, that Husain, our beloved grandson, shall on one occasion put on this shirt and go to Karbalá. There some wicked people shall unjustly slay him, and so this shirt shall get stained on that day.

---

* "The Muhammadans say, after the Jews, that Moses received from Shoaib (Jethro) the rod of the prophets (which was a branch of a myrtle of Paradise, and had descended to him from Adam) to keep off the wild beasts from his sheep; and that this was the rod with which he performed all those wonders in Egypt."—Sale's "Koran," chap. xxviii. p. 319, Note d., ed. 1734.

(*Turning to Salmán.*)—O Salmán, thou art now overbusy with other sad thoughts, yet go into the closet once more, there shalt thou find a sealed casket; bring it quickly to me, for in so doing thou wilt greatly oblige me.

Salmán.—O thou whose praise is beyond the description of any intelligent being's tongue, here is the sealed casket for which thou sentest me.

The Prophet.—O 'Alí, thou who hast no equal throughout the world, unlock this casket, and tell me what there is in it.

'Alí.—In the middle of the casket, O ark of honour, there is a gem—nay, rather, a ring, O thou chief link in the prophetical chain!

The Prophet.—This ring, O 'Alí, is more valuable than all the kingdoms of this world, the whole universe being contained miraculously within its small circuit. This ring,* O 'Alí, was at first with Solomon the Prophet, king of Jerusalem (being indeed fit for a prophet's finger, as it was for his); but thou dost not know, O 'Alí, where its last place shall be; I tell thee, it shall be in the mouth of 'Alí Akbar, thy grandson, when he shall be overpowered with thirst.

---

* It was in virtue of the possession of the seal that Solomon held his kingdom. Respecting Muhammad's ring, Sir William Muir states:— "One party relate that, feeling the want of a seal for his despatches, the Prophet had a signet ring prepared for that purpose, of pure silver. Another party assert that Khálid Ibn Saíd made for himself an iron ring plated with silver, and that Mahomet, taking a fancy to the ring, appropriated it to his own use. A third tradition states that the ring was brought by Amr bin Saíd from Abyssinia; and a fourth, that Muádz Ibn Jabal had it engraved for himself in Yemen. One set of traditions hold that Mahomet wore this ring on his right hand; another, on his left; one, that he wore the seal inside; others, that he wore it outside. . . . Now all these traditions refer to one and the same ring, because it is repeatedly added that, after Mahomet's death, it was worn by Abu Bacr, by Omar, and by Othmán, and was lost by the latter in the well of Aris. There is yet another tradition, that neither the Prophet, nor any of his immediate successors, ever wore a ring at all."— Muir's "Life of Mahomet," vol. i., Introduction, chap. i., p. lxxvii., ed. 1858.

'Alí.—If the candle of thy life be extinguished, O Prophet, by some sudden wind, I shall grope in darkness in the brightest part of my day.

The Prophet.—Come thou, dear Fátimah! O light of my seeing eyes! come, for it is a parting interview, visit me once more for the last time. I have one command which I deliver to thee as my dying injunction. Thou knowest that 'Alí, being a poor man, has no more[*] at his table than two barley-loaves. Thou must be content with what he has in his house; eat a loaf of barley-bread, and live peaceably with him.

Fátimah.—I can be content with having a rough reed mat under my body, if only 'Alí deigns to be pleased with me. I hope, and patiently wait for, the real rest to be enjoyed at the resurrection of the just. This world cannot be, good father, a place of tranquillity for me.

The Prophet.—If, O Fátimah, thou spendest but one day peaceably with 'Alí, thou shalt be exalted in the Day of Judgment above the very throne of God. If ungrudgingly thou bearest with his poverty and need in this world, as soon as thou enterest the grave thou shalt find thyself amidst the meadows of Paradise.

Fátimah.—After thou art gone, O father, I shall have so many sad things to think over, that they will leave no room in my mind for the cares of this world to enter therein. On one hand sorrow for thee, on the other the care of Hasan and Husain; now lamenting for thee, now attending to my children.

The Prophet.—You all must go out of my room for awhile; you all must be removed from the precinct of this holy mountain. For I have some private discourse with my Lord. I have to consult my faithful Friend in regard to my proceedings.

Fátimah.—O Lord God, for the sake of Thy goodness and grace, if it be possible, let me not become fatherless.

---

[*] See note †, p. 55.

Oh! let the sigh of the afflicted have a place near Thy mercy-seat; O Lord God, let it not return thence without effect.

Gabriel.—It has been recorded plainly in the divine register, O 'Izráil,* that a perfect man must this very moment leave the world; go thou then to the earth, and take the soul of the Prophet Muhammad. Let his tossed ship come to anchor in some safe harbour.

'Izráil.—Seeing that none can ever have such access to God as the Prophet has, tell me, then, O Gabriel, in what manner am I to take the soul of such an honourable creature?

Gabriel.—Thou shalt go to the earth, O snatcher of the spirits, with thy best respects, and first knock most respectfully at the gate of that highly esteemed person. If he should allow thee permission to enter, step in obediently; if not, return most humbly to thy station.

'Izráil.—Here is one of the least servants of Muhammad, the king of the faithful. Let some one be kind enough to come to the door, for I have a message to deliver.

Fátimah (at the door).—Who is that knocking at the door? And what can have induced him so to do? Is his thunder-like voice going to strike my soul dead?

'Izráil.—Open the door, O best of women,† it is I. I have come to ask the Prophet a question.

Fátimah.—My body begins to tremble by reason of his terrible words. Oh! what shall I do, my friends? Whose voice might that be?

'Izráil.—Know thou, O daughter of the Prophet, that I am a stranger come from a distant country to receive light from Mount Sinai of Arabia. Be pleased to open the door, and allow me to enter, for I have a knot to be untied inside.

Fátimah.—Nay, young man, have thy knot untied some-

---

* See note, p. 23.   † See note *, p. 42.

where else; better go back to look after thine own business. My father has fainted from illness and is in a swoon; he is not in good mood, and is altogether unwell. Go thy way, it is not time to ask questions now. Stay no longer here, for it is no place for thee.

'Izráíl.—Know, O lady, that my abode is very far distant, and that I have an urgent business with the Prophet. It is out of regard and respect that I behave myself thus; otherwise I can enter any house, though the doors be securely fastened.

The Prophet.—Dost thou not know, Fátimah, who is he that knocks at the door?

Fátimah.—No, father, I am unable to tell who that rough-spoken man is. I can only say that his dreadful voice has made me quite restless.

The Prophet.—It is he who continually grieves the heart of men; he who casts dust of misery on the heads of poor widows. It is he, even the snatcher of the souls of men, jinns,* beasts, and birds; he can command a full view of the east and west at the same time.

Fátimah.—Oh! what shall I do? The time of trouble has after all arrived, the hour of affliction approacheth. Come in, O thou snatcher of souls, and say what thou wishest to do, for thou art permitted by the Prophet to enter.

'Izráíl.—Peace be unto thee, O mighty sovereign! Peace be unto thee, O sun of the world!

The Prophet.—On thee be both peace and honour! thou art altogether welcome. What may thy object or message be? tell us.

'Izráíl.—May I be offered unto thee, O thou king of freedom and liberty! the Creator of the world has sent me on the earth to thee, to know whether it be thy pleasure that I should transport thy soul from thy body to a garden

---

* See note, p. 24.

of roses and jasmines; or whether thou preferest rather to live eternally on the earth. Thou mayest choose which thou likest best.

The Prophet.—In the pleasure-garden of this life every beautiful rose is attended with several piercing thorns, and the treasure of this world has many venomous serpents accompanying it. Thou mayest take my life if thou pleasest; but, O snatcher of souls, wait a minute, for we have somewhat to do in the world.

'Izráíl.—I see thee, O Prophet, looking here and there, and sighing. It appears thou art expecting the arrival of somebody.

The Prophet.—O Lord God, nothwithstanding my illness and disease, wherever I look there is no trace of Gabriel to be found.

Gabriel (appearing).—O thou through whose preaching the world has received new life, peace be on thee! O thou who art crowned with the diadem of T.H.,* peace be on thee!

---

* T. H. are the initial letters at the commencement of Chapter XX. of the Kur'án. Sale's remarks respecting them are as follows:—"The signification of these letters, which, being prefixed to the chapter, are therefore taken for the title, is uncertain. Some, however, imagine they stand for *Ya rajol, i.e.* O man! which interpretation, seeming not easily to be accounted for from the *Arabic*, is by a certain tradition deduced from the *Ethiopic*, or for *Ta, i.e. tread*, telling us that Mohammed, being employed in watching and prayer the night this passage was revealed, stood on one foot only, but was hereby commanded to ease himself by setting both feet to the ground. Others fancy the first letter stands for *Túba, beatitude*, and the latter for *Hawiyat*, the name of the lower part of hell. *Tah* is also an interjection commanding silence, and may properly enough be used in this place."—Sale's "Koran," chap. xx. p. 256, ed. 1734. Hughes, however, speaking of the Kur'án, states that there are "intricate sentences or expressions the exact meaning of which it is impossible for man to ascertain until the day of resurrection, but which was known to the Prophet;" and he instances, in exemplification, the Súra-i-Twá Há (xx.): "He is most merciful and sitteth on His throne," *i.e.* God *sitteth* (Arabic, *istawá*).—Hughes "Notes on Muhammadanism," p. 34, ed. 1877.

The Prophet.—And on thee be peace, O honoured and revered Gabriel. Where hast thou been, brother, since I last saw thee?

Gabriel.—May I be offered for thee! I was just making preparations for thee; for I was ornamenting the garden of Paradise for thy coming; I was bearing good tidings of thy arrival to heaven; I was ordering the fragrant zephyrs to blow gently on thy meadows; I was wiping off dust from thy palaces, and filling them with beautiful nymphs.

The Prophet.—O Gabriel, I do not care so much about Paradise and its beautiful nymphs, as about the happiness of my people; give some news about them to the delight of my soul. I have a great knot, as it were, in my heart with regard to the salvation of my people. May the Lord bountifully untie the same through His mercy!

Gabriel.—Be of good cheer, O Muhammad! there came a voice from the throne of mercy on high, just this moment, saying, "O Prophet of God, rejoice, for the ocean of grace is in its full tide with respect to thy people. In the Day of Judgment I shall make thee the advocate of sinners, and shall encompass thee about with my blessings. Thou shalt see so many of thy people inhabiting Paradise in that day, that thou shalt be quite satisfied.

The Prophet (*to 'Alí*).—O prince of all believers, it is now time for me to give up the ghost; I must make ready to leave for ever this frail, perishable world. After my death, thou must wash my body with thine own hands, and use my own shirt for my funeral garment.

'Alí.—Alas! alas! the seal of prophecy is broken; the door of revelation is shut against all. This occurrence has put the souls of angels in perpetual grief; this event has subverted the foundation of religion.

Gabriel (*to the Prophet*).—O model of true religion, call unto thyself thy son-in-law, 'Alí, the elect, thy daughter Fátimah, and thy two grandsons Hasan and Husain. Now thou art going to depart this life, thou must remember the eternal covenant thou hast with thy God. Stay a few minutes more in this world to ratify thy agreement with everyone of those mentioned above, and then thou mayest die.

The Prophet.—O Gabriel, thou hast truly performed to me the duty of a brother. God be pleased with thee for thus reminding me of the subject. Come thou, O 'Alí, my faithful companion, and solve my difficulty, for thou art the only one to do so.

'Alí.—May I be made a ransom for thee! What is the service? Please give thy commands! May I be offered for the curls of thy musky-smelling hair! let me know my duty.

The Prophet.—After my death, O Alí, thou must voluntarily submit that the petals of thy rose be scattered abroad, that thy head be cloven asunder like the point of a pen. Peradventure thy martyrdom will be the means of salvation to my people, in raising thee to the high office of intercessor for them.

'Alí.—O Prophet, I am ready to be afflicted with all sorts of ills in this life for the sake of thy holy people's salvation.

The Prophet.—O Fátimah (may I be offered to thy good name!), thou must know that thy ribs shall be fractured by a door struck against them. Thou must bear the trouble patiently for my sake, and offer Muhassan, thy miscarried child, a ransom for my people.

Fátimah.—I will bear all these trials most patiently, O father; I will offer Muhassan, my darling child, a sacrifice for thy people. But may no hurt ever happen to Husain, my most beloved son; for if mischief befall him in this world, I shall set up a most heart-rending lamentation for him.

The Prophet.—Nay, my child, give up Husain also willingly in the service of God. Thou must love my sinful people above Husain, thy darling son.

Fátimah.—I will give up Husain, my darling child, for the cause of God too; though I have none else so dear to me, I shall try to do without him.

The Prophet.—Know thou, O Hasan, that after my death people will poison thee, and thy skin shall be turned quite green from the effect of the drug. Art thou willing, my son, to undergo such a terrible trial? Art thou ready that thy very intestines should come out of thy throat?

Hasan.—I am ready, O Prophet of God, that, for the sake of thy poor sinful people, even my very heart should be cut into several pieces.

The Prophet.—O Husain, thou who art shedding blood from thine eyes, come near, my grandson, for thy story is very long. Come hither, for thou art a true, faithful friend to me. Come hither, for thou art indeed my real grandchild. All the inhabitants of the two worlds, whether men or jinns, are sunk in sin, and have only one, Husain, to save them.

Husain.—What is thy order, grandfather? I am quite ready to obey it. What is the service that I must duly perform?

The Prophet.—Dear child, I am going to tell thee the story of Karbalá. Oh! I do not know how to say it, seeing thy afflictions are so many. Tell me, child, wilt thou suffer troubles, or not? Wilt thou go to Karbalá submissively, or not?

Husain.—I will go, not only to Karbalá, but to any spot thou mayest command. But may I ask thee what thou meanest?

The Prophet.—O Husain, thou must voluntarily give thy head to the dagger. When Shimar* shall draw out his dagger thou must stretch thy throat before it.

Husain.—With all my heart. I will give my own head for the salvation of thy people. Nay, I will even make the throat of my infant son, Asghar, a target to the arrow of God's decree for them.

The Prophet.—Thou must give up the two hands of

---

* See note, p. 43.

'Abbás,* thy brother. Though it will grieve thee much, thou must offer thy son, 'Alí Akbar, also.

Husain.—Though it is a hard trial indeed to lose a young brother and a blooming son, yet, for the sake of God, I will most readily do so.

The Prophet.—Thou must leave thy dear home for a foreign land, thou must suffer to be unjustly slain, and remain unburied. Thy sister must not be allowed to see thee beneath the sword. Thou must all the while express thy gratitude to God.

Husain.—O grandfather, may God save thee from all troubles! I am ready to undergo what thou hast said, be it ever so hard.

The Prophet.—O 'Izráíl, I say to thee that thou mayest now do what thou art commanded by the glorious Deity.

Gabriel.—O angel of death, take the soul of the Prophet gently.† Let him suffer no anguish, not so much as the point of a hair.

The Prophet (to 'Izráíl).—My patience is going to leave me altogether, for this thy mode of taking a soul. Unless God's mercy should interpose, if thou shouldest seize my people's souls with the same severity—oh, alas! I do not know how they could bear it.

'Izráíl.—May I be offered for thee, for thy honour, for thy majesty and dignity! I have been very mild to thee, in regard to this matter.

The Prophet.—Oh! let me, instead of my people, suffer the severity of death. Give all the afflictions and sorrows of my followers to me alone to bear, that my beloved followers should not suffer the pangs of dissolution at all when they die, that they may never taste the bitterness of death. Since I am acquainted with all the mysteries of truth, I say therefore, what everybody under the same

---

* See note †, p. 17, and note, p. 8.

† The Muhammadans believe that the better the man the less is his agony at the hour of death.

circumstances will declare, "I bear witness that there is no other God but one true God."

'Alí.—O Husain, put the cloth for mourning around thy neck. O, best among women, Fátimah! beat thy head and lament. Arise, Fátimah, weep for the death of thy father; and, O thou faithful spirit Gabriel, spread thy wings from earth to heaven.

Fátimah.—Oh, woe unto me! I have lost the way to my house; nay, my dwelling has been pulled down, for its owner is dead.

Hasan.—Ah, woe unto me! my back is broken by the weight of this burden of grief. The dust of desolation has, at length, covered my face.

Husain.—My heart within me is sounding like a flute. Wherever I set my face, first or last, there is a Karbalá.

Fátimah.—O Husain, weep not, thou dear child, though thou canst not help it, for I can cry enough, beloved son, for the whole world. Sweet youth, wet not thine eyes at all with tears, thou needst not think of poor 'Alí Akbar.

'Alí (to Gabriel).—Go thou, O blessed Gabriel, to heaven, and bring from Paradise a litter for the king of religion, Muhammad, and transport him to the regions of eternity. Bring also with thee some leaves from the tree Al Túba,*

---

* "Concerning this tree (Túba) they fable that it stands in the palace of *Mohammed*, though a branch of it will reach to the house of every true believer; that it will be loaden with pomegranates, grapes, dates, and other fruits, of surprising bigness, and of tastes unknown to mortals. So that if a man desire to eat of any particular kind of fruit, it will immediately be presented to him, or if he choose flesh, birds ready drest will be set before him, according to his wish. They add, that the boughs of this tree will spontaneously bend down to the hand of the person who would gather of its fruits, and that it will supply the blessed not only with food, but also with silken garments, and beasts to ride on, ready saddled and bridled, and adorned with rich trappings, which will burst forth from its fruits; and that this tree is so large that a person mounted on the fleetest horse would not be able to gallop from one end of its shade to the other in a hundred years. . . . This garden

a casket of camphor, and some water from the fountain called Salsabíl.

(Paradise) is also watered by a great number of lesser springs and fountains, whose pebbles are rubies and emeralds, their earth of camphire, their beds of musk, and their sides of saffron, the most remarkable among them being *Salsabíl* and *Tansím*."—Sale's "Koran," Prel. Disc., sec. iv. p. 96, ed. 1734.

SCENE VI.

THE SEIZURE OF THE KHALIFAT BY ABU BAKR.

This Scene relates to the seizure of the Khalífat, on the death of Muhammad, in A.D. 632, by Abú Bakr, an act which was resented by 'Alí, who refused to recognise the authority of his rival. The Shí'ahs to this day regard the succession as an act of usurpation, and discard Abú Bakr from the list of the Imáms. The tradition alluded to in the text, that consequent on 'Alí's refusal to tender his homage to the Khalíf Abú Bakr, the house of the recusant son-in-law of the Prophet was threatened with destruction by fire, is not considered by Sir William Muir to be well founded.

'Alí.—Hereafter I must suffer many troubles; having lost the rose, I must patiently endure the injuries of the thorn. After the death of the Seal* of the Prophets I must sigh painfully with a wounded breast. No impure eye being able to comprehend the truth, I must put a veil on my face to hide me from the glance of mankind.

Hasan.—O thou who hast abandoned the world and scorned it! thou who hast rejected with disdain the perishable pleasures of this life! thou art he, concerning whom the Holy Spirit has proclaimed to all living, "There is no youth so good as 'Alí."

---

* See note ‡, p. 40.

'*Ali.*—Dear child, the tree of hope is about to produce the fruit of regret. O light of mine eyes! my rose avenue is bristling with thorns. The bewitching spheres are playing wonderfully to produce, by illusion, serpents and dragons from ropes. To-day the sower, Fate, is about to scatter seeds of sorrow in the field of the world, the fruit of which shall be reaped on the Day of Judgment!

Hasan.—O 'Alí, tell me, what seed are the spheres about to sow? In what soil do they scatter the seed, and what will it produce when sown? Thy mysterious sayings make even a fool wise, and thy conversation, O 'Alí, renders the mad intelligent.

'Ali.—Know, O child, that Abú Bakr,* the absolute infidel, will seize upon the Khalífat unjustly, and from this deed a thousand various results shall spring in time.

Hasan.—May I become a sacrifice for thee! Briefly explain the case to me, and tell me what will be the result of this matter; declare it to me, O thou who knowest the secret of affairs, thou by whose instruction the ignorant can reach the utmost limit of perfection.

'Ali.—Dear child, the unmanly villain will occasion endless mischief, the merciless enemy will do against us what his heart wishes; but the Lion of God will submit his neck to the chain of trial, and lay his hand on his heart, the seat of

---

* "It is probable that Ali, while the people were swearing allegiance (to Abu Bakr), remained in his own apartments or in the chamber of death. It is alleged by his adherents that he expected the Caliphate for himself. But there was nothing in his previous position, nor in the language and actions of the Prophet towards him, which should have led to this anticipation. It is possible, indeed, that, as the husband of Mahomet's only surviving daughter, he may have conceived that a claim existed by inheritance. . . . Whether Ali swore allegiance at the first to his new chief, or refused to do so, it was certainly not till Fátimah's death, six months after that of her father, that Ali recognised with any cordiality the title of Abu Bakr to the Caliphate."—Muir's "Life of Mahomet," vol. iv. p. 290, ed. 1861.

truth, and will look on. The prime mover, the root or source of this mischief, is Abú Bakr, O dear child, though outwardly 'Umar* appears to make much noise. The dust of this sedition will first set on Fátimah's face. Zahraht will be the foremost to be infected by this contagious melancholy.

Fátimah (to 'Alí).—May I become a sacrifice for thee! If there be any other trouble so great as my sorrow for my lamented father, let me hear it. No heart remaineth to me to be melted, nor any dust that they should throw it on my head. They may split my ribs by the pressure of the door, but surely, O 'Alí, the spheres have already broken my back!

Alí.—O Fátimah, as long as thou art alive thy soul must suffer trouble; thou hast other things, besides thy father's death, wherewith to be afflicted. At Madínah heaven will turn thy day into night; in the land of Karbalá people will hurt thy Zainab.

Fátimah.—Oh! what will Fate do to me and Zainab? How does Destiny intend to treat the family of the King of Yasrib‡? Why should Heaven hurt us and scratch the face of the rose with thorns?

---

* 'Umar (Omar) was a citizen of Makkah, whose conversion took place at the close of the sixth year of Muhammad's mission. "Omar," says Muir, "had so commanding a stature, that he rose far above the crowd, as if he had been mounted. He was stout and fair, and somewhat ruddy. Impulsive and precipitate, his anger was easily aroused; and men feared him because of his uncertain and impetuous temper. At the period of his conversion he was but six-and-twenty; yet so great and immediate was the influence of his accession upon the spread of Islam, that from this era is dated the commencement of its open and fearless profession at Mecca." (Muir's "Life of Mahomet," vol. ii. p. 171, ed. 1858.) On the death of Muhammad he was mainly instrumental in securing the election of Abú Bakr as Khalíf, and ultimately himself succeeded to that dignity.

† See note, p. 22.

‡ Yasrib was the ancient name of Madínah; the King of Yasrib was Muhammad.

Ali.—Sit down by me, that I may declare unto thee thy sorrow; that I may put thee in mind of secrets not yet told. Come, Zainab, sit thou also by Fátimah, that I may foretell thee also the real state of things. O ye two nightingales of the meadow of sorrow, harken! I will explain to you the sad story of my beloved ones.

Fátimah.—O thou who art overwhelmed with the sorrow of a whole world, speak to us of grief; narrate for my distressed soul the woes of the universe! talk to me of Zainab's* dishevelled locks; tell me a story about the ringlets of her hair, which is curl upon curl.

'Ali.—I hesitate to tell thee sad stories, fearing lest I should hurt thy feelings. O Fátimah! thou art ill; I am anxious lest thou die. Wherewithal shall I then comfort my sad heart?

Zainab (to 'Ali).—Dear father, speak to me thy secrets in private; do not talk to my mother about the sad events that will befall thy beloved ones, but tell them to me. Dear father, it is I that am turned pale like amber owing to pain; thou mayest narrate to me the story of the ruby of Arabia Felix.

'Ali.—Yes, it is thou, O Zainab, who wilt suffer many calamities; thou art she who will experience countless cruelties in Karbala; thou wilt have to throw dust on thy head, and everywhere endure hardships and trials.

Fátimah (to 'Ali).—O prince of believers, declare unto us our condition; let us know what will be our adventures.

Ali.—My nightingale of eloquence and prediction will begin to sing, provided thou agreest, O Zahrah, not to

---

* Zainab was the daughter of 'Alí. The mosque erected to her memory is one of the most sacred of all the Muslim sanctuaries.—Lane's "Modern Egypt," vol. i. p. 303, ed. 1836.

rend thy garments, nor lamenting beat on thy head, and by thy cries set the world of angels in flames.

Fátimah.—Relate thy story, O 'Alí! After I have heard, I will remain patient if I can.

'Alí.—Dearly beloved, I will make known the contents of a sad letter. O Husain, Hasan, Zainab, and Fátimah, arise! for I am about to startle you all.

All the Family.—When thou openest thy mouth thou givest us life; thou makest the dead live by thy Christ-like influence. Tell us, O 'Alí, our adventures; after we have heard them thou wilt see what patience we each of us possess.

'Alí.—Two necks shall be pierced by arrows. Two heads belonging to our family shall droop in chains, O friends. One neck shall to-day bend under a grievous burden. Another neck shall be laden in the month of Muharram. The bond of this neck shall be cast aside in a day, but the burden of the other neck will continue from Karbalá to Damascus.

Fátimah.—O thou whose pleasant speech is so very charming, tell me to whom the two mentioned necks belong? O commander of the believers, sprinkle water on my fire, for my breast is burning with the flames of sorrow.

A'lí.—O thou whose lip is sweet as the water of Al Kauzar,* whose face is blooming like the lofty garden of Paradise; thou in the noose of whose ringlets the nymphs of heaven are entangled lovingly! my own neck is the first neck. To-day heaven is going to put bonds of cruelty round my throat, notwithstanding I am called the strong rope of faith. As for the other neck, let me say that my Husain should hear. It belongs to Zain-ul-'Abid-dín,† the

---

* Al Kauzar is one of the rivers of Paradise which supplies the *Pond* of the Prophet in the regions of bliss.

† Zain-ul-'Abid-dín, or "'Alí the Less," was fourth of the Imáms, according to the Shí'ahs. Escaping the fatal massacre at Karbalá, when

fir tree of the garden of Holiness. O Husain, the bond of my neck is simply a rope, but the bonds placed round the throat of Zain-ul-'Abid-dín, thy future son, shall be of iron.

Fátimah.—Heaven, O 'Alí, shall make thy rose-garden to fade. O commander of the believers, may my soul be a ransom for thy neck! O pearl of the effusion of grace, open thy lips to speak, that I may glean some ears of instruction from the field of thy wisdom.

'Alí.—Hear again! The spheres will make our rose-garden to wither; Fate will hurt two sides belonging to us. The first side is thine, O light of mine eyes! the other is that of Husain, the lion of faith. Listen to me, dear one; thy ribs shall be fractured by a door, but Husain's side shall receive the point of a dagger. Fátimah shall, by the stroke of the door, fall on her face to the ground, but Husain shall turn continually from one side to the other.

Fátimah.—O God, why should my dear child suffer so much trouble? Why should the rose of my garden be injured by thorns to such an extent? O 'Alí, how can my heart bear such a burden? Go on prophesying, O 'Alí, though thou breakest my heart; yet, although thy words increase my sorrow, still I take a delight in hearing them.

'Alí.—Of the household of the Prophet two pates shall be cloven asunder. There will be two splittings of the moons in this firmament. Fate shall part open with the sword two bright crowns of the heads. There shall be cleaved two brilliant brows luminous as the morning.

---

his father, Husain, was slain, he was sent to Damascus, together with his aunt Zainab. The lad 'Alí "had a chain round his neck, but the youth carried himself proudly, and would never vouchsafe a word to his conductors" (W. Irvine's "Mahomet and his Successors," vol. ii. p. 402). The family of Husain were afterwards sent to Madínah, where Zain-ul-'Abid-dín died, A.H. 94 (A.D. 712–713).

Fátimah.—Whose pates are these two which the enemy will split like peas in two parts? Of whose garden shall two roses lose their leaves?

'Alí.—The eternal God has decreed that of this house two persons named 'Alí should lose their heads. I am one whose head they shall cut through with a sword, and the other is Husain's future son, the youth 'Alí Akbar.*

Fátimah.—O Heaven! why shouldst thou cut 'Alí Akbar's head into two parts, and grieve me, the daughter of Muhammad, the full moon of darkness? Why shouldst thou, O Heaven, distract me by destroying my two rose-gardens? Rehearse unto me more of the trials to befall the family of the cloak;† O door of the magazine of mysteries, reveal unto me some more secrets.

'Alí.—O Fátimah, Heaven has closed against thee the window of joy! There are two arms that shall be broken by flogging. Know that to-day they will strike thee on the arm, and break it with a malicious whip; when, too, the day of thy unhappy Zainab shall be turned as dark as night, Shimar‡ will also break her arm.

Fátimah.—The story of Zainab the unhappy has rendered me sad! Methinks I have borne thee, child, for oppression; if thou art sated with life, why dost thou not die in thine infancy, dear child?

'Alí.—Strike thy palms, Fátimah, one on the other, and sigh! they shall cut two hands of ours, and one finger. Beat on thy head, for we are to lose two hands and one finger, for the sake of a ring on it.

---

* See note, p. 8.

† "The 'people of the garment,' so called because on one occasion the Prophet wrapped his cloak around himself, his daughter, his son-in-law, and his two grandsons, thereby separating them in dignity from other Moslems."—Burton's "El Medinah and Meccah," vol. i. p. 314, ed. 1857.

‡ See note, p. 43.

Fátimah.—O 'Alí, tell me every word thou hast in thy heart; say nothing about the finger now, but talk to me of the hand, for if thou explain to me the enigma of the finger and the ring, I fear I shall at once give up the ghost, on account of excessive sorrow!

'Alí.—The two hands appertain to 'Abbás,* my son, who shall be killed on the banks of the Euphrates, after he has lost both his hands. I do not know if I must tell thee the story of the camel-driver and the ring,† or whether I must forbear.

Fátimah.—Oh! do not deprive me of this thy grace and generosity, O liberal one! but inform me of the ring, the finger, and the camel-driver. Thy saying, O 'Alí, has made my heart restless like a featherless bird; tell me something about the finger, and a few words in regard to the ring.

'Alí (holding Husain's finger).—O daughter of the best of God's prophets, a certain tyrant will cruelly cut this very finger with his sword. When thy dear son Husain shall suffer ignominy in Karbalá, they will sever his finger with a sword.

Fátimah.—Ah me! Husain's painful sufferings have put me in great tribulation. I have no heart, O friends, for it is gone from my hand. I do not know how to bear a calamity, the very idea of which is distressing to the mind. Why should they, after all, cut my dear child's finger in Karbalá?

'Alí.—Know that a certain one, following the religion of Zoroaster, will cut this finger for the sake of the ring. Thou dost not know the stone of this ring, nor the metal that encloses it. 'Alí Akbar alone will, in part, know the effect of this ring.

Fátimah.—All that thou hast said, O 'Alí, relates to

---

* 'Abbás, a son of 'Alí, was killed at Karbalá.

† When Husain lay dead on the plain of Karbalá, his camel-driver cut off the martyr's finger in order to secure the ring thereon.

sorrowful events. From beginning to end it refers to overwhelming grief. Every saying of thine implies some sad transaction, to the exclusion of all joyous news. I do not gather anything but mournful intelligence; is there no nuptial feast to talk about?

'Alí.—Except sorrow, there is nothing else sold in our shop; in the market of our obedience gain is supposed to be loss. Two marriages were made among us, but both were turned into mourning. It is ominous for us, O Fátimah, to celebrate matrimony in our family.

Fátimah.—There is nothing in the world but what tends to misery and woe. Please speak unto us of the marriages of the two respective spouses. Who are our two bridegrooms and brides? Which are the two cypresses* of our garden, the two elegant fir-trees of our domain?

'Alí.—Thou art one of the two, O Zahrah,† who have seen in our house nought but distraction, and the other is the bride of Kásim, my grandson (none of those yet born), the particulars of whose marriage thou knowest well. If thy father slew seventy-two animals at thy marriage feast, at Kásim's marriage seventy-two‡ persons shall be sacrificed. All trials of the world are for me alone, in order that it may be well one day with the Shí'ahs, my followers.

Fátimah.—When a person hath the audacity to appear with boldness in the street of love, his head must be severed from his body with the sword. He who wishes to save men from everlasting flames must undergo the troubles of Karbalá.

Husain.—Father, there is no occasion to call those things trials, since all refer to the salvation of our sinful followers. Thou, Hasan, and I, together with my mother

---

* See note, p. 10.
† See note, p. 22.

"Hosein's seventy-two men were killed" at Karbalá.—Ockley's "History of the Saracens," vol. ii. p. 177, ed. 1757.

the virgin,* will accept sufferings according to the best of our ability.

'Alí.—Well, dearly beloved, you must not mourn any longer sorrowfully, nor must you let tears fall like rain from your eyes. Have yourselves all ready, for it is the beginning of sorrow, O ye cruelly oppressed! tyranny is about to commence.

Abú Bakr (*in the pulpit*).—Since I have got me on the top of the pulpit, every secret of my innermost soul is brought to light. The desire of my heart has been granted me at last by 'Umar's frequent importunities day and night.

'Umar.—There is a knot in thy work, O Abú Bakr, with which, as a sincere friend, I must acquaint thee. Thou canst not prosper in thy government until thou makest 'Alí submit obediently to thee.

Abú Bakr.—I stand then, O 'Umar, in need of some assistance from thee; venture forth, kindly, in this hazardous enterprise with good confidence. Do what thou thinkest proper in that respect. If he does not yield peaceably to me, force him to obedience with arms. Shouldst thou find Abú Tálib's son too powerful to be conquered immediately, apply to me for assistance.

'Umar.—'Alí is sitting in his house in a private closet; he has, with cunning and deceit, shut his door against all men. I will come upon him with a countless army, knocking at his gate first, in a respectful manner. If he answers me roughly, I will abandon my faith, and destroy the habitation of Gabriel unjustly. I will cruelly set his house on fire, and enter it without any permission.

Abú Bakr.—Go on acting unjustly, for justice is far off from thee, seeing that even the veriest infidel is not so wicked as thou art. Every place touched by thy hand will certainly come to ruin. He that has the least regard for thee shall see no freedom on the Day of Resurrection.

'Umar (*knocking at 'Alí's door*).—I am one of the favou-

---

* See note, p. 57.

rite companions of God's chosen Prophet; let some one come to the door, for I have an urgent message to deliver.

'Alí.—O Fátimah, the bird of sorrow is fluttering in our house; be prepared for trouble, 'Umar is knocking at the door.

Fátimah.—Oh! my tearful eyes stain my sleeves red like blood. 'Umar is come to push the door against Fátimah's side.

Hasan.—My wounded heart is burning like one that has drunk some deadly poison! My broken heart, cut into a hundred pieces, is dying within me!

Husain.—Thou shouldst say Shimar is to-day striking with his sword on my head, and another wicked wretch is thrusting his dagger into my side.

Zainab.—Zainab is about to dip her head-dress in an indigo jar to make it blue, for she is going to set up lamentations for her six brothers killed.

'Alí.—My breast resounds with groans for the death of the Prophet of God. Who is the man knocking at the door?

'Umar.—Why art thou, O 'Alí, so thoughtful? Why dost thou keep away from Abú Bakr disdainfully? Come and give him the hand of allegiance, and help him to settle the disordered affairs of the people of God.

'Alí.—What enmity has thou with this family, 'Umar? Is not the Prophet's beard still wet with the water with which they washed him before his burial? It is scarcely the third day since the Seal of the Prophets* has died. O origin of all wickedness, why shouldst thou pull the thread, or cause mischief to break forth? Suffice thee to have turned aside from the Prophet's word. Why shouldst thou, 'Umar, trouble me without a cause?

'Umar.—Open the door of thy house to me; if thou refuse (I say it loudly) I will put a rope about thy neck and drag thee on the ground to the Mosque. O Abú-turáb†

---

* See note ‡, p. 40.

† "An instance of the pleasantry in which the Prophet sometimes indulged is here recorded. Ali had fallen asleep on the dusty ground

or father of dust, I will render thy dear Husain despicable and mean; yea, I will send him to Karbalá to be killed.

'*Ali.*—Withdraw the hand of violence from me, for the unclean must not enter the abode of the holy. Hear my advice, if thou art a man (which I doubt); return, O 'Umar, by the same way by which thou hast come.

'*Umar (to his men).*—Be it known unto all of you, that 'Alí will not of his own accord open the door for us. Go ye, therefore, and burn the door of his dwelling, and subvert the foundation of his habitation.

Hasan and Husain.—Alas! O Muhammad, the injustice of these cursed ones; they are pulling down our house maliciously and oppressively!

'*Alí and Fátimah.*—O chosen Prophet, behold what mischief Abú Bakr is doing! What enmity he has with our household!

Husain.—O grandfather, see how greatly I am distressed; behold how I am surrounded by fire like Abraham!* They are kindling flames in thy house, O Prophet! Say to Gabriel, "Behold! thy place is burning."

---

in the shade of a palm-grove. Mahomet espied him lying thus, all soiled with the dust, and pushing him with his foot, called out, 'Ho, Abu Torab (*Father of the dust!*), is it thou? Abu Torab, sit up!' Ali, half ashamed, sat up; and the *soubriquet* ever after clung to him."—Muir's "Life of Mahomet," vol. iii. p. 69, ed. 1861.

* The commentators relate that, by *Nimrod's* order, a large space was enclosed at *Cútha*, and filled with a vast quantity of wood, which, being set on fire, burned so fiercely that none dared to venture near it. Then they bound *Abraham*, and putting him into an engine (which some suppose to have been of the Devil's invention), shot him into the midst of the fire; from which he was preserved by the angel *Gabriel*, who was sent to his assistance, the fire burning only the cords with which he was bound. They add that the fire, having miraculously lost its heat, in respect to *Abraham* became an odoriferous air, and that the pile changed to a pleasant meadow; though it raged so furiously otherwise, that, according to some writers, about two thousand of the idolaters were consumed by it.—Sale's "Koran," chap. xxi. p. 269, ed. 1734.

'Alí.—Dear child, the world by thy burning sigh is turned black. Be not sorry. God's grace is on all occasions thy place of refuge. I am not sorry that 'Umar is setting fire to my house, but the thought of thy coming adversity grieves me. By the flame of enmity now kindled shall thy tent and its furniture be all consumed in Karbalá many years hence.

Fátimah.—Why art thou, O 'Umar, burning this sacred place? Why dost thou grieve the heart of Abú-turáb for nothing? In the hot sun of the Day of Resurrection no doubt thy soul shall be consumed because thou art now burning the heart of the sun of righteousness.

'Umar.—Go and tell 'Alí I have still some respect for him. Let him come out from his room, I have a question to ask him. Tell him to give to Abú Bakr the hand of agreement, and in this way deliver his own dear body from being pulled here and there.

Fátimah.—Why, O 'Umar, dost thou not leave my cousin? and what made thee enter my private apartment without my permission. How is it thou hast no respectful regard for us? Am I not Fátimah, the daughter of the glory of all nations, Muhammad?

'Umar (pressing the door).—Go away from behind the door, O Zahrah, otherwise thou shalt perish by the pressure of the same. Go, go, else the rose of the garden of thy lips shall fade. Thou shalt surely die at length by my forcing the door against thy side.

Fátimah (falls into a swoon).—Alas! woe be to me! My soul is greatly troubled. The bones of my side have been fractured by the blow of the door. O prince of the believers, I am going to dishevel my hair. I am overcome by weakness, I swoon!

Zainab.—O spheres! why should our state be thus? Why should the daughter of God's messenger faint from excess of grief? Dear mother, thy body is hurt, thy side is fractured; thou hast fallen into a swoon; I know it is thy ascension on high.

'Alí to 'Umar.—O impudent wretch! well hast thou respected me! Thou hast cruelly put out the light of my direction! Oh, if I had permission to put forth from my sleeves the hand of vengeance, thou wouldst see what my holiness could do! I would have subverted the foundation of this transitory world, to show thee what thy end would be; but, alas! I must refrain.

'Umar.—O my followers, bring down the heavens to the earth! put a rope roughly round 'Alí's neck; make his elegant stature fall flat on the earth. Pull the ornament of God's throne to the ground!

'Alí.—I cannot but have patience, for I must regard what the Prophet of God has said. O faithful messenger, come out of thy grave and observe how, owing to the proceedings of thy people, the heavens have fallen to the earth! Come and see how a few dogs are making an attack on a lion! how boldly they pursue God's own Haidar!*

Fátimah.—O 'Umar! why knowest thou nothing but cruelty? What has made thee cast off the veil of shame and modesty? What dost thou want, O 'Umar, from the family of the cloak? What hast thou to do with us, who are already oppressed and afflicted?

'Umar.—Get thee away, Fátimah, before I hurt thy feelings; go away, for these words will do thee no good. Go thou and practise patience and meekness. Go and tend thy children, Hasan and Husain.

Fátimah.—O 'Umar, do not hurt me, who am a thornless rose; pelt no stones at my wings, for I am already caught. How can I let thee carry 'Alí from my house, from whose skirts I can never withhold my hands by any means?

'Umar (whipping Fátimah).—Withdraw the hand of thy protection from 'Alí. How long wilt thou, O Fátimah, have tender regards for 'Alí? Let him alone, or I will break thine arm with the whip, and turn thy day black as thy hair.

---

* See note, p. 39.

Fátimah (again swoons).—O God! have mercy on my poor soul, and behold my broken arm. My mournful cry has reached all heaven and earth. Strength has left my heart; sense has gone from my head!

Husain.—Alas! my poor mother is stretched on the ground! She has, like the dust of the grave, fallen on the earth. She has fainted; she is quite unconscious; the whip has cast a flame in her soul!

Zainab (to Fátimah).—See thy dear Husain close by thy side; behold a royal gem falling in thy lap! Let me lay thy sacred head in my bosom, for my cypress tree is felled on the bank of a stream!

'Umar (to his followers).—With his very chain drag 'Alí, the prince of believers, to the Mosque.

'Alí (being dragged along).—I picture Karbalá, Damascus, and the wicked Shimar's doing! The chains of my grandchild Zain-ul-'Abid-dín are present in my mind; but since all is done by God's order, I shall patiently submit my neck to the fetters, although I am called a lion.

Abú Bakr.—Stretch forth thy hand, O 'Alí, and make allegiance to me. Dost thou deny my being a khalíf?

'Alí.—Who has given thee authority to become a khalíf? What demonstrative proofs hast thou for thy khalífat? Art thou a cousin to the lord of the two worlds, or am I? Dost thou deserve to be his successor by right, or do I?

Abú Bakr.—O 'Alí, what proofs hast thou of thy title to become khalíf? Who upon the earth is the witness of this thy claim?

'Alí.—Well, since thou seekest proofs as to my being a khalíf, I shall call the Prophet himself from his grave to be the witness thereof. He will bring to light the truth of thy claims, and subvert the foundation of thy tyrannical government. (*Turning to the Prophet's tomb.*) O brother, the people have taken me for a weak person, and are about to kill me. O Messenger of God, march forth from Paradise and behold the accursed Abú Bakr on the top of the pulpit.

The Prophet (rising from the grave).—O Abú Bakr, dost thou disbelieve in Him who created thee from the earth and made thee a man? Hast thou forgotten what I told thee at the pool of water concerning 'Alí the son of Abú Tálib, saying, "'Alí is the master of him whose master I am?" O cursed apostate, Abú Bakr, truly thou hast stepped beyond thy limits. Thou must not sit on the top of the pulpit, for thou art not the Prophet's successor. Is not 'Alí my cousin, and in reality the glory of the nations? Have I not often in public and private said that 'Alí is the executor of my will; that he who loves him loves me, and he who hates him, or does enmity to him is accursed of God and the law?

Abú Bakr.—O 'Umar, thou hast sifted the dust of calamity upon me since thou didst devise the plan of seizing upon 'Alí's rights. Behold the Prophet here present. I do not wish the khalífat; my strength is not sufficient for me to hold such a position. Let 'Alí, the prince of the believers, go free, O ill-starred man, for he is the true successor of the Prophet, and his vicar.

'Umar.—I think, O Khalíf, thy brain is touched by some illness, and thou art deluded by thine own fancies. 'Alí always practised sorcery and witchcraft. Thou must not lose heart by such magical apparitions.

Abú Bakr (to 'Alí).—Let not the palm tree of thy existence be uprooted from the plantation of the living; be not obstinate in refusing to obey me.

'Alí.—I swear by him who gave me knowledge of all things, and made me his own vice-regent in his affairs, that I will not, of my own accord, pay obedience to thee, though heaven should render me contemptible in the world.

'Abú Bakr.—O 'Umar, thou art both a chief and a commander in my army; go and sever 'Alí's head from his body.

'Umar.—O 'Alí, since thou rebellest against our command, and pretendest to be a king, I am going to crown thee with a sharp sword!

Salmán.—Salmán cannot speak out his mind; such is the

injustice, that he cannot complain or cry out by reason of cruelty. Why should 'Umar fall out with 'Alí? Why should the jackal attack the courageous lion?

Abú Bakr.—O friends, seeing our custom is to oppress and to do injustice, put Salmán, therefore, in bonds in the most cruel manner possible.

'Alí.—O cursed Abú Bakr, it appears thou hast lost thy senses. Didst thou not hear the Prophet say, "Salmán is one of us?" Be ashamed before God, 'Umar, to kill Salmán; let my blood alone be sufficient to appease thy wrath.

Abú Bakr.—O people, have respect for God's Prophet, let Salmán free if he is not yet dead.

Zainab (coming at Fátimah's head).—Arise, O Fátimah, it is time to suffer pains; erect thy body, it is the season of affliction. Arise, dear mother, let us go to the Mosque. Get up, O Husain, it is time to be beheaded.

The family coming to the Mosque, Fátimah says.—My lap is overflowing with my tears! a fire of zeal is kindled in me; 'Alí sitting beneath the sword is stretching his neck to be cut, poor thing!

Husain.—O 'Umar, do not kill my father, the vice-regent of God. This is not the land of Karbalá that thou shouldest act the part of Shimar.

Hasan.—Kill not my father, for whom all things are created, the dust of whose door is an honour and glory to heaven.

Husain.—Oh, kill not the lion of God! I beg thee, do not tyrannically cast black earth on my head.

Fátimah.—O Abú Bakr, I have many complaints against thee. My face is, by thee, turned pale, like amber. Withdraw your hand from 'Alí, the door* of God's knowledge,

---

* It is a tradition that Muhammad, when speaking of 'Alí, said, "'Alí is for me, and I for him. He holds the same position about my person as Aaron did with regard to Moses. I am the city wherein all wisdom is included, and 'Alí is the door."—D'Herbelot, head "'Alí."

for I am much attached to this moon-like sun. Thou knowest, in case thou refusest to hear my word, what evils I can bring on thee by my prayers.

Abû Bakr.—If 'Alí refuses to give me his hand submissively, I will sever his head with the edge of a sharp sword. Go and cleave to thy Lord, if thou hast any, and continue to pray against me, if thou thinkest thy intercessions will be heard.

Fátimah (to her children).—Come, Husain, thou light of mine eyes, make thy head bare; come, Zainab, dishevel thy locks here, I too will hold my curls in my hands, and coo from the heart like a pigeon. With one curse I can destroy the whole world, and the inhabitants thereof, not leaving any trace of heaven, the fixed stars, and the planets. O God! for the merit of the pain my arm is suffering to-day, for the fractures my side has received from the pressure of the door——

The Prophet.—Curse not, dear child; let thy curls fall from thy hands. O cooing bird, sigh not so sadly from the heart. Do not attempt to cut the curling ringlets, nor dishevel them, lest the foundation of the world should be out of course. Know thou that I am greatly distressed for God's creatures in the world. Thou art well aware that I was sent out of mercy to all men. Tell Husain, also, not to dishevel his hair, for a single look from him can give life to the whole world.

Abû Bakr.—O 'Umar, thy tricks after all can have no effect. Thine arrow, O archer, cannot hit the mark; withhold thy hands from 'Alí, and let him go. Thy sword must be sheathed in its case, O 'Umar. Dost thou not see the Prophet Muhammad with all the rest of God's messengers beating their heads on account of thy present cruelty? Dost thou mean to destroy the whole universe? I see, O 'Umar, the edifice thou hast reared is not substantial. O Fátimah, I beg thee not to curse me, for I have an awe of thy effective sighs!

SCENE VII.

THE DEATH OF FATIMAH, THE DAUGHTER OF THE PROPHET MUHAMMAD.

FATIMAH, whose death is here recorded, was the daughter of Muhammad, whom she survived but a few months. She married 'Alí, and bore to him Hasan and Husain, the martyrs of Karbalá. There is a tradition that the Prophet on one occasion said "*That among men there had been many perfect, but no more than four of the other sex had attained perfection;* to wit, Aria, *the wife of* Pharaoh; Mary, *the daughter of* Imrán; Khadijah, *the daughter of* Khowailed (the Prophet's first wife); and Fátemah, *the daughter of* Mohammed" (Sale's "Koran," chap. vi. p. 458, ed. 1734). This Scene is noteworthy as indicating the abhorrence with which the people of the East regard any violation of the seclusion of the female sex. "The Sun," says the text, "is ashamed to show his face while that of Zainab is laid open to view." There is also an interesting enumeration of the *souvenirs* of Muhammad and his family most esteemed by the Shí'ahs.

Fátimah.—O holy Creator of all things, how long must I remain distressed and suffer grief owing to the loss of my father? I am dying; dying, indeed, from the pain caused by his departure. His sad memory has, as it were, poisoned my whole constitution; nay, it has already killed me with its venom. O Lord God, if it be possible, let me be honoured once more with the presence of that royal personage whose motto was, "We have not known Thee, O Lord, but in part."

'Alí.—O Thou whose holy nature is perfectly free from our imperfect qualities, whose essence is beyond the limit of our comprehension, Thou art He by whose universal cloud of mercy roses and lilies, as well as thorns and thistles, receive their existence and nourishment. It is from nearness to Thee that Haidar* has become possessed of the glorious title of "Were it not for thee I would not have created the heavens."

Fátimah (to her maid).—O maid, kindly do me a service, and get me mourning dresses, that I may show my grief for my father. Darken my house of sorrow, and make it jet-black as night; and call all kind-hearted women of Hijáz to mourn together with me.

The Maid.—O Lord, look upon me and see how my heart is bleeding from grief. O congregation of mourners,† the hour of sorrow is come; yea, the time of perpetual anguish has arrived! Hoist up your flag of grief, and blacken your house of mourning. O Fátimah, thou queen of the nymphs of Paradise, I have prepared the things belonging to the scene of affliction and sorrow.

Fátimah.—O father! thou sympathising king of thy nation, where art thou? O thou intercessor of the Day of Judgment, where art thou?

The Household.—O father! thou sympathising king of thy nation, where art thou? O thou intercessor of the Day of Resurrection, where art thou?

Fátimah.—If thou comest, I will give thee my soul; if thou appearest not, grief will kill me. At any rate I die for thee, father, whether thou comest or not!

---

* See note, p. 39.

" The women continue their lamentations, and many of the females of the neighbourhood, hearing the conclamation, come to unite with them in their melancholy task."—Lane's "Modern Egyptians," vol. ii. p. 286, ed. 1836.

The Household.—If thou comest, I will give thee my soul; if thou appearest not, grief will kill me. At any rate I die for thee, father, whether thou comest or not!

Fátimah.—Return, dear father, and put once more the turban on thy head, and let thy holy body be clothed with thy blessed cloak.*

The Household.—Return, dear father, and put once more the turban on thy head, and let thy holy body be clothed with thy blessed cloak.

Fátimah.—Let Bilál,† thy attendant, carry thy carpet for adoration to the Mosque. Begin thou to sing the praises of God, and hold the rod in thy hand, O father!

The Household.—Let Bilál, thy attendant, carry thy carpet for adoration to the Mosque. Begin thou to sing the praises of God, and hold the rod in thy hand, O father!

Fátimah.—After thee, O father, the Hand‡ of God will not set his feet on the pulpit. The Mosque, the pulpit, and the altar respectively derived their lustre from thee when thou wast on earth.

The People of Madínah.—O ye inhabitants of Madínah, both small and great, be it known unto all of you, that the Prophet's daughter is disturbing us not a little by her continual lamentation. Let us go soon to her husband, 'Alí, the Lion of God, and state the matter fully unto him; peradventure he may prevail upon her to keep quiet. (*Addressing 'Alí.*) O prince of believers, we have come to our last breath on account of Zahrah's§ continual weeping and wailing. Forbid her, we pray thee, from crying day and night. Tell her to be quiet either at night or in the daytime, that we may, too, have a period of rest.

'Alí.—Alas! the fire of these your sad words has consumed my heart; the arrow of your petition has bent my back like a bow. You have made me very distressed by

---

* See note †, p. 98.   † See note *, p. 36.
‡ 'Alí.   § See note, p. 22.

your request. How can Fátimah cease from weeping since her mother* and father are both dead?

Fátimah.—Alas! alas! again 'Alí's groanings are heard. Wherefore has 'Alí the deliverer arisen and come forth from the Mosque? Why is Abú-turáb† shedding twilight on the moon? Why does he let fall stars on the sun?

'Alí.—My sun-like face, ● Fátimah, has become a pale moon through thee; my sighs and groans are on account of thy weeping and impatience. Multitudes of men and women are complaining of anguish through thy sad cryings. Have pity on these poor people; they are Musulmans after all.

Fátimah.—O 'Alí, how long wilt thou prohibit a sorrowful creature like me from crying? Dost thou not know that my dear father is dead, and so I mourn for him? Alas! woe unto me! why should it be thought a shame for one in my condition to weep? Is this city so small and limited that a miserable person like me cannot be left alone? O 'Alí, I am in deep distress; it is, indeed, a mighty evil to be an orphan! O 'Alí, I am greatly despised; desolation is most truly unbearable.

'Alí.—How long wilt thou complain of being an orphan, and thus sadly bewail? Who dares say thou art despised, seeing thou art the dearest of the age? But the people are simply complaining of thy piercing cries, and they beg thee, most respectfully, to forbear if possible.

Fátimah.—O 'Alí! if the people of Madínah are tired of my crying—if they are weary of my lamentation and wailing, it is an easy thing for me to leave the city. I offer Madínah a present to its inhabitants; I will go to the sepulchre of the Prophet, and dwell there. Let Madínah be an offering to the followers of the Prophet. (*Turning towards the tomb.*) O thou chief of the creation of God, who art His

---

* Her mother was Khadíjah, and her father the Prophet Muhammad.
† See note, p. 102.

true Messenger, peace be on thee! Hear my grievous complaints of thy followers, O God's Apostle! I have come in thy presence, father, with uncovered head, to express how sadly I am vexed with thy people; for they are truly tired of me. Better take me to thyself in the grave, so that thy people may thereby find themselves happy!

'Ali.—O thou Venus of the Heavens, who art the sun* surrounded by two moons and one star! O thou whose eyebrows are the new moon of the world, look at me and pity me! O Fátimah, cease thy crying and weeping; how long wilt thou shed tears from thine eyes?

Fátimah.—O thou who art higher than the highest heavens, the very floor of whose residence is above the divine throne! thou knowest that since the death of my father, the king of Time, my soul has experienced nothing but oppression and cruelty. My soul lives between fire and water. Even Bilál,† my father's crier, is cruel; why does he not make proclamation for prayers, and seek to pacify my heart thereby?

'Ali.—Since thy father's death, O Fátimah, poor Bilál has been himself, too, between fire and water. Still, however, O watchful black-fortuned Bilál, in whose book of fate there shall be no entry on the Day of Judgment (for nothing shall be written against thee in the volume of thy actions), get up, according to the request of Fátimah, the queen of the morn of resurrection, and cry out for prayers.

Bilál (the crier).—A Mosque wherein no Messenger of the two worlds can be found, what sort of a Mosque can that be? and what proclamation, what pulpit, and what cleanliness can it have? How can I go to the top of the minaret to sing out my proclamations like a nightingale, seeing thorns of affliction have filled my soul with blood, like as it were a rosebud? No heart has remained for

---

* *i.e.* The mother of two sons and one daughter.
† See note †, p. 36.

Bilál after the decease of the Apostle of God. What can he do? How can he cry for prayer?

(He proclaims.)

"God is greater than all! God is greater than all!"

Fátimah.—The nightingale of Muhammad's garden is pouring forth its song. He ravishes the heart and disables it with his melodious notes, depriving it of patience and understanding. Sing on, O ye nightingale, if thou meanest to help me, for I am shedding blood, not tears, from my eyes, on account of my father's absence.

Bilál.—I bear witness that there is no other God but God! I bear witness that there is no other God but God!

Fátimah.—O Hasan, my son, take thou the Kur'án of my poor father; and thou, O Husain, carry the carpet of thy grandfather, the Messenger of the two worlds. Take them to the Mosque, and tell the people to be ready, for the Prophet of God will shortly come to pray. And, O Bilál, go on with your proclamation, and untie the knot of sorrow that is in our heart.

Bilál.—I testify that Muhammad is the Messenger of God. I testify that Muhammad is the Messenger of God.

Fátimah (faintly).—Alas! O Muhammad, my crowned father, father! Alas! O Muhammad, my magnified moon!

Hasan and Husain (together).—For God's sake, O crier, have pity on us, and cry no more; for Zahrah,* the daughter of the Prophet, is already dead. O disturbed mother, wherefore shouldst thou so long lament and weep? Why dost thou not speak to us, and why art so restless?

Fátimah.—May Zahrah be a sacrifice for your elegant bodies, dear sons! May she be an offering for your shining faces, beloved children! *(Turning to her maid.)* Come,

---

* See note, p. 22.

O thou grievously afflicted damsel, O thou fellow-companion of my daughter Zainab, come to me.

The Maid.—O thou, my tear-shedding mistress! O thou rest of my wounded heart! May I be a sacrifice for thy pair of tearful eyes! May all thy pains come to the soul of this thy maiden! What is thy command, O thou who art grievously troubled, that I may obey it with my whole soul and heart?

Fátimah.—Get me ready, O damsel, a hand-mill, to grind.

The Maid.—What art thou going to grind in this state* of poverty?

Fátimah.—I wish to grind some barley.

The Maid.—Leave this toil to me, mistress.

Fátimah.—Yesterday it was thy turn, and thou didst perform it.

The Maid.—Why should I get rest from labour at all?

Fátimah—My father has so enjoined, and I must carry out his wishes.

The Maid.—What were the terms of his command, I pray?

Fátimah.—He said, "Have a regard for thy maid, poor girl."

The Maid.—Why? Handmaids are kept for service only.

Fátimah.—Get me some clay, wherewith to rub the head.

The Maid.—For what is the clay? May my head be offered for thine!

Fátimah.—I want to wash Zainab's head therewith.

The Maid.—Oh! my heart has come into my mouth by this saying of thine!

Fátimah.—Bring me a basin, O afflicted maiden!

---

* See note †, p. 55.

The Maid.—What dost thou want to do with the basin, sad lady?

Fátimah.—I want to wash my children's clothes in it.

The Maid.—Oh! I am extremely troubled in my mind at these thy words.

Fátimah.—Whether I be well or unwell, I have always to work for my children. Pour water, O damsel, though it be from the fountain of thy eyes, that I may wash my husband's and my children's clothes. This very turban, which is now tinged with blood, though its fabric was spun by the beautiful nymphs of Paradise, shall be saturated with the blood of 'Alí's head, in the arched niche of the altar for prayer, through the son of Muljam's* cruel sword. Let me smell this shirt, which has the scent of the rose in it: let me cleanse it well, for it belongs to Hasan, my elder son. He shall put on this very shirt, and hold it close to his heart when suffering the pangs of deadly poison. Let my sighs and groans reach the heavens! I am rinsing the clothes of my younger son, Husain, O friends! This very shirt, woe to me! shall be pierced through, in innumerable places, by the sharp arrows of the daring enemy. This very shirt, which I have washed clean, like snow, shall stick like mud to the horse-shoes of the enemy! O Lord God, Thou alone art aware of the state of my suffering heart, as I am washing now the head-dress of Zainab, my dear daughter. I must clean this rose-leaf, this beautiful head-dress, to be a handkerchief in future for Shimar,† the unbeliever. This head-dress, which I have washed and arranged, shall be pulled off from Zainab's head, and flung away on the ground. She shall ride with uncovered head, on a camel,‡

---

* 'Alí was murdered by 'Abd-ur-rahmán, the son of Muljam.

† See note, p. 43.

‡ "Omar and his troops proceeded towards Kúfah, accompanied by his wretched female captives thrown across the backs of camels."—Price's "Chronological Retrospect of Mahomedan History," p. 408, ed. 1811.

and be carried from Karbalá to Shám* with music and drumming, to her shame and my grievance!

The Maid.—O my distressed lady, look upon my bleeding heart, and allow me, O dear mistress, to turn this mill for thee.

Zainab.—O mother, do not lament and bewail any more, nor so oft shed blood from thine eyes. Oh, let me, for Husain's sake, turn the millstone for thee!

Hasan and Husain together.—O our afflicted mother, who art so solicitous about a whole family's welfare, let us, without any further ado, turn the mill for thee.

Fátimah.—O Hasan, I adjure thee by Husain's soul, leave me for awhile; and I implore thee, O Husain, by the soul of Hasan, hearken to my voice. Thee also, O maid, I beg, by the soul of Zainab, go away for awhile; and thee, O Zainab, by the soul of Fátimah, stop thy importunity: for, by the breath of 'Alí do I swear, I have some secret with the Lord. I want to talk a little with the millstone.† O millstone, thou companion of every afflicted spirit! O millstone, thou friend of my chamber! seeing millstones are generally turned by water, I have furnished thee always with the same from the head-fountain of my eyes! Thou art my witness, O millstone, that I have never stained my hands with henna to make them look red,‡ but always with the heart's blood. Thou art my witness that day and night I have been in want of food and rest, in order simply to support Hasan and Husain, my children. O millstone, if thou wilt not bear witness in my favour in the Day of Judgment, when I shall have to render to God an account of all my actions, they will stop me in the scorching heat

---

* Syria.

† No information respecting this tradition is given in any of the ordinary books of reference.

‡ A bright red hue on the hands and feet is considered very becoming in the East.

of the sun in that day. Oh! how difficult to bear the heat of that day's sun. Oh! my heart is quite faint within me, through feebleness, and the severity of the grief arising from my dear father's death. Oh! alas! alas! all my strength has left me at once. (*Falls into a swoon.*)

Angels in Paradise (one of whom comes forward).—O ye assembly of nymphs inhabiting the celestial garden of Paradise, descend from your delightful abodes to the house of Zahrah, the daughter of Muhammad; for she has fainted owing to excessive grief and distress. You must diligently employ yourselves in her service, and attend on her as slaves on their mistress.

Fátimah.—O ye singing birds of the plantations of Heaven!

The Angel.—Yes, thou queen of the throne and palace of Heaven, what is thy order?

Fátimah.—Who are these that are thus weeping for me?

The Angel.—They are all thy slaves, the nymphs[*] of Paradise.

Fátimah.—Why have they come here all at once?

The Angel.—They are summoned here to attend on thee as servants.

Fátimah.—Do these nymphs act at the bidding of anyone, or of their own accord?

The Angel.—Yes; they belong to the illustrious companions of the Prophet.

Fátimah.—Whose is this bright-faced moon-like creature?

---

[*] "The very meanest in Paradise (as he who, it is pretended, must know best, has declared) will have eighty thousand servants, seventy-two wives of the girls of Paradise," &c. &c.—Sale's "Koran," Preliminary Discourse, sec. iv. p. 98, ed. 1734.

The Angel.—It is Salínah; and she belongs to Salmán.*

Fátimah.—To whom belongs yonder sad angel?

The Angel.—That is Makdúdah; and she belongs to Mikdád, another companion of the Prophet.

Fátimah.—Tell me whose is that sprightly sun-like nymph?

The Angel.—That is called Izár, and belongs to Abazar.†

Fátimah.—I have a question which must be answered fairly.

The Angel.—May we know what is the question of thy highness?

Fátimah.—Are there better nymphs in Paradise than these?

The Angel.—Certainly, O lady of the Day of Judgment.

Fátimah.—Tell me, to whom do they generally belong?

The Angel.—Know thou that they belong chiefly to the sympathisers with Husain.

Fátimah.—On whom else will God bestow such nymphs?

The Angel.—To those who truly weep for Husain.

Fátimah.—Dost thou know anything about the Prophet?

The Angel.—Yes; I saw him sitting sadly at the corner of Al Kauzar.‡

Fátimah.—Has he been ill-treated there by his foolish people?

The Angel.—His sadness was chiefly on thy account.

Fátimah.—Did he not say when Zahrah will be delivered from her sorrows?

The Angel.—Yes; to-morrow thou shalt be with him in Paradise.

Fátimah.—Thanks be to God my Creator, that He thus

---

* See note †, p. 36.

† "Mohammed said that four men were his peculiar friends—'Aly-bin-Abutátalib, Mikdád-bin-ul-Asood, Abuzer, and Salmán-e-Fársee."—Meyrick's "Life of Mohammed," p. 356, ed. 1850.

‡ See note *, p. 96.

permits me to go to Paradise to see the face of my dear father! O my poor maid, who art sick with fever of sorrow, O thou incarnate night of affliction and grief, come hither; for my heart is overflowing with unusual sadness, as I intend to wash Zainab's hair. Go thou, O ill-fated, black-starred creature, and get some rose-water and a comb for me.

The Maid.—O hand of death, come forth and comb with the comb of destruction the curls of my life! May I be offered for thy weeping eyes! Here is some rose-water and also a comb; take them from thy handmaid.

Fátimah.—Come, Zainab; may I be offered for thy hair! Come, let me smell thy musky locks. O Heaven, order thy stars to shut their eyes*, for Zainab is going to uncover her head that it may be washed. And thou, O sun, remain hidden under the earth, that thou mayest not see Zainab's hair uncovered. And thou, O day, be buried in the dark night for ever, for Zainab's face and hair are about to be divested of their usual covering!

The People of Madínah.—O thou lion of the thicket of almighty power! O 'Alí, bring out the hand of Godhead from thy sleeves, and save us! Why should the day be buried in perpetual night? Why does not the sun, the ruler of the day, put on his crown of light and reign? Has Zahrah concealed her face from the world, that the sun should, out of shame, remain enveloped in the clouds?

'Alí (conversing with Bilál).—O Bilál, seeing that the bright day is thus turned into a dark night, and the sun has totally hidden himself from view, one might suppose that Zainab my daughter has unveiled her face, or that they are going to wash her head.

---

* An allusion to the seclusion to which the female sex is condemned in the East by the custom of the country.

An Angel.—O 'Alí, the Lion of God! king of the great empire of faith! central force of the divine system of might and power! thus saith the Lord: "Be pleased to order that Zainab's head should be covered; otherwise the sun will not come out from his dark retreat for ever."

'Alí.—O Zahrah, about what art thou so busy?

Fátimah.—O 'Alí, I am combing my daughter's hair.

'Alí.—Put a veil on her face, that day and night may continue their regular courses.

Fátimah.—I have nothing to do, man, with day and night.

'Alí.—The sun is ashamed to show his face while that of Zainab is laid open to view.

Fátimah.—But, alas! this same Zainab's hair shall become full of blood.

'Alí.—Oh! shall Zainab indeed become acquainted with grief?

Fátimah.—Yes; and this her head shall be broken by the wood of the litter, when led away as a captive.

'Alí.—Will the hand of cruelty be stretched against her?

Fátimah.—Yes; in Kúfah* they will cast stones at her.

'Alí.—Oh! shall she be deprived of the pleasures of life?

Fátimah.—Ah! she shall be spurned by the daughters of Shám.

'Alí.—Will she, truly, be subject to contempt at the hands of her enemies?

Fátimah.—Yes; they will pass her through the bázárs with uncovered head, and so disgrace her.

'Alí.—From whom hast thou heard these predictions?

Fátimah.—From the holy mouth of the Prophet himself.†

---

* See note, p. 9. † See note, p. 58.

'Alí.—O Fátimah! thou worthy companion of mine! thou peace of my troubled spirit! thou hapless, friendless sufferer, the whole of whose body looks sickly, like the eye itself! Thou from every eye-lash of whom a flood of tears continually runs down; tell me, dear wife, what kind of fruit dost thou like most?

Fátimah.—O Lion of God, and the high priest of His people, my father, the Prophet of God, has charged me not to drink water when I am parched, though my heart should burn with thirst. Since my body is seized with a very hot fever, I should like to quench its flames with a little piece of some pomegranates.

'Alí (addressing the people of Madínah).—O God, for the merit of the sigh of the needy, put me not to shame before Zahrah, the daughter of Muhammad. O afflicted companions of God's Messenger, the virgin* Fátimah has requested pomegranates from her poor husband 'Alí.

The Inhabitants of Madínah.—May our heads be strewn under thy sacred feet! May our parents be offered as ransoms for thy soul! None has got pomegranates with him in this town save Simeon the Jew.†

'Alí.—Necessity, O merciful Lord, has obliged the king of faith to go to an unbelieving Jew. 'Alí, notwithstanding his natural abilities, is reduced to great difficulties to-day; so that he must go to an infidel. Yes, the mirror may be in want of ashes sometimes. Come out, O Simeon, from thy house; for 'Alí, the hand of God Almighty, needs thee!

Simeon.—Peace be on thee, O king of the throne of judgment! O solar orb of the heaven of justice! what has made thee, O tribunal of justice and faith, cast thine eyes so bashfully on the ground? O majestic 'Alí, tell me, what is thy request?

---

* See note, p. 57.   † See note, p. 61.

'*Alí.*—The sun has condescended to shine upon an insignificant atom.

Simeon.—Why is the face of thy wishes wrapped in a veil?

'*Alí.*—A certain sick person has requested a thing from me.

Simeon.—What may that request be, and who is the sick person?

'*Alí.*—Fátimah is the invalid, and a pomegranate the request.

Simeon.—Pomegranates are not to be had at this season.

'*Alí.*—It is not good to keep her waiting longer.

Simeon.—O thou, who art the only tree of generosity in the garden of creation! they brought me some pomegranates lately from Táif,* but I sold the whole, since people were eager to buy them. I do not sew bags in which to preserve pomegranates.

'*Alí.*—O Jew, go and make diligent search. Thou hast got still two loads of pomegranates left thee; get me one pomegranate therefrom, please.

Simeon.—O 'Alí, God knoweth that thou art aware of all things. Thou hast well spoken, indeed, and uttered what is true. I confess with shame that I said falsely; so I penitently ask thy pardon. But the pomegranates thou mentionest had been stolen, and stored up somewhere by my wife against my knowledge; and so I am partly right, O thou collyrium of mine eye. Be it as it may, thou mayest take this pomegranate from me, and carry it as a present to Zahrah thy wife.

---

* Name of a town in the vicinity of Makkah, which it supplies with fruit, &c. "Táyif is remarkable as the only place where a strong demonstration of popular feeling attended the fate of any of the idols of Arabia. Everywhere else they appear to have been destroyed without sympathy and without a pang."—Muir's "Life of Mahomet," vol. iv. p. 207, ed. 1861.

'Alí.—Praise be unto God, the sole Creator of all things, who would not suffer me to be put to shame before Zahrah.

A blind man wandering in a desolate place.—O woe unto me! my spirit burns within me, in consequence of fever; my very bones are in a glow for the same reason. Blindness, poverty, destitution, illness, and the misery of privation are all gathered around me! O Lord God! for the sake of the solitude of the lonely, in the corner of ruined places and prisons, have mercy on me, and bring here to me 'Alí, the prince of the believers, the sympathising friend of the Shí'ahs, that I may forget my pain for a while!

'Alí.—What is the cause of this dreadful noise, this solicitation, this entreaty? Who is this that cries so sadly, and mourns so bitterly? O thou that groanest so painfully, where art thou? Art thou a stranger or an acquaintance?

The Sick Blind Man.—I am a blind man without any resource; a stranger far from his home and companions; a man deprived of all things; a sick person, having none to pity him or take care of him, except God. I am quite helpless, indisposed, unable to do anything. Have mercy on me, O inquirer! I am yet young.

'Alí.—Alas! these last words remind me of a sad event which will take place hereafter, namely, the end of 'Alí Akbar,* my grandson, in Karbalá. For whenever I see a young man distressed I cannot but remember the youth's melancholy death. Yes, yes, O young man, I am coming to thee; I am a key to the lock of thy difficulties. Come, lay thy poor head on my lap, and sigh no more so sadly.

The Blind Man.—Who art thou that holdest my head in thy kind lap, and wipest off the tears from mine eyes?

---

* See note, p. 8.

'*Ali*.—I am 'Alí, the prince of the faithful, the king of this and the next world, O young man.

The Blind Man.—O my lord 'Alí, may I be offered unto thee! May I be sacrificed to thy goodness and kindness! I am burning, O 'Alí, with fever and thirst. I would prefer death to such a miserable existence.

'*Ali*.—Thou puttest me in mind, O young man, of Husain's dreadful thirst in the plain of Karbalá. Come, then, O broken-hearted, miserable sufferer, place thy head gently in my lap; for I will be a kind physician to thee. Tell me which kind of fruit thou likest best; quinces, grapes, dates, pomegranates, or apples?

The Blind Young Man.—Oh! may I be offered to the dust of thy feet, O 'Alí! May my soul be a sacrifice to thy faithfulness! My heart has no inclination for any fruit save pomegranates, which I believe cannot at this time be had in any bázár. The fire of fever has inflamed my heart, O 'Alí; quench it, if possible, with some juice of pomegranates.

'*Ali*.—Be not troubled, young man; I have got thee a pomegranate which will change thy autumn into verdant spring. Put thy head, poor young man, in my lap, that I may squeeze out the juice of the pomegranate into thy mouth. But, O thou who art blind as regards the body, but whose mental vision is unimpaired, half of this fruit must be thine, and the other half 'Alí's.

The Blind Man.—Oh! may I be offered for thee, the intelligent king! How nice this delicious piece of pomegranate tastes! If thou wilt be so kind as to grant me the other half too, I am sure the fever will at once flee away from my body.

'*Ali*.—Take the other half also, and eat it, poor stranger; sit on one side, that 'Alí, thy lord, may sweep the place under thee. Alas! O Lord God, I am put in mind of the prisoner of Shám, my grandson, Zain-ul-'Abid-dín.*

---

* See note *, p. 96.

The Blind Man.—Why are thine eyes filled with pearl-like tears?

'Alí.—Oh! I was reminded of another poor patient.

The Blind Man.—Who is that patient, O king of noble birth?

'Alí.—It is Zain-ul-'Abid-dín, the prisoner of Shám.

The Blind Man.—Whose offspring is he, O thou light of mine eyes?

'Alí.—He is the future offspring of my son Husain.

The Blind Man.—Tell me, where shall his destination be?

'Alí.—In the solitude of Shám with feverish body.

The Blind Man.—What shall be his diet in that solitary place?

'Alí.—Blood from the heart and tears from the eyes.

The Blind Man.—May I be offered for this thy great humanity! and may my soul be a sacrifice to thy favour and benevolence!

Angels bringing pomegranates for Fátimah.—O Lord God, angels' hearts are broken in consequence of excessive grief! How long shall Zahrah suffer pain in expecting 'Alí's return? Come along, ye large-eyed,* beautiful nymphs of Paradise, with salvers on your heads bearing pomegranates to your mistress Fátimah, the mother of Husain. O ye servants of the court of him† whom the angels serve with joy, let one of your number come behind the door and open it for us!

Fátimah (to her maid).—O damsel, I heard a voice at the door; hasten and see if it be not 'Alí, Zahrah's husband.

The Maid.—Who is he that knocks outside at the door? What is his name? Why does he so, and what may be the news?

---

* Large eyes are esteemed a sign of beauty amongst the Persians.
† *i.e.* 'Alí.

The Angel.—I am a porter of this court, a home-born slave of God's defender;* and have come from him with pomegranates for Zahrah his wife. Be thou pleased to take them from his servant.

The Maid (to Fátimah).—Dear lady, may my soul be offered for thy head! Thy husband has sent thee pomegranates.

Fátimah.—O damsel, since my lord and husband is not present to partake of the same with me, the pomegranates do not seem agreeable to my palate.

'Alí.—O Fátimah, thou matron of Muhammad's family! thou queen of the palace of Arabia's divine king, good news! thy companion is come; but tell me, whence didst thou get these pomegranates?

Fátimah.—O 'Alí, this very moment, when I was in the midst of hope and despair, there came some one and knocked at the door, saying, "Take these pomegranates, sent by Zahrah's husband, 'Alí the most high."

'Alí.—Rest awhile, O most faithful Zahrah, and do not make sighs and lamentations any more; for that was Gabriel,† the sweet angel of revelation, who came and knocked; and these pomegranates are from the garden of Paradise.

Fátimah (to her maid).—Come, O damsel, take this plate of pomegranates to keep for my poor children, who are soon about to become orphans. And thou, O 'Alí, go to the mosque, there to pray for us, and to think awhile about our painful state of mind.

'Alí.—How can I voluntarily go away from thy happy presence, or how can I leave thee alone in the house? O Lord God, for the merit of Hasan and the soul of Husain, forgive thou the sins of the followers of the latter.

Fátimah.—Come to me, poor Zainab, apart from the others.

---

* 'Alí.   † See note, p. 15.

Zainab.—What is thy object in thus speaking, O sorrowful mother?

Fátimah.—Hold my arms and help me to get up, child.

Zainab.—Oh! may God put an end to the days of my life!

Fátimah.—Carry me, and leave me near that box, girl.

Zainab.—Mother, thou turnest my bright day into dark night.

Fátimah.—See that Husain be not about, either far nor near.

Zainab.—His moon does not shine in the room, which is consequently dark.

Fátimah.—Take this key from me, and unlock the box.

Zainab.—I have done it; what are thy further orders?

Fátimah.—Take this casket, but keep it carefully.

Zainab.—What can there be in it, good mother?

Fátimah.—There is in it the Prophet's tooth, which was knocked out in the battle of Ohod.*

Zainab.—Let me kiss it; for fresh blood still gushes therefrom.

Fátimah.—Hold this casket also in thy hand.

Zainab.—What is in this again, mother? for my eyes begin to shed blood as soon as I hold it in my hands.

Fátimah.—In it is the evidence of Husain's blood.

Zainab.—What evidence, O thou brightness of the two worlds, is this?

Fátimah.—It is an evidence with which I shall succeed in the last day in making intercession for the sins of our people.

---

* Battle of Ohod, Jan. A.D. 625. "A stone wounded the Prophet's under-lip and broke one of his front teeth."—Muir's "Life of Mahomet," vol. iii. p. 172, ed. 1861. So, again, Sale: "He (Muhammad) lost the day, and was very near losing his life, being struck down by a shower of stones, and wounded in the face with two arrows, on pulling out of which his two fore-teeth dropped out."—"Koran," chap. ii. p. 50, ed. 1734.

Zainab.—Oh, how happy such a people; how blessed!

Fátimah.—Take out the third casket, daughter.

Zainab.—What can be in that, dear mother?

Fátimah.—Nothing but the ring that was on King Solomon's* finger.

Zainab.—Why hast thou hid it here in a casket?

Fátimah.—Because my dear grandson 'Alí Akbar† will suck water out of it when thirsty in Karbalá.

Zainab.—Oh, may I die! for my soul has become restless.

Fátimah.—Husain shall wear this ring on his finger.

Zainab.—Will anybody take it from off his finger?

Fátimah.—Yes; a camel-driver shall cut Husain's finger,‡ and take off the ring.

Zainab.—Yes; see how his friends weep on this sad occasion.

Fátimah.—Take out that bundle of clothes from the box.

Zainab.—My heart overflows with blood at the sight of this bundle.

Fátimah.—Look at this shirt, torn into pieces.

Zainab.—Let it be a burial shroud§ for Zainab.

Fátimah.—This is the shirt of Husain my son.

Zainab.—O Lord! see the sad state of my Husain.

Fátimah.—When my Husain shall prepare himself for the field of battle——

Zainab.—Oh, tell me what to do at that time, mother.

Fátimah.—Kiss his dear throat, and remember me.

Zainab.—Oh! mother, kill me at once, that I may not see such a thing.

Fátimah.—Come and open for me the other box, girl.

Zainab.—What is in this one, O dear mother?

---

* See note, p. 81. ‡ See note *, p. 99.
† See note, p. 8. § See note, p. 27.

Fátimah.—Take out the three bottles filled with camphor.

Zainab.—I have done it; but for what dost thou intend them?

Fátimah.—When I die thou must sprinkle one over my body.

Zainab.—What shall I do with the remaining two?

Fátimah.—One of the two belongs to Haidar,* thy father.

Zainab.—Say, whose is the third, dear mother?

Fátimah.—That is for Hasan, thy elder brother, dear.

Zainab.—Where is Husain, my helpless brother's, share?

Fátimah.—Husain's body shall receive no washing,† no lotus leaves' powder, and no camphor when he dies.

Zainab.—But why, dear mother? What is his fault?

Fátimah.—His camphor shall be the dust of Karbalá.

Zainab.—O ye Musalmans, weep on for him.

Fátimah.—Go away, dear daughter, and let my maid come to me now.

Zainab.—Come, thou suffering, broken-hearted damsel, Fátimah, my mother, the best among women,‡ wanteth thee.

The Maid.—What dost thou desire, O crown of my head? Declare it to me.

Fátimah.—Look at me, and prepare for me camphor

---

* See note, p. 39.

† "The ordinary ablution preparatory to prayer having been performed upon the corpse, with the exception of the washing of the mouth and nose, the whole body is well washed, from head to foot, with warm water and soap, and with *leef* (or fibres of the palm-tree); or, more properly, with water in which some leaves of the lote-tree (*nubck* or *sidr*) have been boiled. The nostrils, ears, &c. are stuffed with cotton, and the corpse is sprinkled with a mixture of water, pounded camphor, and dried and pounded leaves of the nubck, and with rose-water. Sometimes other dried and pounded leaves are added to those of the nubck."—Lane's "Modern Egyptians," vol. ii. p. 288, ed. 1836.

‡ See note, p. 42.

and funeral garments. There is a shroud of mine in that closet, with some camphor of paradise placed on it. Run quickly, my poor damsel, and bring it at once to me.

The Maid.—Alas! woe unto me, from the injustice of time! My mistress is going away from us for ever. My Hasan will be in great affliction and sorrow, and my Husain will have no one to take care of him. Dear lady, may my head be given a ransom for thee! Here is the winding-sheet and the camphor; take them.

Fátimah.—O heaven, thou hast at length begun thy torments! Thou hast thrown me suddenly from a close union to distant separation! Thou takest away Hasan from me, and buildest up a wall of partition between me and Husain! O dear Hasan, may I be made a ransom for thy soul; a sacrifice for thee and thy tearful eyes! And, O Husain, may I be offered for thy head, and be made an oblation for thee and thy throat! What is thy sin, child, that it should happen to thee to be deprived of all, and fall naked before the hot sun in the plain of Karbalá? O great God, I leave this world never to see it again, having experienced no pleasures in my short life, which consists only of eighteen years; and am going cheerfully to the Messenger of God, my father in heaven. Therefore do I bear witness that there is no real God besides the true One.

SCENE VIII.

THE MARTYRDOM OF ALI THE SON OF ABU TALIB.

'ALI was assassinated in a mosque at Kúfah, Jan. (about 26th) A.D. 661. "Just as he was entering the mosque, Werdan, one of the accomplices of Eben Múljum, all of whom lay on the watch for this opportunity, made a stroke at the person of the Khalif, but, missing his aim, his scimitar took the side post of the entrance. Eben Múljum, with more fatal precision, gave the devoted prince a cut on the head, exactly on the scar of a former wound, which, in the action of Ekhraub, he had received from Amrú the son of Abdoúd. On feeling himself struck, some words dropped from Ally expressive of his resignation to the will of Him, who is Lord of the Kaaubah, and summoning resolution to meet his fate. Being immediately surrounded by the people, to their inquiries as to the author of this sacrilegious assault upon his person, he replied, that God would soon overtake the miscreant. . . . The Khalif then addressed him (the murderer), and demanded if he had not loaded him with benefits, and what motives could have induced him to such an ungrateful act of perfidy. Eben Múljum did not deny his obligations, but alleged that for forty days he had been employed in whetting his sword, and had importuned heaven with his prayers to permit him to make a sacrifice of that man who was the most sinful of his nation. He was now consigned to the attendants, with a charge that if the Khalif's wound proved mortal, he should be put to death without torture. Others further relate that the assassin was consigned to the particular care of Imaum Hussun, with strict injunctions that he should not be doomed to suffer either hunger or thirst; and that if the Khalif should perish of his wound, the criminal should be executed by a single stroke, intimating that he might not suffer the aggravated punishment of a lingering death. Accordingly when Ally had breathed his last, the traitor Eben Múljum was carried to a summary execution in the manner which had been enjoined; though his detestable carcase was wrapped up in mats, and consumed to ashes, by the the afflicted friends of the departed monarch." — Price's "Chronological Retrospect of Mahommedan History,".vol. i. p. 361, ed. 1811.

'Alí (addressing the Almighty).—O beneficent Creator! Lord of jinns * and men! look upon Thy humble servant 'Alí, who seeks continually for Thy grace, and boasts of Thy loving kindness and protection before the inhabitants of the world. I adjure Thee, by those arms of mine which tore the dragon in pieces when I was yet an infant only four months old, and lay in a cradle, to forgive the sins of my followers the Shí'ahs, for whom I am greatly concerned, O ineffable Being!

Kulsúm, his daughter (to her sister Zainab).—O thou queen of the palace of faith! thou most respected amongst the family of the Prophet! thou light of the eye of Zahrah† his daughter! may I be a ransom for thee! I intend to invite to my house to-night the king of men, the successor of the Prophet, the pillar of faith, 'Alí our father. Tell me, may I be offered unto thee! what dost thou think of that?

Zainab.—Dear sister, thou light of my sorrowful eyes, what thou hast already said is quite right in itself. Our father is very kind to us, his afflicted daughters, and sympathises with us in all our troubles and pains. Most certainly he will accept this thy request; go, then, and state it humbly to his lordship.

Kulsúm (to 'Alí).—O light of nature's eye, may I be a ransom for thee! O glory of the inhabitants of the world, may I be a sacrifice for thee! O father, let it please thee to condescend to come to my humble hut this evening, and partake of the same meal with me, thy broken-hearted

---

* See note, p. 24. † See note, p. 22.

daughter; rest in my eyes for awhile, as it were the light.

'Alí.—May I be an offering for thy soul, O my chosen daughter! thou pacifier of my heart and light of both my eyes! Return home and prepare what thou hast got; but take care not to be extravagant in God's gifts. In the evening, when I shall have performed my duty to the Lord, I will come to the house of my well-behaved, beautiful-faced daughter, and take my first meal.

Kulsúm.—Come to me, O my worthy sister of laudable character; for in a moment or two the glory of our father and his majesty will appear. Have the goodness to help Kulsúm, thy favoured sister, in preparing a repast agreeable to his blessed palate.

Zainab.—May I be offered for thee, O my poor labouring sister! May I be a ransom for thee and for thy affecting condition, dear Kulsúm. Be not troubled, sister; everything is quite ready for our father, even the bird of ours, if he should require to have it roasted. I am sitting here anxiously awaiting his arrival, to see what time the lord of heaven and earth will arrive.

Kulsúm (to 'Alí).—May I be a ransom for thee, O thou enlightener of heaven and earth! Thy poor daughter Zainab is in anxious expectation for thy coming. May it please thee to honour the humble hut of thy helpless, miserable daughter Kulsúm.

Zainab.—Welcome, O glory of 'Irák and Hijáz! May the souls of Zainab and Kulsúm be cast at thy holy feet! Think not that we two are thy dear daughters; God is the witness that we consider ourselves thy slaves. The dust of thy feet is the collyrium* of Zainab's eyes. Come, take thy seat, thou king of noble birth; be pleased to pardon Kulsúm's boldness for the trouble she has given thee, and condescend to eat what she has humbly set here before thee.

---

* Eastern ladies are much addicted to the use of antimony and other drugs, which they rub into the eyes to improve their appearance.

'Alí (to Zainab and Kulsúm).—O ye brightness of the eyes of Haidar* the warrior! if you wish I should take my meal at this table, remove from it everything except bread and salt, and trouble me not to eat the other things.

Kulsúm.—What has happened, O my chosen father, that thou art not inclined to eat anything? Why shouldst thou this very night, when it has pleased thee to honour me, be so much disturbed in thy mind?

'Alí.—What shall I say, dear child, in answer to thy inquiry? Thy father is going to have an end of his sorrows. Seeing the time of my martyrdom is drawing very near, for this reason I do not feel inclined for any kind of food.

Zainab.—If it be so, then it is better thou shouldst take a little rest. Come, sleep on in this bed which is spread for thee. The adversity of the journey to Nahrawán† has broken thee down. Yea, afflictions of the age have rendered thy body extremely weak.

'Alí (to his two daughters).—O my two afflicted daughters, whose eyes continually shed tears, you must go to bed too, dear ones, and that this very moment; but mind to awake me early in the morning for prayer.

Kulsúm (to Zainab).—My poor oppressed sister, may I be a ransom for thee! Come and sleep, O helpless, wretched creature. Come and sleep, thou reflex of Fátimah,‡ the best among women. May God never lessen thy shadow from our head!

The Prophet (appearing to 'Alí in his dream).—This is a wonderful night; for when its evening shall be changed into morning, 'Alí's beard shall be stained with the blood of his head. To-night Zainab is sitting quite

---

* See note, p. 39.

† Nahrawán is a position on the Tigris, some leagues above the confluence of that river with the Euphrates. It was the scene of one of 'Alí's battles, A.D. 659.

‡ Mother of Kulsúm and Zainab; see note, p. 42.

happy in the company of her father; but to-morrow she will be mourning over the dead body of a parent. Hasan and Husain are happy, but only for to-night; for to-morrow the dust of mourning shall sit on the head of both. O my dear cousin 'Alí, open thine eyes kindly towards me, before I suffer grievously from separation from thee.

'Alí, in his dream, speaks to the Prophet.—O seal* of the prophets of all ages, how unbearable is this separation! My soul has come to my lip owing to my earnest desire to see thee. After thy death, O Prophet of God, the wicked, through envy and hatred, agreed together to oppress me. They tied my hands behind my back, and broke the ribs of the Prophet's daughter Fátimah. These hardships have made me miserable, and my patience has left me altogether. Graciously call me, O Prophet, to thyself; for thy cousin can no longer live in this world!

The Prophet.—O 'Alí! O my sweet soul, awake a little! O 'Alí! O my former companion, awake a little! Open thine eyes and behold thy cousin, whom thou art desirous to see. Good luck is attending on thee at thy pillow; thou shouldest open thine eyes.

'Alí.—Peace be on thee, O thou fountain of generosity and beneficence! Thou art welcome; may thy feet be placed on my tearful eyes! How strange it is that thou hast deigned to come and visit me. May my sweet soul become an offering to the earth of thy path! Think not, O Prophet, that I am a dear cousin to thee; I swear by the dust of thy feet that I am but thy slave.

The Prophet.—On thee be peace, O my successor† and cousin! On thee be peace, O thou my companion in all my afflictions and sorrows! Though my abode is now in the delightful garden of Paradise, yet Heaven without thy rosy cheeks is but a prison to me. I am aware of thy

---

* See note ‡, p. 40.   † This is the Shí'ah tradition.

condition, knowing well that since my death thou hast been tyrannized over by my cruel people. My heart is full of grief and sorrow on thy account; I cannot lift up my head before thee, nor open my eyes in thy presence, I am so much ashamed.

'Alí.—O cousin, thy people, after thou wert gone, had no regard for thee. A certain dog* stretched forth the hand of cruelty and injustice, and made a breach in thy house. He disregarded my nobility and merits, and took the Khalífat from me by force. He aimed at 'Alí's disgrace, in that he put a rope round my neck. He burned the door of thy house with fire,† and in so doing grieved thy holy children.

The Prophet.—O 'Alí! 'Alí! I am undone! Complain no more, for I cannot bear to hear it. I am consuming away as a burning candle by reason of thy sad condition; I am terribly concerned on thy behalf. O 'Alí, I swear by the Lord, the Creator, the mighty God, that I am heartily weary of such people, who have not regarded nor honoured thee. By the Lord, I am an enemy of such a nation. Be not sorry; I will advocate thy cause in the Day of Judgment.

'Alí.—When thy feet, O Prophet, trod the threshold of Paradise, how shall I say what injustice and cruelty I afterwards suffered? The burden of separation from thee has weighed so heavily on my heart as to make my groans reach the heaven of heavens.

The Prophet.—Be not troubled any more, dear cousin, seeing that the end of our separation is near at hand; the dark night of sorrow is about to be followed by bright pleasant morning. Sigh no more so deeply, nor shed tears so plentifully; the day of affliction draws to its close, and thy pain will obtain a cure.

'Alí.—Say, O Prophet, who will help me in the matter?

---

* Abú Bakr.   † See introduction, scene vi. p. 92.

How long must I remain confined in this prison? At what time shall I be delivered from this despicable world and its vain toils? When shall I have the honour of being in thy company in heaven?

The Prophet.—Be not impatient, for the day of separation is far spent; blessed fortune is going to appear. Thou hast but a brief time to sojourn in this perishable abode. My most wicked people, not regarding me at all, whilst thou art praying shall smite thee on the head with a sword. This very night thy moon-like face shall be encompassed with a halo of blood. And shortly after thou shalt be with the Prophet, and in Paradise shalt enjoy the companionship of my child the virgin.*

'Ali.—This good news, O cousin, deserves that by reason thereof I should instantly cast my head at thy feet. Oh! I shall be delivered at once from many troubles and sorrows when I shall have closed my eyes for ever on the things of this mortal life.

The Prophet.—Sleep on, dear cousin, in thy bed, having laid thy head for awhile on my lap; for this is thy last slumber in the world, death having already laid wait for thee.

'Ali (awaking).—I was just now in the presence of Muhammad the Prophet. Why was his glorious light removed suddenly from my sight? O Messenger of God, why didst thou not take me with thee on thy departure? Why should I continue in affliction and sorrow any longer?

Zainab.—Again I hear my father's sad voice. I am much disturbed by the groanings of my parent to-night. O Lord God, what may be the cause of all this sighing and crying? The piteous cries of my father have made my soul reach the tip of my lip.

'Ali.—This night has become almost a year in regard to length! Methinks the morning cocks have become dumb

---

* See note, p. 57.

or the king of light must have trampled under foot the army of darkness.

Zainab.—Oh! why does my father complain so much to-night in his bed? What has made him noisy like a ringing bell? O Lord, what shall I do to my poor father to keep him quiet? My heart is beating within me owing to his sad voice.

'Ali.—O night, art thou not to be followed by happy morning? Why art thou unaware of my miserable condition? O sun, put forth thy face from behind the curtain. 'Alí is fully determined upon resignation and acquiescence.

Zainab.—Oh! why does not my father sleep to-night? Why does he grieve my heart so much by his mournful utterings? He has nothing on his tongue but words of separation to-night. I fear the stone of his sorrow will one day break my wings.

'Ali.—Show forth thyself, O sun, out of the bosom of the east, and be not sorry for Haidar's death. Shine on the surface of the dark world and make it bright, and care not so much about my murder.

Zainab.—To-night my father's complaints are very bitter, his eyes tearful, and his face pallid. Why does he complain of the length of night? It would appear— God forbid!—he has some pain.

'Ali.—Come out, O morning, from the bosom of the east, and be not sad owing to Haidar's murder. It is decreed that before dawn my head shall be cloven asunder with the stroke of a scymetar, and my moon-like* face be washed with my own blood. But let God's will be done; it is for the Shí'ahs that I suffer all this.

Zainab (addressing 'Alí).—May I be a sacrifice for thee, O my chosen father! May my soul be a ransom for thee, O thou brightness of my two eyes! O thou heaven of glory, what has happened to thee that thou art so sad?

---

* See note, p. 7.

Oh! tell me, thy poor daughter, why now thou lookest towards the earth, now towards heaven. At one moment thou sheddest tears down thy cheeks, at another thou bowest down and fallest prostrate on the ground.

'*Alí.*—May I be a ransom for thee, my poor sore-hearted daughter! In a few short hours I intend to have a journey to Paradise. The chosen one of the glorious God appeared to me in a dream, and invited me to his happy banquet. The time has come that my beard shall be stained with my own blood by the cruel sword of the son of Muljam,* the accursed wicked dog.

Zainab.—May God never decree this, dear father! May I be offered unto thee! Never can people act so cruelly towards us! Thou art the asylum of the poor, the ointment of the wounded in heart. Why shouldst thou conceive a bad omen against thyself, dear father?

'*Alí.*—Shed not tears down thy poor cheeks, O my daughter; grieve me not in so doing, dear child. Get me some water soon, that I may renew my ablutions, for the time of prayer is come; the dawn has appeared on the horizon.

Zainab (*bringing water*).—Come, here is water for the renewal of thy ablutions. Perform the ceremonies, thou Lion of the glorious Creator! Make thy ablutions. May the God of the world be thy refuge! May my midnight prayers direct thee in the right way!

'*Alí* (*making his ablutions*).—O great God, for the merits of Muhammad the Arabian, the king of Thy prophets, the director† of the right way, for this head of mine which shall be cloven asunder with the sword of tyranny, and for the sake of my body, which shall roll to-morrow in its own blood, forgive Thou mercifully the sins of my Shí'ahs and in the Day of Judgment pardon Thou all them that love me. I am going now to the Mosque to perform my prayers, and serve my Creator with supplication and intercession.

---

* See note *, p. 117. † See note, p. 72.

Zainab.—O father, I most humbly entreat thee not to go to Mosque. Remain at home and perform God's service here.

'Ali.—How can I forbear going to the Mosque to serve there the Lord of all creatures? Whatever happens by God's decrees, I cannot, dear child, but assent thereto.

Zainab.—Order then, O honourable father, please, my brothers Hasan and Husain to accompany thee whither thou goest, that they may defend thee, if necessary, from the mischief of the enemy during the hours of prayer.

'Ali (about to depart).—Dear daughter, light of my tearful eyes, how can I take them with me? It is decreed, dear child, that my beard should be stained with the blood of my head in the Mosque, and I cannot avert it.

Zainab.—May I be offered for thy elegant stature, O father! come, let me show my readiness to die for thee. How can I soothe the pain of separation from thee? How can I bear the hard calamity of being an orphan? If a thorn happens to prick thy foot unawares, I would rather have it in my eye than see it hurt thy foot.

'Ali (to his water-fowls).—O ye water-fowls,* why are you all so sad, and why put ye your heads under your wings mournfully? You seem to lament the death of some honourable creature—nay, by our Lord, ye are mourning for me!

Zainab (to 'Ali).—May I be a ransom for thee, O thou central orb of the constellation of truth! pray tell me what art thou saying to the water-fowl? Why are they hold-

---

* "As he quitted his own door, a flock of poultry, which was at hand, raising a loud outcry at his appearance, one of the attendants attempted to beat them away with his cudgel, but was desired by Ally not to molest them, since they were the mourners of his death."—Price's "Chronological Retrospect of Mahommedan History," vol. i. p. 361, ed. 1811.

ing the skirts of thy garment with their bills, and making such a sad noise at this time? They are all running round thee, and saying, "'Alí, 'Alí!" they are encompassing thee around as holy pilgrims, hoping by thee to be made happy.

'Alí.—The water-fowls of our house, dear child, are all mourning affectionately for me. It appears they have been informed of my approaching murder, and are, for this reason, holding the skirts of my garment.

Zainab.—No doubt it is most ominous to keep water-fowls at home. They have, at any rate, brought innumerable evils upon me by their ill-luck. I am much troubled in mind at the ceaseless noise of these creatures, and shall therefore break their wings with stones, and turn them out from the house at once.

'Alí.—Strike not, dear girl, the water-fowls of the household of faith. Pelt not stones at the nightingales of the garden of lamentation. Break not, dear daughter, the wings of these poor birds, these lapwings of the city of Sabá.*

Zainab.—O what shall I do? the murder of my poor father is about to be accomplished, for birds and beasts are mourning for him. We shall, ere long, become fatherless in the world. O Lord God, look mercifully upon us.

'Alí (in the Mosque, proclaiming for prayer).—God is great! God is great! God is great! God is great! I bear witness that there is no other God but God!

---

* "And he (Solomon) viewed the birds, and said, 'What is the reason that I see not the lapwing? Is she absent? Verily I will chastise her with a severe chastisement, or I will put her to death, unless she bring me a just excuse.' And she tarried not long *before she presented herself unto Solomon*, and said, 'I have viewed *a country* which thou hast not viewed, and I come unto thee from Saba, with a certain piece of news.'"
—Sale's "Koran," chap. xxvii. p. 310, ed. 1734.

The cursed Katámah*.—My address is to thee, O son of Muljam the traitor, awake and arise quickly from thy sleep, for 'Alí has come most pompously to the Mosque. Dost thou not hear his proclamation for prayer? Hold this sword in thy hand, and run soon to the Mosque and kill 'Alí, if thou lovest me and intendest to make me glad and happy. Deliver me, my dear friend, from the great pain which troubles my heart, and render Fátimah's children fatherless at once. In no other way canst thou please me except in murdering the Prophet's successor. My heart will not rejoice until I see Hasan and Husain putting round their necks the shawl of mourning.

'Alí (finding the son of Muljam sleeping in the Mosque).— My address is to thee, O Ibn Muljam the traitor, awake thou for the service of the great Lord! If I would I could put thee to shame by disclosing what thou hast concealed carefully under thy cloak. Arise from thy place, it is time for thee to be cheerful, for it is the night of my decease and the day of thy revelry.

Gabriel† *(to the Angels).*—Be it known unto you, O ye heavenly hosts, that his lordship 'Alí, the Lion of God,

---

* "On his arrival at Kúfah, Eben Múljum became acquainted with, and violently enamoured of, a woman whose uncommon beauty and attractions he was unable to resist, whose name was Kettaumah, and of whom, adds our author, might justly be said, that her face was like the glorious reward of the virtuous, and the tresses which adorned her cheek like the black record of the villain's guilt. This woman had belonged to the faction of the Khouauredje, had lost a father, brother, and husband, or, according to others, an uncle and husband, in the conflict at Neherwaun; and to the solicitations of her lover she now replied that there would be no obstacle to the attainment of his wishes provided he would undertake, on his part, to discharge himself of the terms which she should propose as the price of her hand; these she stipulated to be three thousand dirhems, a male and female slave, and the head of Ally the son of Abútauleb."—Price's " Chronological Retrospect of Mahommedan History," vol. i. p. 357, ed. 1811.

† See note, p. 15.

has gone to the Mosque to pray. The sign of God's mercy has descended in the niche to offer his obedience to his Maker. Let us go down to imitate that high personage and offer our souls to the dust of his holy feet. It being the last prayer of the Lion of God on earth, let us descend once more, to take a lesson from him before we lose the opportunity.

The Angels.—Woe unto us! it is the last day of 'Ali's life! Alas! it is his final prayer! This very hour the sword of Muljam's son, the accursed, shall touch the crown of 'Ali's head. Whom shall we imitate hereafter in God's worship, seeing the first Imám is going to be killed? Come on, O ye angels, all of you; it is time to bid adieu to the king of true religion.

The Son of Muljam (smiting 'Ali).—For the sake of Katámah, the cursed, treacherous woman, I strike on 'Ali's* head, maliciously, the sword of cruelty!

'Ali (smitten down).—In the name of God, by His order, and in His way! O religion of the Messenger of God, Muhammad! the blessings of the Lord be on him and his family!

Angels announce 'Ali's death.—Alas! alas! the high priest of God's religion has been murdered by the sword of the enemy! Alas! alas! the prince of the faithful has been cruelly slain! The successor of the chosen Prophet has been killed with the sword of injustice, and blood has gushed out of the Lion of God's head! Alas! alas!

Zainab (awaking).—O Lord God! what fire of tumult is

---

* "Little is left of Kufa but the mosque where Ali was assassinated, a plain edifice, in the form of a square, with a court in the centre, surrounded with a cloister. There is but one entrance, through an elegant gateway, and the walls being high, and flanked with bastions, give it more the appearance of a castle than of a place of worship. The Mahomedans hold in high veneration the spot on which this mosque has been built."—Kinneir's "Persia," p. 285, ed. 1813.

flaming without! What news is this which has heaped up sorrows on my heart? Merciful God! what is this commotion among the angels of Heaven! Oh! their sighs and cries are disturbing my mind in a manner I cannot express! Methinks my poor father has suffered martyrdom; if so, Zainab is reduced to the lowest degree of misery.

Gabriel.—Be it known unto you, O ye household of faith, that 'Alí's spirit has flown like a bird to its heavenly nest in Paradise. A head, whose umbrella was the chapter of the Kur'án entitled "The Sun,"* yea, such a glorious head has received from the sword of malice a blow of a nature to cleave it asunder like the bosom of a rose-bud. He is like a red lily rolling in his own blood through the stroke of Muljam's son, the cruel unbeliever.

Zainab (to Kulsúm).—Woe unto me! What was the voice which reached my ear so suddenly? Is—God forbid!—the Lion of God slain? Come, dear sister, let us go lamentingly to Hasan and Husain's bed-room to awake them.

Kulsúm (to Hasan).—O Hasan, may Kulsúm be offered for thy head! awake thou! Thine enlightened father is slain; awake, dear brother!

Zainab (to Husain).—O brother, thou brightness of my tearful eyes, awake from thy sleep! We have at length become fatherless; dear brother, awake!

Hasan and Husain.—Distressed sisters, why are you making such an ado? Wherefore do tears run down your cheeks? Dear sisters, your sighs and groans are burning

---

* "By the sun, and its rising brightness; by the moon, when she followeth him; by the day, when it showeth his splendour; by the night, when it covereth him with darkness; by the heaven, and Him who built it; by the earth, and Him who spread it forth; by the soul, and Him who completely formed it, and inspired into the same its faculty of distinguishing, and power of choosing wickedness and piety," &c. &c.—Sale's "Koran," chap. xci. p. 492, ed. 1734.

my very inward soul. What is the cause of this mournful noise?

Zainab.—Dear brothers, our father went to the Mosque to say his prayers and to bless the people. Now there reach my ears continually the voices of the holy ones of God, saying, "'Alí is killed." They seem crying between heaven and earth, and saying plainly, "'Alí, the high priest of religion, was killed in the general Mosque." It is better both of you should run to the sacred place and see what is become of our dear father there.

Hasan and Husain.—Woe unto us! Why is our father wallowing in his blood? Why is the crown of our head fallen in the niche of prayer? Father, may we be offered for thy blood-stained face! May we be sacrificed for thy rose-coloured, moon-like visage!

'Alí.—Welcome, dear sons! do you come at such a time to see your father? The end of my troubles is at hand. The time has come that I should be saved from the miseries of this world, and go to Paradise to visit the Prophet of God. You may take me home at once from the Mosque; there is no occasion for my miserable family to weep.

Hasan and Husain together.—Alas! O our followers, Haidar is slain! The cup-bearer of the tank of Al Kausar* is no more! Mourn on, O ye mourners; for thy sons have become orphans!

Zainab (to 'Alí).—May I be a ransom for thee, O thou lion of the thicket of God's creation! May the soul of Zainab be offered a sacrifice for thine! What cruel, irreligious infidel has smitten thee with the sword on thy holy head? Open thine eyes compassionately on us, for God's sake, and for the afflicted soul of Zainab thy daughter.

'Alí.—Be not sorry, dear child, on account of my martyrdom; for so was it decreed as regards me that I should thus be killed. Lamentations and weepings do not avail

---

* See note, p. 96.

me at all. Do something, if thou canst, to alleviate awhile my pain.

Zainab (to Hasan and Husain).—O ye two princes, may I be a ransom for your souls! Prepare black clothes for me that I may put them on. The king of the throne of the Imámat* is leaving the world for ever; make ready for him funeral garments and things pertaining to mourning. I am about to rend my clothes in pieces through excess of sorrow. Oh, what am I to do? My father is going out of my reach so suddenly.

Kulsúm (to Hasan and Husain).—O ye brightness of the eyes of the age! O ye plants of the rose-garden of 'Alí, dear Hasan and Husain, behold in what state the pillar of faith, our father, is. Run and call for him Na'mán the surgeon,† that he may see the wound of the supporter of religion; peradventure he will be able to cure him.

Hasan and Husain (to Na'mán).—We beseech thee, for God's sake, O Na'mán, to come to our house and see how the Lion of God, the king of men, feels. Look pitifully on the sad state of us, the orphans of the pillar of faith, and treat the wound of 'Alí, the royal priest.

Na'mán, the Surgeon.—May I be a ransom for you, ye two tender plants of the Prophet's garden; ye ornaments of the bosom of Muhammad, the Arabian. Be not grieved, O ye Hasan and Husain! I am coming just now to treat Haidar the warrior's wound. Go ye in haste to that king of piety; I am coming after you to see if I can cure him.

Hasan (to Zainab).—O dear sister, sadly afflicted with grief by reason of thy father's mortal wound, go on one side, and hide thy face carefully, for a stranger is about to enter. Behold, Na'mán is coming to examine the wound of Haidar the brave.

---

* Priesthood.
† Probably an ideal name for a surgeon.

Na'mán.—O ye chosen family of the Messenger of God, peace be on you! O ye household of the elect of God, peace be on you! Ye tender plants of the rose-garden of religion, drooping from the blast of the tempest of God's decree, peace be on you!

The Family.—O thou votary of the law of God's Apostle, on thee be peace! O thou lover of the possessor of the crown and standard, on thee be peace! See, O Na'mán, how the blooming garden of faith has suddenly withered through Time's unjust proceedings! Have thou mercy on us poor children, and treat well the mortal wound of the model of piety.

Kulsúm.—O surgeon, for the sake of the living God and Judge, see the wound of the head of my father, the cup-bearer of Kausar! Look if his wound be mortal, for I am very anxious for my dear father. If I hear good news from thy mouth, I will go to thy children and show my readiness to bear their painful calamities.

Zainab.—O Na'mán, I adjure thee by the veracity of Muhammad, the chief of God's religion, to pity me, a sad, miserable creature, and to lay my desponding soul under a great obligation to thee, by treating my father. Take me as one of thy slaves bought with money, and pity me. Do it for God's sake, and have compassion on me and these poor children. I am still in mourning for Zahrah my mother; how can I bear the additional burden of separation from my father?

Na'mán (to 'Alí).—Peace be unto thee, O glory of heaven and earth! O Imám of the two worlds, and director of the followers of truth! Why is thy face immersed in blood? Why should the phenomenon of the moon's splitting be reproduced in thy forehead? Who has felled the tree of faith to the ground? Who has plunged in blood the pilot of the deluge?

'Alí.—What shall I say, O Na'mán? Alas! when I went to the Mosque, and stood up there for prayer, toward the niche of faith, as soon as I fell prostrate on the

ground, the cruel sword of the traitor alighted on my head whilst thus bowing myself, and cut down as far as my forehead.

Na'mán, probing the wound.—Alas! let me see what heaven, the supporter of the faithful, has done to the noble cousin of the Prophet? Alas! alas! mayest thou be subverted, O heaven! Mayest thou be plunged in the ocean of blood like the head of the Lion of God! For the pate of 'Alí, the equal of Aaron, the son of Imrán,* is cloven asunder, and the unjust blow has reached down to the forehead.

Hasan.—I adjure thee by the living God, O Na'mán, to cure the wound of our father the priest of the age. Let not the two tender plants of 'Alí be rooted up by overwhelming sorrow, but deliver them from the bonds of desolation, if thou canst.

Na'mán (to the family).—Wash your hands at once of Haidar's life; have no more hope of his recovery. 'Alí will be but for one hour more with you, his dear ones. O children of the Lion of God, you will ere long become fatherless. Read the Kur'án over your father, for he is gone. Prepare for him winding-sheets, and do not leave him alone. Tell Zainab to put on black, and mourn for her father.

'Alí's Family, crying and lamenting.—Make us not fatherless, O Lord, O God! Shall we be orphans and sorrowful ones, O Lord, O God? Take our souls instead of his, O Lord, O God! Make us not tearful-eyed, O Lord, O God!

'Alí (to his family).—O my poor, sad family, gather ye yourselves together around me, like the constellation of Pleiades about the moon; and you, O brightness of my eyes, Hasan and Husain, come near me for awhile, dear sons; and come thou, Zainab my daughter, see thy father's

---

* See Sale's "Koran," chap. iii. p. 38, ed. 1734.

face, for the time has arrived that thou shouldst put on black on account of my death.

Hasan.—May I be offered unto thee, O thou glory of the people of the age! I am Hasan, thy poor orphan son. Thou art greatly desirous to go to Paradise, the abode of the just, and hast, therefore, forgotten us altogether.

'Ali.—O thou tender plant of the garden of Time's glory, thou brightness of my tearful eyes, Hasan, come to me, that I may commit unto thee the secret knowledge of the Imámat, or priesthood. Come, let me put my lips to thy delicate lips, and deliver the mystery of religion in this way to thy heart. Thou art the guide of men after me, O my successor! Perform the rites of Imámat for the people after my departure.

Hasan.—What shall I, thy oppressed son, do when thou art taken away from us? To whom shall I look hereafter for comfort and solace? May Hasan be offered for thy parched throat, O father! Come, let me put my lips to thine as thou didst order me to do.

'Ali.—Oh, my poor helpless, weeping family, leave me alone in the room for awhile; for I have to speak my secrets to my Creator, and make supplication to Him, before I leave this world.

Hasan.—O ye, my brothers and sisters, go out all of you from this room, with tearful eyes, and let everyone put a copy of the Kur'án on his head, and pray earnestly to the holy Creator for the recovery of our father and protector.

'Ali.—O thou beneficent Creator, the sole, the almighty God, I adjure Thee by Thine own glory, O Thou who art without any equal, and by that pearl-like tooth* of Thy chosen and glorious Prophet, which was knocked out with a stone in the battle of Ohod; and by the disappointment of his child Fátimah, and by the fracture which she

---

* See note, p. 129.

suffered in her side; and by the tearful eyes of his distressed family; and, lastly, by this blood-stained beard of mine, to forgive, O eternal, ineffable Maker, the sins of 'Alí's followers in the Day of Judgment. Now I depart this life with the desire of meeting the Messenger of God in the next world. I do therefore bear witness that there is no God except God. (*Dies.*)

Zainab, perceiving that 'Alí is dead.—Why has thy mouth ceased from speaking, dear father? Has heaven thrown black dust on our head to make us miserable? Alas! his honour, the Lion of God, has departed this life! He is gone to the garden of Paradise to visit Zahrah! Dear ones, inform 'Alí's afflicted servant of his master's death, that he may cover Haidar's mule "Duldul"* with black.

Hasan and Husain together.—Come, let us put shawls of mourning round our necks. Come, let us groan and make a sad noise. Come, dear sisters, dutifully close our father's eyes.

Zainab and Kulsúm together.—Alas! our father is, after all, gone! Alas! he is gone as an arrow out of our hand! Come, let us put on black; let us dishevel our hair over his corpse.

'Alí's Servant, leading the mule "Duldul" draped in black.—Oh! they have killed the owner of "Duldul," 'Alí, the prince of believers! Alas! they have slain the chief, the Lion of the Lord of all creatures! The master of the crown and standard has suffered martyrdom by the sword of Muljam the traitor! They have destroyed the all-wise successor of the chosen of God.

Hasan and Husain.—O "Duldul" of our lord, where is our father and thy master? Where is our chief and

---

* "Duldul, one of Muhammad's mules, was given to 'Alí by the Prophet while the latter was alive, that no one might quarrel about it after his death."—Meyrick's "Life of Mohammed," p. 370, ed. 1850.

our prince? Where is our dear supporter and protector? Where is the lustre of the Prophet's religion? Where the husband of Zahrah the virgin?* O poor creature, thy master has been killed by the insensate populace.

---

* See note, p. 57.

SCENE IX.

THE MARTYRDOM OF HASAN, THE SON OF ALI.

HASAN was murdered at Madinah, A.D. 670. This event is thus described in Price's "Chronological Retrospect of Mahommedan History," vol. i. p. 369, ed. 1811 :—" Hussun had, however, been suffered to live without apparent molestation for some years at Medeinah, when the impatience of Mauweiah to declare his son Yezzeid successor to the empire, hastened the destiny of this unfortunate prince. For conceiving that his favourite object was not to be conveniently carried into execution while Hussun survived to claim an observance of the faith of treaties, Mauweiah resolved to relieve himself from the embarrassment, and was perhaps not over-scrupulous in his means. It is, however, mortifying to learn that an instrument to secure the accomplishment of his treacherous design against the existence of his unsuspecting victim, was to be found in the very sanctuary of domestic peace, while it furnishes another deplorable example of that foul depravity by which a vicious and unprincipled female has been sometimes led to stigmatise the character of her sex. The person whom Mauweiah selected on this occasion for the perpetration of his purpose was no other than the wife of the devoted Hussun, Jaidah, the daughter of Aishauth, the son of Keyss, whom he prevailed upon to undertake the destruction of her husband, by the promise of a sum of money and of being united in marriage to his favourite Yezzeid. The method which she adopted for its accomplishment is not less remarkable than the consummate perfidy of the design. While yet warm from her embraces, and with a napkin, which she had previously impregnated with poison for her purpose, she rubbed the person of her husband all over. The subtle preparation soon pervaded the frame of Hussun, and speedy and inevitable death was the consequence. . . . Her only compensation for the foul parricide, by which this wretched woman consented to consign her name to eternal infamy, was a sum of fifty thousand dirhems (equal about £1,146), which Mauweiah remitted for her use. . . . Before he expired, the much-injured Hussun had signified to his brother a request that he might be buried by the side of the Prophet, provided this could be done without effusion of blood; otherwise that his body might be consigned to the earth in the public burying-ground of Medeinah. The former request Hûsseyne was prevented from carrying into execution by Ayaishah and the party of Othman, who unaccountably opposed it. The body of the deceased Imaum was therefore conveyed to the ordinary cemetery, where it was deposited in the earth near the grave of his paternal grandmother."

Hasan.—The days of my youth have been all spent in anguish and sorrow; Thou art aware, O God, of my miserable condition. And now, O friends, I know that the time is come, when my enemies shall put poison in my drinking-water, not knowing that whosoever seeks his happiness in my destruction shall experience great misery.

The Messenger of Mu'áwiyah, the Governor of Syria (to Marwán, the Governor of Madínah).—Be it known unto thee, O Marwán, that I am sent from Shám* unto thee; yea, from the city of Syria to this holy territory. Mu'áwiyah has despatched me to thee with a written order and a verbal message, the purport of which is, to kill Hasan, the son of 'Alí, as soon as possible, with some mortal poison, and in this way cast down the star from its heavenly station, and eclipse the solar orb.

Marwán.—You must conceal this matter, O my dear friends. None besides yourselves must come to know it. Listen attentively to what I say to you; it is a secret, it must be hidden from all strangers. Call unto me soon Saudá, the procuress.

Marwán's Servant.—Come, O Saudá, Marwán is calling thee! he has a secret errand on which to send thee, and it can be transacted well by none save thyself.

The Procuress.—Why art thou so perplexed in thy proceeding? Tell me, O Marwán, what is thy errand?

---

* Damascus.

Marwán.—I have a secret errand to be transacted by thee; as it is a delicate case, thou must use thy best contrivances in bringing it about. My heart, O Saudá, is greatly vexed within me on account of Hasan's existence. While he is alive I am not sure of my Khalífat. Go thou, cunningly, to his consort, Ja'dah, and tell her Mu'áwiyah has sent her his best compliments, saying, that Yazíd his son having fallen in love with her, he is almost mad for her, and has no rest day and night. If she can manage to kill Hasan she may be sure Mu'áwiyah will take her for Yazíd, and make her the great queen of his palace.

The Procuress.—I beg thee to have me excused in the matter; for I think I cannot do such a thing. How can I resist that holy person's will, and bring such trials on him? Is not Hasan the ornament of God's glorious throne? Did he not have the privilege of riding on the Prophet's shoulder on the feast-day? How then can I commit such a wicked action?

Marwán.—Hearken unto me, good woman, and give up these stories of thine; here is a bag of gold coins to dispel thy pretexts. Take these strings of pearls too, and give them to Ja'dah, letting her know that these are presents to her from Yazíd.

The Procuress.—I fear neither God nor the Day of Judgment, since I have such a bag of gold coins in my possession. I will at once go there, and devise all possible sorts of contrivances to have Hasan killed and Zainab made brotherless.

Hasan.—Come to me, O my heart-rent Zainab, and thou, O Kulsúm, who art acquainted with grief. I am heavy from excessive drowsiness; put my bed in order that I may go to sleep. My tree of life seems stripped of its fruit and leaves, and this sleep appears to me to be the slumber of death. Go ye also, dear sisters, to your own closets, and rest in your own beds.

Kulsúm (spreading the bed).—May nought but joy and

pleasure ever enter thy heart. May thy sister not see thy place vacant! Come, my bright moon, thou delight of Kulsúm's soul, sleep in thy bed.

The Procuress (to Ja'dah).—Peace be unto thee, fair lady! I am come from a distant place to thee with an urgent errand, and expect a kind reception from thy angelic highness.

Ja'dah.—On thee be peace, my lovely newly-arrived visitor! Thou art welcome, be thy auspicious feet placed on my eyes! What is thy errand, thou cunning woman? Dread nobody, but declare the whole unto me.

The Procuress.—Thou must know that thy beauty and elegance are, now-a-days, the subject of conversation in all kingdoms. How many a heart that is bound fast in the chains of thy curling locks, never seeking deliverance! Prince Yazíd is one of the many captives and prisoners who are suffering the torments of love, not having yet seen thy charming face. If thy aim miss not the butt, I am sure thou wilt have conquered 'Irák and Egypt but with one darting glance of thine.

Ja'dah.—What thou hast said is the utmost of my desire, yet, seeing I am married already to Hasan, such a thing cannot possibly be done. God knows how earnestly I yearn after Yazíd; yea, I am melting for him as a candle, yet, owing to Hasan, this honourable union cannot be obtained. If thou art truly my friend, as I doubt not, teach me then kindly how to do away with Hasan.

The Procuress.—Wise contrivances are not uncommon in our age; though the case appears very serious, still, thank God, it is not irremediable. The prince has already sent thee some presents too, namely, a bracelet of gold and a string of pearls. He has given me also some diamond powder, a subtle poison, that thou mayest make Hasan take it when thou findest good opportunity.

Ja'dah.—Go to thy house in peace. I will soon poison him, and, making an end of his life, let you quickly know all about it. (*Puts poison in the jug.*) O Lord God, let nobody learn this secret, nor put me to shame in this world for what I do. For if this thing be known, I lose my object; having already thrown aside my religion, I shall fare ill in this world too.

Hasan (drinking the poisoned water).—Alas! woe unto me! heaven's eye has at length darted its malignant influence. Alas! this water has put my heart on fire. Dear sister Zainab, arise from thy bed; I am parched! I was very thirsty, so I drank a drop of this water; but it is burning me! Come, poor troubled Zainab, thou wilt lose thy Hasan, thy very brother. Both my sons will at a stroke become orphans.

Zainab.—Why art thou drenching thy lap with the tears of thine eyes? Why art thou turning the house with thy groans into the plain of the Day of Resurrection? Why hast thy head fallen from the pillow on the ground? Thy sister will surely perish through excess of grief.

Hasan.—Come, sister, time has undone Hasan thy brother. It has poured in my mouth an unpleasant poison. Prepare for me winding-sheets and some camphor,* for I shall carry thy love with me to the grave.

Zainab.—God forbid that the tree of my hope should be fruitless! The Lord will never suffer poor Kásim to be fatherless. The Almighty will surely not turn my joy into sorrow, or separate Hasan and Husain the one from the other!

Hasan.—Oh! I have many complaints, sister, of heaven's cruelty and oppression. I have a flame in my heart which it is difficult for me to conceal. Go thou, dear, and awake Kulsúm from her pleasant sleep. Tell her to come and see me once more.

Zainab (to Kulsúm).—My poor sighing sister, awake a little, thou art become brotherless; O desolate creature,

---

* See note *, p. 131.

awake! Mournful sister, thy brother is going out of thy hand. Awake, gardener! thy beautiful rose is fading away.

Kulsúm.—Tell me, dear sister, what has happened? Let me know if heaven has rolled up the carpet of our life. Has Husain, my brother, gone armed to battle? or has Hasan drunk poison from the jug?

Zainab.—Dear sister, rend thy garments for this manifest misfortune; fling earth on thy head, for thou hast become brotherless in the world. Our brother Hasan, having been poisoned, is rolling there on the ground in agonies, like a half-killed fowl.

Kulsúm (to Hasan).—Incomparable creature, why dost thou seem so confounded? Why art thou speechless and silent? Thou hast closed thy mouth, and dost not converse with thy sister. The enemy has at length succeeded in his designs. Open thy lips and speak, sweet-voiced nightingale; let me hear a few words from thy mouth, O my spirit of life!

Hasan.—The burning sensation within me hinders my tongue from speaking. God knows what things pass through my brain. Go, sister, commence thy shrieking; go in the tent of Kásim and inform him of all. Awake also my other poor child, and bring both of my afflicted sons here.

Kulsúm.—Awake a minute, dear Kásim; I am thy aunt. Thy nightingale has fallen sadly in a corner of the cage; awake, and see what is the matter with him. And thou, O son of Hasan, give up sleeping; thou hast lost thy father and protector, poor thing; awake! The head of the caravan is gone, it is time to depart; my breast is ringing like a bell. Awake, dear little thing, awake!

Kásim.—Dear aunt, why like a spring bird art thou pouring forth thy sad notes? Why art thou so mournful and restless, thine eyes being also full of tears? I see thee continually sighing and weeping; and thou hast, too, dishevelled thy hair; tell me the reason, why art thou so?

Zainab.—Dear nephew, may I be a sacrifice for thee! we are in a great difficulty; the bird of our heart is caught in a snare of sorrow and grief. Beloved one, thy father is suffering grievously from deadly poison; get up and help him, otherwise thou shalt be fatherless and I brotherless.

Kásim (to Hasan).—Father, make us not miserably helpless with thy unexpected death; thou hast a dear Joseph, why shouldst thou put him in the prison of affliction? Open thine eyes and look once more on my poor pallid face; deliver me from the painful torment of being an orphan.

Hasan.—Heaven deemed it proper to put me to shame before thee, dear Kásim. Come, let me once more inhale thy perfume. I am much ashamed, thou unhappy Kásim, for not having had thee married before my death.* Go now, both of you, dear ones, to your venerable uncle Husain, my brother, and tell him to come to me, for it is time to give one another farewell. Tell him, "Come, father has many things to speak to thee."

Kásim (to Husain).—Uncle Husain, awake! observe how the sea of trouble is encroaching on us. Arise, behold thy afflicted family!

Kásim's Brother (to Husain).—Dear uncle, awake! Hasan thy brother is poisoned. Open thine eyes! behold the destroyer of rest and quietude!

Kásim.—Zainab, Kulsúm, and Kásim, all three are beating their own heads. Arise, uncle! behold the commotion of the Day of Resurrection!

Husain (to Kásim and his brother.)—Why are you so disturbed, O ye two beautiful rose-plants? Why are you like nightingales chanting out your sad notes? Why have you put your shawls around your necks, and why are your garments so rent to pieces?

---

* Kásim, the son of Hasan, was espoused to Fátimah, the daughter of Husain, but was killed at Karbalá the same day on which the marriage was celebrated.

Kásim.—I have no mouth to speak to thee uncle, for heaven has made me an orphan. Time has pelted the bottle of my heart with cruel stones! Thy brother Hasan has drunk mortal venom; he has given up all hopes of living any longer.

Husain.—O thou cruel and obstinate heaven, hast thou thrown earth on my head! Hast thou, by way of tyranny, made me brotherless? If my brother gives up the ghost in this sad calamity, I am sure Zainab my sister also will die through grief. Dear sorrowful sisters, why are you shedding tears from your eyes? Why has Hasan fallen fainting in his bed? Let Husain, your brother, be fully informed of the matter.

Kulsúm.—While I was in my own bed sleeping, I was suddenly aroused by the groans of Zainab, which burned my sorrowful heart within me. When I opened my eyes I beheld Hasan rolling on the ground, and Zainab bewailing in anguish of heart.

Husain (to his brother Hasan).—O flower of the meadow of the chosen Prophet of God, peace be on thee! O thou who art bound fast with the chains of affliction, trials, and sorrows, peace be on thee! Thou hast fainted brother; thou art wretched thus lying on the ground. Tell me what thou hast seen in thy sleep. What may that dream be, the interpretation of which points to death? What was that apparition, the result of which was this sudden swoon? Why art thou unkind to thy brother Husain? Why dost thou not answer his questions?

Hasan.—Let me, dear brother, lay hold of the skirt of thy garment. Come near, that I may hang awhile on thy neck. The pot of my life has ceased from its natural ebullition; the burning candle of my life has at length gone out.

Husain.—O thou who art the joy of the heart of Fátimah, the daughter of the faithful Messenger of God! O thou by the brightness of whose face the gallery of God's palace is illuminated! thou fruitful tree of the garden of the lord of the two worlds, Muhammad, relate thy case kindly to Husain thy brother.

Hasan.—Dear brother Husain, I was dreaming that I was with the Prophet, conversing with him on a particular subject. When I awoke I felt extremely thirsty, so I took the jug of water from the stand and drank some drops. As soon as I had finished, my heart, dear Husain, began as it were to burn.

Husain, taking up the jug.—O thou jug, thou hast become the cause of trouble to Hasan, in the month of Safar.* Thou hast made Husain brotherless, and Kásim a fatherless vagrant. Let me drink this same water, and put an end to my life too. What matter should 'Alí Akbar my son become fatherless like Kásim my nephew.

Hasan.—Do not drink the water; put away the jug from thy mouth, for it is not proper that thy rose should be turned into a water-lily. Do not now destroy the foundation of thy health by drinking the water of this jug. Thou shalt, too, ere long, meet thy fate; but it is not necessary to be in haste. When thou shalt have arrived at Karbalá, Shimar,† thy murderer, will offer thee water in the day of thy slaughter. Go thou, O sorrowful Zainab; for God's sake take the jug from the hand of Husain, the lord of the martyrs.

Zainab (to Husain).—Give the jug to me, brother, and let me drink, and so be delivered from this miserable life. Zainab alone is weary of her existence; death is necessary only for this sister.

Hasan.—My unhappy Kásim, though thou too art tired of thy life, yet, dear child, take the jug from thy poor aunt.

Kásim (to Zainab).—Do not take water from this jug,

---

* Name of the month in which Hasan was poisoned.
† See note, p. 43.

poor aunt, for I, who am an orphan, deserve to drink it. Whoever becomes an orphan, better for him to take some poison at once. He who happens to be fatherless, death is certainly preferable for him than life.

Hasan.—O thou mother of Kásim, come out from the corner of thy tent, and behold what thy son is doing. Come out awhile from thy abode, and see a new Karbalá! Come quickly! snatch the jug from thy son's hand. Is thy child indeed weary of his life?

The mother of Kásim.—Give the jug to me, son; have compassion on my darkened days and unfortunate life. Why shouldest thou drink poison? What is my fault, dear son?

Kásim.—By our lord, dear father, to become an orphan is an intolerable calamity. It is a sad pain to be fatherless, grieved at heart, and going from gate to gate for want of shelter and help. After thy death, which will ruin my house altogether, what prospect can I have of prosperity in this life?

Hasan.—If Hasan, dear son, is poisoned and dies, a protector, Husain, survives, who is to thee much kinder than thy father. Be not sorry, nor beat so much on thy head and breast; Husain my brother will be a parent to thee.

Hasan's younger Son.—May I be offered for thee! I am thy oppressed orphan boy; be pleased to look at me. Bid my dear uncle Husain, when thou shalt be hidden under the veil of the grave, to kindly remove the burden of thy sorrow from my heart by burying me close to thee in the same spot.

Hasan.—Come, come, dear child, I am greatly sorry for thee. Come near me, thou my happy and blessed son. Mourn not, my pretty rose, nor grieve; for in the eternal abode of Paradise I will prepare a wedding-chamber for thee.

Zainab.—O heaven, why bringest thou always new troubles upon me? Why dost thou add scar to my scars, by making every now and then a rosy one to pass away from my family? Dost thou intend to cut off the posterity of Zahrah,* the Prophet's daughter? Art thou not afraid of the consequences of my sighing and crying?

Hasan.—Let me address you, O my relations and friends, and demand one thing from you. It is my wish that, since I am in this troubled and distracted state, you should carry me kindly to the sepulchre of the Messenger of God, that I may not miss the honour of visiting it while yet alive, and paying it my best respects. (*They carry him there.*) O Apostle of the whole creation, and guide of the universal right way, peace be on thee! O thou end and final cause of the creation of all objects, peace be on thee! It is I, thy grandson Hasan, come to thee in a most piteous condition. Look upon me, dear ancestor; may my spirit be offered to thee! My heart is inflamed by deadly poison; think about me, O my ancestor! This very moment I am going to leave the world; pardon thou all my faults.

Zainab.—Alas! O Messenger of God, for the cruelty of thy people! Woe me! Tongue cannot describe the oppression and tyranny of thy followers. Look graciously on us, thy oppressed ones. Know our misery, O Messenger of God, and help us!

Hasan.—Wail no more, and rend not your clothes any longer. Take me soon home from the sepulchre of my grandfather. I plainly see death at my pillow, and am reminded of my blooming son, Kásim.

Husain.—Alas! alas! my spring has become suddenly autumn! My beautiful cypress† tree is stretched on the ground! To-day I am bereaved of my dear brother! Woe unto me and to my hopeful heart!

Hasan.—Come to me, O thou brightness of my tearful eyes! I have three requests to ask of thee, dear brother. When thou shalt experience thy great trials, thy conflicts

---

* See note, p. 10. † See note, p. 10.

in Karbalá, when all thy handsome, blooming youths shall be killed, do me then the favour of receiving Kásim my child as thy son-in-law, by giving him one of thy daughters in marriage.

Husain.—May I be offered unto thee, O thou glory of time and eternity! Be pleased to tell me what thy second request is.

Hasan.—My second request, thou brightness of my tearful eyes, is this. When the bird of the soul shall have flown away from its bushy nest, the body; when I am no longer in the world, order thou 'Alí Akbar, thy son, and Kásim, my child, to put black shawls about their necks. Tell them to weep for me, and read the Kur'án with a loud voice over my grave.

Husain.—Thy affecting words, brother, break my heart! Now tell me what thy third request is.

Hasan.—My third request is this, thou light of my eyes! when, on the tenth of Muharram,* in Karbalá, Shimar, thy cruel murderer, comes forward to cut thy throat, my poor son, not being able to bear the sight, will run and fall on thee to prevent the wicked tyrant from his design. What shall I say on behalf of my child in this contingency? I beg thee not to withhold thy mercy from him at such a time. Tell Shimar not to strike my child; tell him not to prick the youth with the point of his dagger.†

Husain.—O heaven! thou never pitiest my grievous sighs, nor art thou ashamed that Husain is without refuge.

Hasan.—O Zainab, thou who hast seen nought but trouble and sorrow in the world, come to me, sister!

---

* The first month of the Muhammadan year; Hasan was murdered on the 10th of Muharram.

† "At the same time a little nephew of his, a beautiful child, with jewels in his ears, came to embrace him, and had his hand cut off with a sword; to whom Hosein said, 'Thy reward, child, is with God; thou shalt go to thy pious forefathers!'"—Oakley's "History of the Saracens," vol. ii. p. 175, ed. 1757.

I have a request to make to thee also. Go thou, O afflicted one, into that chamber, and fetch me thence a parcel, wherein is a winding-sheet.

Zainab.—May I be offered for thee, O thou who art deprived of life by poison! Here is the thing thou hast requested.

Hasan.—Come to me, Zainab, and bewail for what I am going to say. Take this winding-sheet, and keep it carefully. When Kásim my son's marriage-time shall come, before the desire of his heart be fulfilled, his joy shall immediately be turned into sorrow. At that time, kind sister, put this winding-sheet on thy disappointed nephew Kásim, instead of his bridal or nuptial dress.

Zainab.—Heaven, why hast thou, without cause, brought so many evils upon us? Why hast thou stripped me of all my joys and pleasures? Thou takest away Hasan from me, rendering Kásim at the same time fatherless; and thou also intendest to turn the joyous existence of my poor nephew into sad misery.

Hasan (to his family).—Go out for some minutes from this room; I want to untie the blood-stained knot of my painful heart. Come to me, Ja'dah, my treacherous companion. Come hither; for it is time to reveal the secret of thy perfidy.

Ja'dah.—How shall I come to thee, seeing shame has covered my face? Alas! what shall I do to be saved from this whirlpool of sin?

Hasan.—Why didst thou poison me, thou cruel woman? Wherefore didst thou make my sweet Kásim fatherless? Have I not loved thee truly, and have I ever ceased to honour thee? What more could have been done for thee that I have not done? Wherefore shouldst thou grieve my sisters by my death? What wrong had I committed against thee to deserve this treatment at thy hands?

Ja'dah.—O thou sweet-tempered husband, I have done wrong in that I have poisoned thee. I am heartily sorry for the sin I have committed, though sorrow does not seem to benefit me. I repent of my misdeed; may I be cursed for this my act. Look at my tearful eyes and pity me; I have no face with which to remain, no feet wherewith to go away. May nobody ever be in such a miserable state!

Hasan.—Depart from before my eyes, thou perfidious woman. May God disappoint thee in all thy prospects! Depart from my presence, thou cause of so many mischiefs. Go away; go! Thou shalt never prosper in thy life. But as for thee, O mother of Kásim, thou mayest approach me without any apprehension of annoyance. Come, let us deplore together the sad state of Kásim, our poor son. The time has come, dear faithful companion, that I should put off this corruptible body. Pardon me, dear wife, if I have done thee any wrong during life.

The Mother of Kásim.—O thou who shalt soon be invested with the green* robes of Paradise, thou crowned prince of heaven! O disembarking Noah of the present generation, whose ark shall soon be wrecked on this shore! What am I to do after thou art gone, good husband? How shall I deal with these little ones, these broken-hearted orphans of thine?

Hasan.—Be not anxious about my orphans, dear wife; God their Maker will care for them and keep them. I have committed my family and their concerns to the merciful Lord, and carry the thought of Kásim's wedding with me to the grave.

The Mother of Kásim.—Alas! Hasan is gone out of my hand, and I am left helpless. I have no hope whatever, either from the fixed stars or planets. Hereafter I alone must bear the heavy burden of keeping the little orphans. I must dedicate my broken heart to the toilsome care of the children.

---

* "They are to be clothed in the richest silks and brocades, chiefly of green, which will burst forth from the fruits of Paradise, and will be also supplied by the leaves of the tree *Túba*."—Sale's "Koran," Preliminary Discourse, p. 99, ed. 1734.

Hasan.—Come, Zainab, rend thy clothes and show thy heartfelt grief. My breath comes but by spasms; I am certainly dying. Come, sister, kindly close my eyes, and stretch my hands and feet towards Kiblah,* the universal Muslim cynosure.

Zainab, closing Hasan's eyes.—Heaven has indeed distressed and troubled me! Come, let me close thy beautiful black eyes, Hasan. By our Lord, I am weary of such a miserable existence! O God, do graciously take away my life! O women, Zainab is altogether undone. A woman whose brother is dead is assuredly in a wretched condition.

(*The Family sing elegies, and carry the body out to be buried.*)

'A'yishah, the Wife of Muhammad, meeting them in the way, says to Husain.—May I be offered unto thee, O thou priest of all the nations! Wherefore hast thou put a black shawl about thy neck to signify thy grief? Why art thou shedding tears so sadly? Whose coffin is this which thou bearest on thy shoulders?

Husain.—Know thou, O wife of the Prophet, that Hasan, the ornament of my bosom, is dead; and this is his body which I am carrying on my own shoulder. I am taking him, according to his own bequest, to the sepulchre of the Prophet, to have him buried there.

'A'yishah.—If this is what thou intendest to do, thou must give it up at once; for it is impossible. I will never suffer thee to do this thing, for the house wherein the Prophet is buried is my own.

Husain.—Do not say such things, 'Áyishah! Hear me; do not create new troubles, thou mischievous woman. Is not Hasan a flower of the garden of the Prophet? Is not

---

* Kiblah is the Point of Adoration towards which the faithful turn when worshipping. "The corpse is then placed on its back in the grave, with the head to the north and feet to the south, the face being turned towards Mecca."— Hughes' "Notes on Muhammadanism," p. 191, ed. 1877.

he a member of the body of Muhammad, the seal of all the prophets? Hast thou forgotten, worthless woman, how Hasan had the indulgence of riding on the Prophet's shoulder on feast-days?

'A'yishah.—Do not speak any more so reproachfully to me. Return to your houses quietly, without any further words. Come on, O my faithful followers, and help me to shoot the body of Hasan; make it a butt for your arrows.

Zainab.—Do not hoist up thy flag of mischief, O wicked woman! Let not Hasan's holy body be a target for thy arrows. Allow us, for the sake of God's Prophet, to bury the grandson near his grandfather.

'A'yishah.—O amiable and dear Zainab, it is better for thee to go to thy house. Had it not been for thy glorious grandfather, my husband, I would order my attendants to put thee to death. I would hew thee to pieces with their swords.

Kulsûm (*to 'A'yishah*).—Humble thyself, ambitious woman that thou art! Now thou ridest on a mule, now on a camel! Why dost thou not abandon this thy unjust contention? Let us know what rights thou hast in this house.

'A'yishah.—Who art thou, that thou shouldst speak so impertinently to me? What dost thou say by way of reproach? Art thou sad on account of thy brother's death? Go home and lament for him; I am not answerable for what thou feelest. In the house of thy grandfather there is a place for a sepulchre, but I intend it for myself. Hasan's holy body may be buried in the graveyard of Bakía',* outside the town.

---

* "There is a tradition that 70,000, or, according to others, 100,000 saints, all with faces like full moons, shall cleave on the last day the yawning bosom of El Bakia. About 10,000 of the Ashab (companions of the Prophet) and innumerable Sayyids are buried here. Their graves are forgotten, because, in the olden time, tombstones were not

Muhammad Hanífah,* another son of 'Alí (to Husain, his step-brother).—Give me permission now, O great Imám of all mankind, to draw out the sword from its sheath, and falling upon this wicked people, to extirpate them from the face of the earth.

Husain.—Nay, my brother; it is better to have patience with them for awhile; for thus has Hasan enjoined, saying, "You must take care not to excite the people, or provoke them to jealousy, lest there should be bloodshed over my bier." Let the coffin, therefore, according to the order of the highly-exalted Imám himself, go to Bakía' to be buried there. Come, let us depart; for what God has willed, that must be done; and what the Prophet has said, that must be fulfilled.

---

placed over the last dwelling-places of mankind. The first of flesh who shall arise is Mohammed, the second Abu Bekr, the third Omar, then the people of El Bakia (amongst whom is Osman, the fourth caliph), and then the incolœ of the Jannat el Maala, the Meccan cemetery. The Hadis, 'Whoever dies at the two Harams, shall rise with the secure on the Day of Judgment,' has made these spots priceless in value. And even upon earth they might be made a mine of wealth. Like the catacombs at Rome, El Bakia is literally full of the odour of sanctity, and a single item of the great aggregate here would render any other Moslem town famous. It is a pity that this people refuses to exhume its relics."—Burton's "El Medinah and Meccah," vol. ii. p. 31, ed. 1857.

* "Mohammed Ben Hanefiah is the name of the third son of Ali, but not born of Fatimah the daughter of Mahomet, as was the case with Hassan and Houssain. All three descended from one father, but Mohammed Ben Hanefiah was born of a second wife, named Hanefiah, whom Ali married after the death of Fatimah. In consequence of this difference in regard to his mother, this personage is not included amongst the number of Imams, since he was not of the blood of Mahomet."—Translated from D'Herbelot, head "Mohammed ben Hanefiah."

SCENE X.

THE MARTYRDOM OF MUSLIM, THE ENVOY OF HUSAIN.

The advisers of Husain were persistent in their endeavours to dissuade him from going to Kúfah (A.D. 680) till he had ascertained to what extent the fickle inhabitants were willing to support him. "To this Husseyne at last assented, and Mosslem, the son of Aukkail, being the person chosen for the purpose, was directed to proceed immediately to Kúfah, there to remain in private until he should have made himself sufficiently acquainted with the number and resources, and engaged the fidelity of the friends of his cause; of all which he was to transmit the necessary information, when, if it appeared advisable, Husseyne, at the proper period, would not fail to join him . . . . In the meantime Mosslem, the son of Aukkail, becoming apprised of what had happened, endeavoured to secrete himself under the protection of Hauny, the son of Orwauh, the most distinguished of Husseyne's adherents. While Obaidullah Zeiaud, having called together the principal inhabitants on the following day, told them, without reserve, that the design of his visit to Kúfah was to extirpate, without exception, all who had acknowledged the authority of Husseyne, of their attachment to whom he desired it might be understood that he was well informed. Then, addressing himself particularly to Hauny, the son of Orwauh: 'I have heard,' said he, 'that Mosslem, the emissary of Husseyne, is at thy house.' And Hauny, denying the circumstance, was called upon by Obaidullah to swear it, which he had accordingly no sooner complied with, than his person was secured, while some of Obaidullah's attendants were despatched to his house. There they seized the unfortunate agent, and brought him immediately to the presence of their chief, by whom he was placed in safe custody, together with his protector. The palace being, however, soon after surrounded by a concourse of the inhabitants, to the number, as it is said, of fifty thousand men, in consequence of the detention of these two persons, Obaidullah, with his usual decision, took a very short course of suppressing the tumult; he caused both his prisoners to be conducted to the roof of the palace, where their heads were immediately struck off, and thrown among the multitude, which, thus scared like a flock of sheep, as immediately dispersed in every direction."—Price's "Chronological Retrospect of Mahommedan History," vol. i. p. 391, ed 1811.

Shári', a principal person in Kúfah.*—O Husain, how greatly do we long to see thee in our country! Everyone with whom I am acquainted seems to seek after thee in this valley. I, who am Shári', desire earnestly to hear with my own ears the mystery of truth from thy sweet lips. I have no other desire in my heart, nor any request from my God, except to be enabled to see thine honourable countenance.

Hání, another principal man in Kúfah.—O Husain, come hither; for thy place is vacant with us here! Blessed be the hour when I shall lay my head at thy feet! Poor Hání has no other desire but that of casting his fond glance at thy beautiful eyes!

Shári'.—Arise, O messenger, quickly; and go to Madínah with these letters addressed to Husain, the king of the age. Tell him they are from principal men in Kúfah, the capital of 'Irák 'Arabí; and make good mention of every one of us there before him.

Hání.—Arise, O lapwing,† and begin to flutter in order to ravish the heart, and carry the message of Solomon the Prophet to the queen of Sheba! If anyone should ask thee who have written these letters, name thou Khaulí, Hání, and the impudent fellow Shimar.‡

The Messenger (having returned from Madínah).—Good tidings, O friends! Rejoice ye, and make yourselves cheerful, because Muslim, Husain's cousin, is coming to

---

* See note, p. 9.   † See note, p. 143.
‡ See note, p. 43.

Kúfah as his forerunner. Go forth to meet and receive him.

Háni (addressing Muslim).—Many thanks to God, who has made us see thy smiling lips, thy braided ringlets and curling locks! I will lay my head, according to the manner and custom of enthusiastic lovers, on every spot of ground where thy noble horse has trodden! Thy efficacious breath healeth all manner of diseases among men with a single word; and the inhabitants of our country are dying with impatience to see thee!

Muslim.—There is, O Hání, much ignorance in the world, and little or no knowledge; and the people of Kúfah are, almost all, careless and indifferent. I have traversed the whole city of Kúfah, O Hání, but have found not even one faithful man in all the town.

Shári'.—As for us, O Muslim, we are ready to suffer even death rather than break our word or promise. We are prepared to give up our lives and all we have in the cause of God. If thy favour be the waterer of the flower-garden of our hope, we shall both grow in peace, and spread our branches everywhere, bearing, by God's help, at the same time most excellent fruit.

Muslim.—I fear, O Hání, lest I be maltreated by the people of Kúfah. I am alarmed lest, before my heart rejoices in the prospect of good success, the inhabitants of Kúfah shall occasion me grief and disappointment. I am afraid, Hání, as soon as Husain shall have arrived at Karbalá, you people of Kúfah will fight against us with these very swords now in your hands to defend us!

Hání.—Be assured, O Muslim, that we are not as thou hast suspected us. We will make even now a solemn covenant with thee, and enter into an oath never to disobey thy orders. We pledge our treaty, our oath, our faith, our word with thee, our chief, never to swerve from thy commands, be they as they may.

Muslim.—Now I have begun in some degree to rely on your words; but still I fear you will break your covenant and annul your treaty. It is better you should renew your covenants, and make a fresh agreement, that my mind may be at ease and my confidence increase.

Shári'.—Again do we bind ourselves to obey thee with all possible sincerity. Once more we give thy highness our hands and make our solemn agreement. We are always true and upright in our dealings with all. Heaven may revolve crookedly, but our integrity may be depended upon!

Muslim.—Thanks be to God that He has heard our prayers, and made us successful and prosperous. Glory be to the Lord, who, for the sake of Husain, has again rendered us famous in the world.

Shári'.—Arise, O messenger, and carry this letter to our beloved; deliver the message of this sad nightingale to the happy rosebud; bear Muslim's letter to Husain.

Muslim.—Tell him personally to bring an army with him when he comes. Bid him fetch the weapons of war belonging to the Prophet. Let him also take his sucking child; make him a mark to be shot at by the archers.* Let him bring with him 'Abbás, his brave lion-like brother, also, that he may become a water-bearer for his thirsty children.

The Messenger.—If thou hast any other grief or sorrow in thy heart, give vent thereto. If thou hast ought to say or explain to thy cousin, say on.

Muslim.—Let this one word, O messenger, be like a ring to thine ear, and be always remembered by thee. Let this

---

* " Quite tired out, he sat down at the door of his tent, and took his little son Abdollah upon his lap, who was presently killed with an arrow. Hosein took his hand full of the child's blood, and, throwing it towards heaven, said, 'O Lord! if thou withholdest help from us from heaven, give it to those that are better, and take vengeance upon the wicked!'"
—Oakley's "History of the Saracens," vol. ii. p. 175, ed. 1757.

saying, I pray thee, be never forgotten by thee. Tell Husain to bring with him the chief essence of sorrow, even Zainab, his poor sister, that she may weep and lament; that she may embrace the dead bodies of the martyrs, and cry over them; that she may be our chief mourner henceforth and for ever!

The Messenger.—O friends, this is the beginning of the spring season of Karbalá! This is the first tender herbage of the ever verdant meadow of Karbalá!

Muslim.—I feel I have got into a great difficulty, for my heart has already failed me. May God, of His bountiful grace, facilitate this embarrassing affair! Where have you prepared a lodging for us in this foreign town, that we may there await our destiny?

Hání.—Honour us, if it please thee, by taking thy lodging in this thy servant's humble house. Let thy servant's head reach the heavens owing to this glorious exaltation! Let his beggarly hut be turned, by thy condescension, into a royal palace!

Muslim.—Arise, O Hání, let us go to thy dwelling; let me enter, like a guest, thy hospitable house for a short time. Be glad and cheerful, and free from all sorts of care as to the treasure that is going to put up in some corner of thy ruins. (*The party accompany Muslim to Hání's house.*)

Hání.—The dust of thy feet has raised me to a glorious height! My house may now vie with Paradise in splendour and excellency!

Muslim.—You may go now, O people, every one to his house. If anything should take place, we shall immediately let you know. If you hear that I am in great distress, you may run forth to my assistance. In time of adversity and misfortune I expect to be helped and cheered by you.

Hání.—Thank God, we have seen thee residing in the city of Kúfah! Praise be to the Lord, that the town is now at thy disposal! The government of this place, and the chieftainship of this country, are, indeed, a fit robe, suiting thy comely stature.

Muslim.—Know, O Hání, that the men of Kúfah are unsteady and fickle in their disposition. They are all perfidious in their dealings with others. It is true, they have now entered into a covenant with us, but I am sure they will not keep it until the end. Know of a certainty that they prefer infidelity to faith, and that they are very prone to sell the latter for the former.

Muhammad, the son of Muslim.—Father, I see thee weeping in secret like one in great trouble! Wilt thou tell us what office thou hast obtained here in Kúfah? We want to know if thou hast already achieved thy object: if the desire of thy heart has been fully granted thee.

Muslim.—Yes, dear child, the desire of our heart has been fully satisfied. I am invested with the office and title of a commander-in-chief. But instead of the honourable robe of investiture, I must put on, dear child, a rose-coloured coat, and appear on the scaffold!

Ibráhím, another son of Muslim.—Dear father, I feel extremely sad in this town of Kúfah. Though there may be no occasion of anxiety, I am quite sorrowful. I am very sad and melancholy in heart, without any apparent cause! I seem to be in a continual conflict with heaven and earth. Oh! I am tired of this town, father; let us go out a little for an excursion. Take me, please, to the bank of the river for recreation.

Muslim.—Yes, death certainly warns men beforehand of its own approach. When anything is about to befall a man, it previously makes, as it were, an impression on his mind. Arise, dear ones, both of you, and let us have a walk outside the town. This lengthy story will ere long be abbreviated.

The Children.—The bank of this river, father, seems to be a pleasant play-ground for us. Yea, the side of the river looks to us like our abode, or home. When we die, dear father, let our burial-place be here on the banks of the Euphrates, for this place is extremely agreeable.

Muslim.—Aye, dear sons, in this very spot you will receive the honour of being beheaded! You will indeed play in this river, for, having tenderly embraced each other, you will afterwards be cruelly killed! Oh! let me draw my last breath, and not think of these sad events! Come children, come, let us return to our home before we are overtaken by night.

Ibn Ziyád* entering the city in disguise, and subsequently disclosing himself.—Who am I, O people? I am 'Ubaid, the son of Ziyád. I am a reprobate person, more wicked than Nimrod,† the mighty hunter before the Lord! I

---

* 'Ubaidullah, the son of Ziyád, was, on his father's death, appointed by Mu'áwiyah governor of Khurásán, and subsequently the government of Basrah was added to his authority.

† "Some tell us that Nimrod . . . . . cried out that he would make an offering to the God of Abraham, and that he accordingly sacrificed four thousand kine. But, if he ever relented, he soon relapsed into his former infidelity, for he built a tower that he might ascend to heaven to see *Abraham's* God, which, being overthrown, still persisting in his design, he would be carried to heaven in a chest borne by four monstrous birds; but, after wandering for some time through the air, he fell down on a mountain, with such a force that he made it shake, whereto (as some fancy) 'a passage in the *Korán* alludes, which may be translated, *although their contrivances be such as to make the mountain tremble.* Nimrod, disappointed in his design of making war with God, turned his arms against *Abraham*, who, being a great prince, raised forces to defend himself; but God, dividing *Nimrod's* subjects, and confounding their language, deprived him of the greater part of his people, and plagued those who adhered to him by swarms of gnats, which destroyed almost all of them; and one of those gnats, having entered into the nostril, or ear, of *Nimrod*, penetrated to one of the membranes of his brain, where, growing bigger every day, it gave him such intolerable pain, that he was obliged to cause his head to be beaten with a mallet, in order to procure some ease! which torture he suffered four hundred years; God being willing to punish, by one of the smallest of His creatures, him who insolently boasted himself to be Lord of all."—Sale's "Koran," chap. xxi. p. 269, ed. 1734.

pretended to be Husain when I entered the town; but everybody knows that I am not. I am, on the contrary, the destroyer of his peace and happiness. Go on beating drums and proclaiming a feast-day, and let all the people say, "God save Yazíd* the King!"

Muslim.—O poor, miserable Hání, what does this sound of trumpet mean? Why, there are tumultuous noises on all sides! Why, the city is become full of confusion!

Hání.—May I be offered for thee, O thou honourable Amír! I think the army of Shám† has entered Kúfah. I believe the son of Ziyád, that mighty general and commander, is come against us. If it be so, Kúfah will certainly be set on fire!

Muslim.—Alas! woe unto me! My house will after all be ruined! My joy and happiness will be brought to an end! I am surely ruined! Oh, why did I take these children away from home!

Ibn Ziyád.—Go forth, and proclaim throughout the city of Kúfah that my highness is appointed by Yazíd to be the governor of this place. Tell them, whoever shall act contrary to my order shall never find the way of peace. I will punish him with most severe tortures, and extirpate his family from the land of the living.

Muhammad-i-A'shúftah goes forth to proclaim.—The Amír has ordered that you must take care and not provoke us to anger with your seditious doings. Whoever shall prove rebellious, I will surely cut his throat, and hurl down his star from its heavenly station!

The Son of Ziyád.—The time has come, O my soldiers, that you should take counsel together how to proceed in order to make the inhabitants of Kúfah quiet and submissive. My advice is, that you should first search out Muslim and seize him, if you can.

Muhammad-i-A'shúftah.—O General, though art very

---

* See note ‡, p. 17. † Damascus.

lucky, and fortunate indeed; for none can boast of prosperity and success, now-a-days, as thou. I can tell thee where Muslim, Husain's cousin, has concealed himself. Behold, he is in the house of Hání!

The Son of Ziyád.—Let a rough-looking, rude-speaking soldier go to the house of Hání and sit in a menacing posture at his gate. Nay, let him take Hání forcibly, and drag him to my court, for I intend to seek occasion against him to-day.

Muhammad-i-A'shúftah, having undertaken the work, says to Hání:—Be it known unto thee, O well-behaved Hání, that the Governor of Kúfah has summoned thee to his presence. Arise from thy place, and repair to the court of his highness the son of Ziyád. Have no fear of thy life, come what may!

Hání (addressing the Governor).—O thou who hast always been addicted to sedition and error, tell me why hast thou called me, or what dost thou want from me?

The Son of Ziyád.—Why dost thou offend us, Hání, with thy abusive behaviour? Thou art altogether mistaken in thy opinions concerning us. I have been told by some that thou hast invited Muslim to thy house. How long wilt thou defend 'Alí's party in opposition to us?

Hání.—O 'Ubaidullah, thou art always troubling us without reason. If thou dost not do us any good, cease, at least, from injuring us. Muslim, it is true, came to my house the other day, but he soon went away again. My roof was not worthy that he should take shelter under it.

The Son of Ziyád.—I am sure, O Hání, thou art playing with thy life. It is not a difficult thing with us to sever an old man's head from his body. Take this seditious man to prison, and put a heavy chain about his neck, for he has lost his reason, and a madman must be enchained.

A certain Inhabitant of Kúfah.—Arise, O Muslim, from thy seat, and make thy utmost endeavours to save thy party. Behold how the city is full of commotion and disturbance! They are going to kill Háni this very day, merely because he has received thee in his house! Arise, young man, from thy place, and see what thou canst do for him!

Muslim, (mounting his horse).—Alas! woe unto me! My daylight is overtaken by darkness: Zainab's hour of lamentation and mourning draws near! Come on, O my friends, it is time to prepare an army for defence. It is time, dear companions, to fight the best battle of faith!

Muslim's party (gathering together around him).—O Muslim, we will cut off thine enemies' heads to prove our allegiance to thee! We will drink cups of blood from the skulls of thine enemies! We are men of fidelity, O Muslim; we are not faithless, like others. We are citizens, and not the inhabitants of deserts, that we should not know what is right. (*The number increases.*) Be not distressed, O Muslim! to-day we shall make such an uproar, and fight so valiantly, that we shall fill this land with the bodies of the slain! We shall set fire to the world with the edge of our glittering swords! We shall put the line of the enemy to confusion for the sake of thee, our friend.

Muhammad-i-A'shúftah.—Know, O Amír, that the matter concerning Muslim has become serious: he is already proclaimed Governor of Kúfah, and is received as such by all. He has raised a great army, with the resolution to fight with thee and to turn thee out. In a word, he has got forty thousand men with him.

The Son of Ziyád.—O Muhammad, I have appointed thee commander of the army. Take with thee an innumerable multitude, and march against the people of the town; lift up the standards of war everywhere, and make a stir and uproar.

Muhammad-i-A'shúftah.—To-day I am going to bring down the pride of the inhabitants of Kúfah! I am going to turn the light of 'Alí's party into darkness! O people of Kúfah, break your treaty with Muslim; I say this because I am your well-wisher.

A certain Inhabitant of Kúfah.—O people of Kúfah, the army of the son of Ziyád has come forth to fight against you. I am sure we shall not be able to stand before them. We are not sufficient for such a task as this; nor is it proper for us to behave so. I advise you, therefore, to put your swords in their sheaths; it matters not to break one's own covenant, or act contrary to one's own word or promises, when occasion requires. (*The people disperse themselves.*)

Muslim.—It is decreed that my head shall be severed from the body! It is fated that my throat shall be cut here where I am in exile. O ye covenant-breakers, wanting in both zeal and humanity, is it good in you to break off so soon, and leave me alone in the midst of a powerful, cruel army?

Muhammad Muslim's son.—O people, why do you bring such a calamity on us? Is this what we expected from you, our friends? Come back and assist my poor father; make not yourselves contemptible by leaving him alone to fight.

Ibráhím, Muslim's youngest son.—O people, I humbly beg you to return and help us. Now is the time your number should increase. Pity my tearful eyes, and abandon not my poor father, in this conflict, to his fate.

Muslim.—Do not put me to shame on such a day, O ye assembly! Why do you disobey my orders? Have compassion on us, for God's sake! Why did you bring us to Kúfah if you were resolved to leave us to ourselves?

Muslim's son Muhammad.—Alas! alas! Will heaven render me an orphan? Woe unto me! I am distressed and miserably afflicted! Alas! the cruelty of time, the illtreatment of heaven! I am greatly perplexed in my affairs.

Muslim.—Dear son, moan not so sadly, lest thou set fire to my heart! Time has at last, dear child, put me to shame. You are at length entrapped, dear ones, in the city of Kúfah. Well indeed have I led you to pleasant walks and beautiful rose-gardens!

Muhammad.—Honourable father, may I be offered for thy conversation! Who will help thee in this foreign country?

Ibráhím.—Oh! who will wipe off the dust of exile from thy moon-like* face?

Muhammad.—Oh! who will comb and brush thy helpless children's hair in the land of strangers?

Ibráhím.—Oh! the nest of the two singing-birds of thy pleasure-garden shall be blown away by the wind in this state of exile!

Muslim.—Oh! these two flutes of mine play such sad tunes to-day, that it grieves me to hear them! I do not know where to carry my complaint or who will listen to me!

Muhammad.—Take us away from here secretly, dear father. Carry our colourless pearls to some better sea! We are weary of 'Irák. Take these natives of Hijáz to their native city, Bat-há.†

Muslim.—Dear children, I will do just what you like. I will take and conceal you somewhere. Come along with me. O Shári', I have come to thy hospitable house to-day to beg thee receive my children under thy kind protection.

Shári'.—Be at ease, Muslim, I will try to get thy children home as soon as I can. Be not troubled any more about them. I shall plant them and let them thrive in their native soil.

Muslim (taking Shári' aside and whispering).—O Shári', come along with me; I have a secret to disclose to thee, which is just this—my unfortunate children will be miserably slain on the side of this river; and the poor things do not know it! A shroud will be their connubial dress: mind they are not buried with bare bodies!

---

* See note, p. 7.

† "Bat-há" signifies a "pebbly watercourse," or the "channel of a torrent." It is, however, frequently used to designate the country around Makkah; but the allusion in the text is apparently to Madínah. See p. 192.

Muhammad.—Dear father, seeing alms avert calamitous events, and sacrifices prevent pending misfortunes, offer, then, thy two sorrowful sons to the living God as acceptable sacrifices, that thy Lord may have mercy on thy youth and spare thy soul from death!

Shári'.—May I be a ransom for you, poor, sad things! you two afflicted, oppressed, helpless little ones! Come into my house, and cry no more. Come in quickly; I am afraid the enemy will overtake you, and make you prisoners.

Muslim (to his children).—Walk slowly, even though the danger be better escaped by going faster. Oh! you have gone, and by your departure my back is indeed broken! Alas! Heaven has dealt cruelly with us in separating us from one another. Pity it is the last time I shall see you! It is verily our final meeting! Draw near unto me, dear ones, that I may kiss you once more!

Shári'.—Enter the house, disconsolate creatures! Do not throw dust on your heads any longer. It is night, go to bed, without moaning any more. Go to bed, and take your rest.

Muslim.—O Lord, look upon my exile and misery! how I have even no place in which to lodge! Where shall I go in this dark night, to be delivered from such unbelieving people? I have none, in this state of exile, to protect me! If I die I have not a soul here to mourn for me. Where is my sister, *she* would lament my death, and cry like a mother for me?

Táwah, a pious old woman.—Who is there, groaning for want of shelter and hospitable reception? Who is he that has set fire to my soul by saying "he is homeless?" (*Addressing Muslim.*) O man, who art thou? Dost thou not know there is commotion in this city? And dost thou not hear the confused murmur of combatants? Go, hide thyself somewhere, and take care of thine own soul at such time of disturbance. How is it thou complainest continually of exile? why moanest thou so sadly, like a melancholy nightingale?

Muslim.—What shall I say to thee, O poor compassionate woman? I am complaining of my own misery and solitude. Kind soul, I am a wretched, powerless person, banished from my own home, helpless and houseless! I have no abode, no place to shelter me, no legs wherewith to walk. Yea, I do not know what to do in this dark night. I should not wonder if, pitying a poor stranger, thou would'st kindly receive me, and hide me in some corner of thy house?

Táwah.—Oh! most readily will I receive thee in my house, poor stranger! I will keep thee like the apple of mine eye. When I see a stranger, like thyself, in an afflicted condition, I am ready to offer my body and soul for him, to make him comfortable. Come to my house, and abide cheerfully there, free from all care, anxiety, or trouble.

Muslim (in Táwah's house).—Oh! I do not know what has become of my children at this time, or how my helpless, broken-hearted offspring are passing the night!

Muhammad.—I do not know what has become of our father to-night in this country. How long shall I sit waiting for him to-night?

Muslim.—O Lord! what must two little children feel, not knowing anything about the town, and wandering in the streets of Kúfah? I do not know what they have eaten to-night, or where they have slept.

Muhammad.—I cannot tell whether my father got any place to lodge in to-night, or whether he was caught by the enemy and put in prison!

Muslim.—O ye groans, be my companions awhile, that I may deplore the miserable condition of my children to-night!

Táwah.—May I be offered for thee! Why art thou so sad to night? Why dost thou shed such an abundance of tears from thine eyes? Be pleased to rest a little; here is thy bed, go and sleep in it.

Muslim.—How shall I sleep, O woman? how can I refrain from shedding blood-coloured tears? I have two dear sons in this place, who are concealed somewhere, through fear of this malicious army. How can I, without my beloved children, lay my head for rest on the pillow?

Muhammad.—O Ibráhím, better not sleep in bed, dear brother, for that becometh not an orphan. A head without a father, and a body without a home, have no connection with soft mattresses and pillows of gold cloth.

Ibráhím.—May I be offered for thee! thy words are right and proper. Come, then, let us go out of this house, and enter the old Mosque close by. Let us go to that ruined, solitary place, and lie down there on the ground, like poor desolate creatures. (*They seek shelter in the ruin.*)

Muhammad.—O my dear brother, thou light of mine eyes, rest of my mind, and spirit of my body, sleep on, and let me sit holding thy head on my lap!

Ibráhím.—No, dear brother, thou afflicted youth, my beautiful cypress,* my elegant fir tree, my most beloved, that will not do, it cannot be; better thou sleep, and let me sit up awake!

Muhammad.—Since we have no home, are acquainted with sorrow, are scarred with grief, and are both mortally wounded in heart; let us each go, and, fetching a brick, lay it, instead of a pillow, under our head.

Ibráhím.—Alas! alas! woe to us! woe to us! we are banished from home; our lot is affliction; we are poor sojourners! miserable travellers! The brick of exile has at last become our pillow!

Muslim (*in the house of Táwah*).—Oh! my children cannot sleep to-night, seeing that they have no kind attendant, and that my hands are not under their heads!

Muhammad.—I only know that I am groaning without having fever or any other malady, laying my head on a rough brick, neither awake nor asleep.

---

* See note, p. 10.

Muslim (finding his children).—Oh! may I be offered for these heads and these curls! What passed in your little heads to induce you to make pillows of earth and bricks on which to repose? Oh! may I die rather than see you thus! I am so sorry, dear ones, that I brought you to Kúfah; but what is the good of regretting? it is now done!

Muhammad (awaking).—May I be made a ransom for thee, thou poor afflicted father! We pray thee, do not separate us from thyself!

Ibráhím.—O dear father, make me not, I pray thee, a wanderer in this land of exile: send me, I pray thee, back to Madínah.

Muslim.—It is difficult for you, dear sons, to go to Madínah, for there are innumerable obstacles in the way, unless God should, of His mercy, facilitate the difficulty. Get out of this mosque, and proceed straight to your proper lodging, without showing signs of anxiety or fear of the enemy. I am also about to start for my own home.

The Old Woman's Son (to the Governor).—Good tidings, O Prince! I have discovered where thine enemy is concealed, and am therefore come, as quick as lightning, to thy court. Come on, for thy game is lying hid in our house: he is sitting quietly there.

The Son of Ziyád.—The star of my luck has made a fortunate appearance in the east! My dark night has become as bright as the morning beams! O ye brave companions, hold your swords in your hands, and, running to the old woman's house, hunt out this entangled game.

Muslim (commencing to fight).—In the name of God, the gracious, the merciful! This is the beginning of battle! In the name of the Most Compassionate Lord, this is the commencement of war! and it is a shame to live. How long shall I hide myself while death is, like a wolf, pursuing me? Is my heart a stone? Be it as it may: In the name of God, the gracious, the merciful! (*Making a second onslaught.*) Heart's blood is the pleasant red wine in our tavern! Arrows and lances are wings for our flight homewards! Oh, dear cousin Husain, I am in contempt and suffer much from exile. Thou knowest not how strangely we are treated here! (*Making a third attack.*) Thirst, O friends, is burning my inward parts! My heart has failed me through excessive thirst! Oh! if you give me a few drops of water to drink, you shall have the reward of the righteous, and make the cup-bearer of Al Kausar* be pleased with you! O people of Kúfah, have the goodness to give water to a thirsty soul!

Táwah (offering him water).—Drink water, poor man, for thy heart must be inflamed. Drink water: may I be a sacrifice for thy tearful eyes! Thou thirsteth after water to drink, as well as after thy children to see them, poor thing! (*Muslim puts the cup to his mouth, whereupon the water becomes blood; he therefore spills it.*)

Muslim.—Methinks it is decreed by God that I should be distressed above measure; that I should drink my own blood at the time I am going to die!

Táwah gets him another cup.—Do not pour floods of tears from thine eyes, good man, nor complain of the cruel heavens, O thou who art drenched with thine own blood! Drink this pure, pleasant water I have brought thee, and stain not my cup another time with the blood of thy melted heart. (*Muslim's tooth having fallen in the water, he spills it.*)

Muslim.—Oh, dear me! again my wine-glass has become broken in this house! Again my pearl-like tooth has been knocked out with stones!

Muhammad-i-A'shúftah.—Aim at his life, O ye archers, and turn his liver into blood with arrows! Make his forehead a mark for your shafts, and shoot volleys at him from your bows!

Muslim.—O heaven! thou didst make me a butt for

---

* See note, p. 96.

arrows! Enough of tyranny. Leave me to myself awhile! I am sore troubled for want of a kind friend to pity my condition! Wherever I turn myself, behold a flight of arrows dart against me!

Muhammad-i-A'shúftah.—O brave soldiers, put Muslim to-day to complete discomfiture. Throw stones at his head and break his sacred skull.

Muslim (fainting).—Alas! Lord God, I do not know where to go, or what to do. Whithersoever I turn, my body receives showers of stones pelted against it.

Muhammad-i-A'shúftah.—Pour down hot ashes and embers on his head from the terrace; for he has already fainted from the wounds he has received.

Muslim.—Oh! abandonment of my own country has brought all this evil upon me! I suffer all these torments from exile. A stranger, though he be a king, is contemptible; he is not received with respect by anyone. Oh, the misery of exile has been at last allotted to me! I am an exile! an exile! an exile! I have none to help me but God, and besides Him there is no protector!

Muhammad-i-A'shúftah.—O ye troops, Muslim has fallen on the ground in a sad plight; he is not able to rise again. Whoever from among you wishes to receive a brocade robe of honour, let him fall on this wretch, and tying his arms behind his back, make his companions mourn for him. (*Dragging Muslim to Ibn Ziyád.*) O highly exalted prince, may thy fortune be ever wakeful; the wretched Muslim is made a captive by our soldiers; he is in custody outside, with his tearful eyes, to know thy highness' orders.

The Son of Ziyád.—Why didst thou not, O Muslim, pay me due respect? Why didst thou disdain to salute me? What inordinate self-esteem and pride thou hast! Dost thou still entertain the vain desire of becoming a great leader?

Muslim.—I receive the chastisement of my divine Lord with humble gratitude. O impudent wretch, am I afraid to die, that thou reproachest me thus? There is a point in salutation, but thou art too stupid to know that! The salám is a mark of address amongst Muhammadans, and is not proper to be offered to any but those who are truly such. What share hast thou, infidel, of Islám, that I, called Muslim, should proffer thee a token of respect?

Ibn Ziyád.—Come here, O wicked blood-thirsty executioner; sever the head of Muslim from his body!

The Executioner (to Muslim).—Make thy confession, that I may sever thy head from the body, and put an everlasting separation between the two.

Muslim (addressing Husain).—O chief of the caravan of Karbalá, peace be on thee! O rose of the flower-garden of the best amongst women,* peace be on thee! Come and see how fares thy cousin—how he has become a captive, a helpless creature! I am going voluntarily to Muhammad the Messenger of God, I therefore say that I am bearing witness to the truth that there is no God but the one God!

---

* See note *, p. 42.

SCENE XI.

MURDER OF THE SONS OF MUSLIM.

AFTER the death of Muslim, 'Ubaidullah, the Governor of Kúfah, ever anxious to inflict injuries on any of the adherents of the unfortunate Husain, threw the sons of the murdered envoy into prison. The gaoler, however, taking pity upon them, allows them to escape, whereupon the son of Ziyád enjoins that diligent search shall be made for the missing youths, and promises to any one who may find them "good rewards for his trouble, namely, a horse, a dress of honour, a purse of gold, all by way of bounty and munificence." Captivated by the offer, a man steps forward and undertakes the task. While he is in search of the lads, his wife's maid, going to the Euphrates to fetch some water, accidentally meets with the sons of Muslim, wandering about homeless and desolate. She at once apprises her mistress, who thereupon gives them shelter in her house. Her husband, shortly returning, is surprised to find the object of his search concealed in his own house; whereupon, violating the sacred rites of hospitality, so inviolably respected in all Eastern countries, he basely murders the hapless lads; to secure the "prize of gold and silver" he hardened himself against "the darkness of the grave, and the terrible punishment of the Day of Judgment," and added two more to the list of martyrs whose memory the Shí'ahs delight to reverence and honour.

Ibn Ziyád.*—Praise be to God, that the country has been brought to a state of peace; that sedition has been appeased, and our government well established. Thanks

---

* See note *, p. 177.

be to the Lord, that Muslim, Husain's cousin, has been beheaded by our party, and buried in this land.

Shári', the Guardian of Muslim's Sons.—Why, O heaven, dost thou so much oppose the household of God's Prophet? If thou viewest them not with favour, why at any rate shouldst thou maltreat them? Thou didst cause Muslim and his sons to come to Kúfah; but, behold, what hast thou now done to that poor man? I know if people receive intelligence about his two sons, who are here with me, they will frighten me to death, and kill these poor miserable orphans!

Muslim's Children.—O our protector Shári', peace be on thee! O our sympathising friend, peace be on thee! We were delivered to thy care by our dear father, and acknowledge that thou hast been the best guardian to us.

Shári'.—On you be peace, my dear ones! On you be peace, my poor exiled creatures! You are not a trust, but a rest for my soul. You are my two beloved little guests.

Muslim's Sons.—O pious Sir, we beseech thee not to hide it from us if we have unfortunately lost our father. Tell us whether our father died a natural death, or whether some one cruelly killed him. Please let us know in what manner he lost his life. We do not know why Muslim, our father, does not appear: we only hear thee often making sad mention of his name.

Shári'.—O ye poor guests of Shári'! O ye light-givers of his eyes! what shall this grieved and perplexed creature say to you? Shame has covered my face! Yes, poor things, your father, the palm of your victory and hope, was cruelly beheaded by the tyrannical inhabitants of Kúfah.

The Sons of Muslim.—We are fatherless and miserable, O dear parent! We are estranged from our native town! We are surrounded with affliction and grief, O father, father! Our sorrows are great and innumerable.

Shári'.—Dear friends, lamentation and mourning will

not do you any good, I am sure; pour no more such a flood of tears down your pretty cheeks. Your sad noise is so loud that it reaches the heaven! I am afraid your enemies will come to know that you are in my house; if so, they will doubtless shed your blood too with the edge of their swords, and throw dust of grief, anew, on my head.

Muslim's Sons.—O good chief, do something, then, for us; we beseech thee, deliver us; for if the enemy receive notice about us and kill us, our blood will be on thy head! Our poor mother must be even now very anxious for us; she must be eagerly expecting our return to Madínah. O honourable chief, do this one favour to us orphans, we pray thee. Send us, please, to Madínah, our native city.

Shári'.—Come along, my faithful guests; come along, ye broken-hearted exiled creatures! Yonder caravan is going to Madínah, they have nothing to carry but bales of trouble and sorrow! All of them are sincere adorers of the Prophet, and faithful followers of God's command. You may accompany these good people to Madínah, ringing your sad knell all along with them!

Muslim's Sons.—Good-bye, kind Sir, we are going, and request only thy kind blessing to prosper us. By our Lord, had it not been for thy pious zeal we could not escape from danger! We are, however, very sorry to leave thee, owing to the kindness with which we have been treated in thy house; more sorry still that we are deprived of the opportunity of serving thee in return.

Shári'.—God preserve you, ye poor sons of Muslim! I wish you prosperity, ye brightness of my tearful eyes! You are quitting me, and my soul will lament your sad absence. Go in peace to your country, though your departure will be much felt by your old friend.

Muhammad, the elder Son.—Dear brother, let us make haste to go. We have no companions except your sighs and cries. Since we must be the ringing bells of the caravan with our sad lamentations, let us endeavour, then, to overtake it soon.

Ibráhím, the younger brother.—Dear brother, light of mine eyes! the caravan is hidden from my view; behold, I am so tired that no more strength is left me, and the caravan, too, cannot be seen.

Muhammad.—Open thine eyes well, dear brother, and examine this road, for it has already branched in different directions. This is a dangerous place indeed: behold, I see two paths before me. Oh! always some new troubles arise ready to overwhelm us! Which of the two roads shall we now take?

Ibráhím.—Brother, thou art not alone in thy calamities; both of us are cruelly treated and suffer wrong. We have lost our father, and are far removed from our mother; we have indeed now become vagrants, wandering perplexedly in this wilderness. But patience seems to be the only remedy. What dost thou think of this turning, brother?

Muhammad.—It is not a road at all, dear brother; let us go back—let us take counsel together what we must do to alleviate our pain. Groan thou sadly, and let me sigh. Thou shalt go by that way, and I will try this, to see which is better.

Ibráhím.—O brother, besides death there is nothing left! No exiled wanderers like us have ever existed! Groan thou sadly, and I will sigh! Take thou that road, and let me toil along this.

Muhammad.—Go on, God be with thee! but thou must not proceed far, nor betake thyself a long distance from me, dear brother. Thou shalt call out to me when thou art in any difficulty, to let me know.

Ibráhím.—Brother, here is a terrible perplexity indeed! What shall I say, or how shall I describe it? There seems to be nothing but gardens and plantations. There is not one road here, but several. What dost thou see, dear brother? As for me, I am sitting here weeping!

Muhammad.—Dear brother, my way has become hard

too. The ground is covered with thorns and thistles. Oh! what was that noise? Return! return! Oh! where art thou gone? Come back, come back!

Ibráhím.—Dear brother, dost thou not see that I have lost the way? I am in a very pitiable condition, brother; help me! How can I return, thou rest of my soul? I have fallen into great distress here.

Muhammad.—Where hast thou fallen, dear brother? May I be offered for thee! Oh! may God make me a sacrifice for thy dear voice! Where art thou? May I be made an oblation for thy head! Why art thou hidden from my sight?

Ibráhím.—Run and save me, brother, for I am altogether undone! I am entangled amongst prickly bushes, and am already much hurt! If I were concealed from thy view—may it never come to pass—I should soon be lifeless without thee!

Muhammad.—Art thou going to become lifeless, dear brother? I am already dead, as it were, owing to the abundance of care I have had for thee!

Ibráhím.—Come and see me, dear brother, before I breathe my last; for I see Muslim my father and 'Ákil our grandfather before mine eyes, and this is a sure sign of death!

Muhammad.—What shall I do, dear brother, to get myself to thee? I cannot find out the way, seeing all the plain is covered with plantations and fir trees.

Ibráhím.—Oh, may I be offered for thy voice! hasten and relieve thy poor brother, who is at the point of death.

Muhammad, coming to Ibráhím.—Arise from thy place, O thou my twin companion in sorrow, that at any rate we may proceed on our journey. Let us hasten to see our mother once more.

Ibráhím.—Dear brother, my feet are deprived of sensation; I cannot walk with them any longer. Leave me here to myself, and go thou on thy way. Let me die here groaning and sighing.

Muhammad.—Do not talk so, darling little brother;

arise from thy place, and let us be going. There is no habitation here, and we have no provisions with us. How can we live if we stay in so solitary a locality?

Ibráhím.—I beg thee, dear brother, let me alone, and leave me altogether to my own misery. The dust of death has already settled on me, on account of the many thorns with which I am pricked. My feet are become inactive through the same cause.

Muhammad.—Every thorn that has punctured thy feet has pierced my heart, as it were, with a dagger. Come, dear brother, sit in my lap, that I may take out the thorns that have injured thy feet in such a cruel manner. Oh! we are much fatigued with the journey! Come, brother, let me carry thee on my shoulders.

The Patrol, meeting the children.—O two poor children, who are you, and what are you doing in this solitary place? I see you crying and weeping; would you tell me the reason of your sadness?

The Children.—O young man, we are strangers in this country. We are sore oppressed by the inhabitants of Kúfah,* of whom we are complaining. We are the two orphans of poor Muslim, who was lately beheaded. This is the chief cause of our misfortune, and this is why we are wandering in this sad plight.

The Patrol.—Thanks! that the good fortune of 'Ubaid, the son of Ziyád, has ensnared these young sacred gazelles in my trap so easily. It is vain to wander from country to country in search of wealth. That is true wealth which can be acquired without any labour whatever. I will take both of these children to-day to the Court of the Prince, that he may shed their blood with the edge of the sword as cruelly as he likes.

The Children.—O young man, we humbly beseech thee not to take us to the Prince; and do not cause innocent blood to be shed, for we have done no wrong; we have

---

* See note, p. 9.

committed no fault to be thus treated either by thee or by him.

The Patrol.—God forbid that I should let you go out of my hand! There is no other alternative for you but death! Do not, in vain, make supplications to me, or beseech me so hard, young children. I must now bind your hands fast behind your backs with this chain.

The Children.—O young man, have compassion on our poor old mother, who is looking for our return. If thou art determined to destroy our life, kill us here with thine own hand. We are terribly afraid of the Prince, O young man! We dread the cruel Amír a great deal!

The Patrol (to the Son of Ziyád).—O Prince, I see thy government is going to be established for ever! I see the throne of thy dominion will be fixed eternally! These two children, whom thou see'st so pitilessly bound with chains before thee, are most assuredly the orphans of Muslim, the son of 'Ákil. I caught the poor things outside the town, and brought them bound before thee.

The Son of Ziyád.—Thanks be to God that heaven has assisted us—that the desire of our heart has been granted us! O patrol, take these two children to prison, and deliver them into the hands of the gaoler. Tell him he must feed them sparingly with bread and water, and must take care they do not escape from the prison.

The Patrol.—O Mashkúr, thou keeper of this prison, thou watchful guardian of the captives, thus saith the great Prince: "Take these two children, and drag them to prison." Take care not to be deceived by their sad looks, and never be negligent in regard to them, for they are apt to run away if a fitting opportunity present itself.

Muhammad.—Heaven, why hast thou put us in the gaol of affliction? Why hast thou brought so many trials and evils upon us poor orphans? What is the cause of this thine enmity against us, O heaven? Why shouldst thou without cause remove us far away from our home and mother?

Ibráhím.—O heaven, wherefore hast thou made us captive and prisoners in Kúfah? Why didst thou separate us from our companions and friends? We two nightingales had a nest of security in Hijáz our native land; why shouldst thou take us far away from our abode?

Muhammad.—Dear brother, I feel extremely sad in this prison; there is no one but God to have compassion on us poor things. Come, dear brother, let us arrange some plans for our deliverance from this dungeon.

Ibráhím.—Dear brother, listen to me attentively for a minute. Why should we be kept in this prison, like nightingales in a cage? If thou thinkest it proper, let us acquaint the gaoler with our sacred lineage as quietly as possible.

Muhammad.—Come near, O gaoler, for God's sake! I have a few short questions to ask thee. Dost thou know Muhammad, the elect of God? Art thou acquainted with his cousin, Haidar* the warrior? Let me know if thou recognisest their superiority, or acknowledgest their pre-eminence.

Mashkúr, the gaoler.—I know well who Muhammad the elect of God is. I know also his cousin Haidar, the champion of faith. Their esteem is very great in the sight of God. One of them is the intercessor for us in the Day of Judgment.

Muhammad.—Dost thou know who we two children are, and why we are put in this prison? We are the two sons of Muslim the helpless; we are the captive prisoners of a cruel, unbelieving people. How can it be lawful that we should be so cruelly treated—not even bread and water being ever allowed us by thee?

Mashkúr.—May I be offered for you, O two miserable astonished ones! May I be made a ransom for your souls, ye perplexed little things! I am one of the least attendants of your threshold; one of the friends and loving followers of your holy family.

---

* See note, p. 39.

Muhammad.—Do not afflict thy soul, poor man, so sadly. The holy spirit of the Prophet is well pleased with thee now. Instead of the molestations we have received at thy hand, be pleased to set us free and deliver us from this prison. Take these heavy chains from off us; let these chased game have their freedom to go where they like, that we may, if possible, betake ourselves to our country, and be able once more to see our poor mother.

Mashkúr.—Oh! may my hands be broken for what I have done to you, dear little things! Arise ye from your place, young saints; would to God my two hands were cut off when they were lifted up against you! would that my blood were shed instead of tears!

The Children.—Seeing that thou hast been so kind as to release us poor orphans from the heavy chains of imprisonment, and that thou hast shown tokens of love and affection towards us, we pray that it may please the Lord to receive the Prophet's intercession in thy behalf; that it may please Him to make the arm of 'Alí, the conqueror of the fort of Khaibar,* thy saving help!

Mashkúr.—May I be offered for you, ye two helpless wanderers! I beg you to receive these loaves of bread and this skin of water, for use on your road. It may be you will require the one and be thirsty for the other, while in the desert. And please forgive me the harsh treatment you received from me whilst in prison.

Muhammad.—Go in peace, man. May God make thee prosperous, just as thou, having pitied us, hast made us free from all care!

Ibráhím.—Since thou hast delivered us from the bonds of affliction and misery, may the gracious Lord preserve thy family and ever deliver it from troubles!

Muhammad (to Ibráhím).—Urge forward, dear brother,

---

* See note *, p. 45.

let us lose no time, lest the enemy come to know of our escape and pursue us.

Ibráhím.—Death is travelling with us all along the way; what farther fear can we have of the enemy, dear brother?

Muhammad.—We shall die, beloved brother, most miserably, having neither a mother at our head, nor a sister!

Ibráhím.—Oh! we are at a loss how to proceed on our journey. Oh! the happiness of our bonds, and the delight of our imprisonment!

The Gaoler (to the Prince).—O Prince, I am sorry to report that the two miserable, wretched boys, brought to prison lately, ran away this evening, I do not know how.

The Son of Ziyád.—O ye military men of war, let diligent search be made for the sons of Muslim, for they have by stealth run away from prison. Whoever of you shall bring them bound here in my presence will be sure to receive from my highness good rewards for his trouble, namely, a horse, a dress of honour, a purse of gold, all by way of bounty and munificence.

Háris.—I am going to search them out, depending on the good fortune of 'Ubaid the son of Ziyád, our Prince. Let thy highness grant his servant what he deems proper. I will destroy these two blooming sons of Muslim; if I do not so, I will give up the religion of Islám, be it as it may.

The Wife of Háris (to her maid.)—O maid, go quickly to the Euphrates and fetch me some water to bathe. The time of sleep is past, it is the hour of prayer. I must get up and make ablution for the service of God. I must set my face toward the temple of Him who is self-sufficient, and pray to the Lord who seeth me when I rise.

The Maid, on the banks of the Euphrates, meeting Muslim's sons.—O ye who shine here brilliantly as great stars, doubtless you are brightness to every eye. You look as splendid as the moon in beauty, but I wonder why you shed star-like tears. You resemble the nymphs of Paradise in handsomeness, yet strangely you mourn. You are two lights, or rather two great luminaries. When I saw your shadow in the water I fancied I beheld the sun in a looking-glass! I perceive that you belong to a noble family, but will you declare to me your glorious pedigree?

The Children.—Know thou, O happy and fortunate maiden (if thou art one of those who adore the family of God's Prophet), that we are two poor wanderers, two broken-hearted creatures of Háshimite* origin, two tender plants of the garden of Muhammad the Arabian Prophet. We are two afflicted children, cruelly treated and handled by time. In short, we are the orphans of Muslim the son of 'Ákil, who was lately murdered in Kúfah. I am called Muhammad, and my brother's name is Ibráhím.

The Maiden (returning to her mistress).—Good tidings, O mistress, I saw the water of life in the river! I found Enoch† and Elias, like lights shining in darkness. Though I am as dark as night, yet I can tell thee I have with me a sun and a moon. I mean I can say where Muslim's two sons are. Notwithstanding my black skin, thank God! I have received a light within me that has made my mind shine brightly. If thou, O mistress, seekest to see a beloved friend, then come along with me.

The Wife of Háris.—Good news indeed; but I hardly know what present to give thee to make thee cheerful. There is nothing better than to make thee free, and grant thee thy liberty. Well, henceforth thou art free from slavery, though I cannot forget thee for the kindness thou hast done me in informing me about these two beloved

---

* Muhammad was descended from the tribe of Háshim.

† "Enoch, the great-grandfather of Noah, who had that surname from his great *knowledge,* for he was favoured with no less than thirty books of divine revelations," &c.—Sale's "Koran," chap. xix. p. 253, ed. 1734.

"They suppose Al Khedr (Elias), having found out the fountain of life and drank thereof, became immortal, and that he had therefore this name from his flourishing and continued youth."—Sale's "Koran," chap. xviii. p. 245, ed. 1734.

objects. Come along, and lead me where they are. Be my guide in this pleasant enterprise, for without thee I cannot attain my object.

The Maiden.—Make haste, mistress; yonder is a wanderer. Run fast, the desire of thy heart is not far! If thou seekest to see the two sons of Muslim, behold them in that garden; show them motherly love and care. Behold, here are the fatherless children!

The Lady.—May I be a ranson for you, ye light of mine eyes, ye strangers of Kúfah! But my dear newly arrived guests, where are you, and where is Madínah, and where Kúfah? How far is the one from the other? Who took you out of Madínah, poor things? Come on, however, to this your humble servant's house, and let me have the honour of being at your service.

Muhammad.—Dear lady, know that I am quite weary of this life! But, alas! why should I complain, since what is done is done by God's decree!* When, however, we set out from Madínah, having been deprived of our relations and friends, we came to Kúfah, and were tried there with a hundred sort of afflictions. We had a father with us whom they first ill-treated, and subsequently cruelly cut his throat. After the ill-luck of our father, we mourned much and lamented long, and then left the town for Madínah. But with much labour and fatigue we have come here on foot.

The Wife of Háris.—My dear Muhammad and Ibráhím, it is better you should go to bed, for you are both tired; and I fear also lest some one, getting to know that you are in this house, may, through enmity, render my labour vain, and the tree of prospect fruitless.

After the children have retired, Háris enters, and says to his wife.—Alas! the trouble and fatigue I have undergone

---

* "The sixth great point of faith which the *Mohammedans* are taught by the *Koran* to believe, is God's absolute decree and predestination both of good and evil."—Sale's "Koran," Prel. Disc., sec. iv. p. 103, ed. 1734.

in searching for the children of Muslim! But all in vain, for I could not find them, I could not chase out the two sacred gazelles. Woman, make haste and prepare me a morsel of meal, for I am very hungry. My strength is altogether exhausted; but I should like first to have a nap.

The Wife of Háris.—Ill-luck is manifest in thy wicked countenance! Here is food for thee, take it; may it be poison of asps within thee !

Muhammad (addressing Ibráhím in their bedroom).— Dear brother, I saw our father in my dreams. I beheld a splendid sun in my bed! But my dream has made my heart to palpitate within me. Surely we shall both die or suffer martyrdom to-day.

Ibráhím.—Tell me, dear brother, what thy dream was which made thee suddenly start from sleep. Tell me, I am getting anxious about the matter.

Muhammad.—Brother, as soon as I slept I saw the lord of men and demons, the mediator of the Day of Judgment, the glorious grandfather of Hasan and Husain, namely, the Prophet Muhammad, who, turning to my father, said, " Muslim, why hast thou left thy poor orphans behind when thou camest to me ? " He answered that angelic being, saying, " Behold, they are just behind me; this very minute my two children are about to come ! "

Ibráhím.—Dearly beloved brother, I swear by the elect lord himself that I saw the same thing in my dream a moment before I awoke! I am certain both of us will be killed, and registered in the book of the martyrs. Seeing our mother will not be present the hour we die, to mourn for us, dear brother, let us weep for ourselves. Begin thou to think of our poor mother, and let me call to mind our father; groan thou, and I will scatter dust on my head to signify our trouble.

The Two Children.—Come, it is time to bid adieu to one another! We have no mother in this place, and our father is gone from us! We are strangers, we are miserably despised by all! we have lost our father and have none to take care of us, none to sympathise with us, none to pity us!

Háris.—I hear plenty of noise in this house; some persons appear to be singing sad songs to one another. Is there a melancholy singing bird imprisoned in this cage-like house? I perceive from the mournful voice that some orphan boys are crying. Doubtless there are some fatherless children somewhere in this abode; for wherever I listen I hear lamentations and weepings. Listen attentively, you will hear the same sad tone of the sufferers that I do.

The Wife of Háris.—Sleep, man, there is no wailing in this house at all. This noise may be from the habitation of some neighbours. Never must thou be found troublesome or offensive to any friend. What hast thou to do with the people, whether they cry or not?

The Children.—To-night is the evening that precedes the day of our destruction. May the nine spheres pour down blood for this sad event! O thou gentle zephyr, blow on the side where we are, and passing hence to the holy monument of the Prophet, or to Madínah, salute our dear mother in our name, and deliver to her the message of our love!

Háris (surprising the children).—O ye wing-tied nightingales, whose delight of the soul are you? How did you get yourselves into this place? And whose beloved ones are you? At this midnight am I dreaming of a sun, of a moon, or of both? Tell me plainly of whose family are you?

The Children.—Know thou, O inquirer, that we are two strangers who have here no protector. We are the two miserably afflicted sons of Muslim. We were removed accidentally from Madínah, our native town, and came to Kúfah, where we were delivered to a cruel party, by whom we have been sadly ill-treated.

Háris (beating the children).—The object of my heart is

at home, and I wander in search of it here and there! The beloved of my soul is before my face, and I look for her in different directions! The heart, for years, used to demand of us the mysterious cup of Jamshíd;* strange to say, it is the very thing that itself possessed.

Ibráhím.—O Háris, fear God, and blush with shame before 'Alí His chosen! remember the torments of the Day of Judgment, and dread the mournful complaint of the best amongst women† before the Lord. Please leave us.

Háris.—I never blush before God, nor do I fear 'Alí His lion. I neither care for the curses of the Prophet, nor have I the least dread of Zahrah‡ his daughter, styled by you the best amongst women. I will kill you now immediately without any feeling of compassion. I do not mind the darkness of the grave, nor the terrible punishment of the Day of Judgment.

The Wife of Háris.—O Háris, leave these poor oppressed things alone, for they are destitute strangers, scarred in their hearts. None, beside thee, ever ill-treated a guest! There is a Day of Resurrection; there is an account for actions done by man; there is a responsibility.

Háris.—Get thee hence, wife; I must kill this sacred game maliciously. I cannot voluntarily lose the prize of gold and silver. I will kill both of them at once, for I am obstinately set against them. I have no compassion, no humanity, no feeling of kindness.

Muhammad.—Nay, good man, appease thine anger, stop thy wrath, and humble thy pride. Have mercy on our destitute state, for we are poor orphans, and in exile! Consent not that our innocent blood be shed. If thy design is to get money, or to be rich in perishable things,

---

* "Jamshíd is said to have possessed a cup in which were depicted future events."—Wollaston's Translation of the "Anwár-i-Suhailí," p. 83, ed. 1877.

† See note, p. 42.   ‡ See note, p. 22.

why, thou needst not add grief to our grief. Thou mayest shave our dear curls at once, and put rings of serfdom in our ears, and then pass us for slaves in the market for sale. I am sure thou canst be enriched by our price.

Háris.—I am not abashed before your grandfather in killing you, nor have I any feeling of mercy in my heart. My soul is harder than stone, and not in the least degree soft. I know my abode will be in the bottomless pit.

Muhammad (to Háris' wife).—We poor sorrowful destitute creatures have but one request to make; we hope thou wilt be kind enough to listen, and grant our request. When we shall have been killed, take thou our two blood-stained shirts, and send them to our poor mother in Madínah. Let her know that we have been cruelly slain, and are no longer in the enjoyment of life, and that these are the best memorials we could send her.

Ibráhím.—Another favour is this—after we have rolled in our blood, thou shouldst kindly inform Shári', our guardian in Kúfah, of what has happened, that he may come mournfully here, take the bodies, wash them most carefully with tears, and after he has prayed over them ceremoniously bury them in some spot.

Háris.—Away with your nonsensical bequests and unnecessary wailings! Make yourselves ready for slaughter! I shall sever the heads of both with this my glittering sword, and throw the dead bodies in the river.

Ibráhím.—Come here, thou unbelieving tyrant; sever first my head from the body, and show thy excessive malice and hatred, for I cannot bear to see my elder brother killed before mine eyes.

Muhammad.—Nay, dear brother, let him first kill me; peradventure, after he has slain me, his anger will be appeased, and so he may give up the intention of spilling thy blood. Come, thou knave, make first a martyr of me, for I cannot bear to see my younger brother killed before mine eyes.

After his brother is killed, Ibráhím mournfully says :—O

brother Muhammad, may I be offered for thee! may I be sacrificed for thy love and faith! may I be an oblation for thy curling locks, and a sacrifice for thy tearful eyes! O brother, how can I see thee killed and myself live? How can I see thee rolling in thine own blood?

SCENE XII.

THE DEPARTURE OF HUSAIN FROM MADINAH, ON HIS WAY TO KUFAH.

HUSAIN, the son of 'Alí, deeming himself in danger at Makkah, withdrew to Madínah; he steadily "refused to take the oath of allegiance to Yezid. A messenger was sent to him from Koufa, entreating him to come to that city. The whole population, he was assured, were eager to espouse his cause, and pronounce the deposition of the Bani Ommaya. At first Hosain was distrustful of these advances, but such a number of invitations kept pouring in, with long lists of the chief men of the city, all of whom had taken a solemn oath to die in his defence, that he ultimately resolved to make the venture. His friends vainly counselled him not to do so. They urged that if the people of Koufa were so bitter against Yezid as they affirmed themselves to be, they could revolt without him being actually in their midst. When Hosain turned a deaf ear to these solicitations, they entreated him at least to go alone. But here also they failed. Hosain started (September A.D. 680) on his perilous expedition, accompanied by all his wives, his brothers, and his children, and escorted by forty horsemen and one hundred foot soldiers."—Osborne's "Islam under the Arabs," p. 123, ed. 1876.

Husain.—Troops of gloom have made a sudden invasion on the heart, the capital of the human soul; they have plundered all her property—patience, resolution, and fortitude—and laid waste her fortifications. Fate has become a guide to the commander of the caravan of faith, and Doom is crying out ever and anon, "Bind up your litters, and start." We must one day set out, my soul, from this transitory abode, and travel onwards to our eternal home.

Zainab.—Muharram* has come; this is the period when Moroseness encamps in the front of the heart, when the armies of Grief get their barracks appointed for them, when the Vintner of Time fills his cup to the brim with the wine of anguish and sorrow, and the tale of Karbalá becomes the talk of every entertainment. Abandon thy tyranny, O heaven! Hast thou no fear of the Living Judge? for with God all impossibilities are possible.

Husain.—O memorial of Fátimah, O my beloved sister! O my miserable and oppressed Zainab! it is time to prove thy sisterhood. Come, then, faithfully, like a dear soul, to Husain, thy brother. For the olefactory organ of my soul ever detects in thee the fragrant perfume of Fátimah, my mother, for thou art indeed like her.

Zainab.—O thou by whose name the exalted throne of God has received its glorious height, and the dust of whose court is a crown of honour for the head of Gabriel† the faithful spirit! Husain, dear brother, may thy sister Zainab never live to see thee sad in heart owing to the outrages of Time! Why is thy mind in the same condition as Zainab's dishevelled hair? why do red corals drop pearls on the surface of the jasmine flowers? why dost thou weep? O light of my sight! thy presence is indeed to me the source of all my future happiness, since my grandfather, father, and mother's death.

The Imám.—Dear sister, I am sore vexed in mind on account of the vexations of Time. How can I escape with my life from the malevolent designs of seditious men? If I remain at home in Madínah, I am not secure from the mischief of the enemy, for they seem to be in ambush everywhere to take my life. The family of Abú Sufiyán‡

---

* See note, p. 74.   † See note, p. 15.

‡ Abú Sufiyán was a leader of the Kuraish, and for many years one of Muhammad's bitterest opponents; but after the capture of Makkah

think if I continue to remain here that I shall create disturbance in the affairs of Yazíd's* government. Lest I should become a ruling khalíf myself, they are distressing me on all sides, making life bitter to me.

Zainab.—May sorrowful Zainab die rather than see her dear Husain so distressed and oppressed with calamities and misfortunes! He has retired into a corner, he has withdrawn from the world, having washed his hand from the khalífat, or government, and no longer covets a throne; still they do not let him alone at Madínah, nor at Makkah. Where or to what country shall this miserable brother of mine go, then? poor thing!

Husain.—Cry not, dear sister, now; the time of thy wailing is not yet come! the hour of thy lamentation and weeping will soon be at hand! The land of Karbalá is made only for cries of grief; have patience now, and sob not till the hour shall have fully come. That time is fit for mourning and bewailing, when one shall smell (as it were) the odour of roasting from the livers of those burning with thirst!

Zainab.—Alas! dear brother, as soon as thou didst mention the name of Karbalá, thou didst bring on me worlds of affliction and grief. The mere name of Karbalá kindles a flame in my soul, which causes so many tears as to immerse me in the sea of annihilation! Is Karbalá a mine of sorrow and moroseness, a source for pains and anguish of heart, that its very mention has brought abundance of grief to my mind?

Husain.—Zainab, poor broken-hearted sister, the brightness of my tearful eyes! thou hast not yet seen Karbalá,

---

by the Prophet, the chief in question, and others of the tribe, " who had till then been inveterate enemies to the Moslems, embraced the same faith, and became their friends and brethren."—Sale's " Koran," chap. lx. p. 447, ed. 1734.

* See note ‡, p. 17.

thou art still resting peaceably at home; the groans of the thirsty have not yet reached thine ears, to make thee quite unconscious. Why shouldst thou have an awe of this name Karbalá? why shouldst thou, O sister, be thus beforehand acquainted with grief?

Zainab.—Well, brother, what does Karbalá mean, where I must suffer so much trouble? I do not suppose any such thing will happen to me as long as I am under thine auspicious protection. Who dares, when one has a dear brother like thee, do me, or any of us, the least harm?

Husain.—I will tell thee a story. I will explain to thee the misfortunes of the plain of Karbalá. This Husain, whom thou canst not see sad or sullen, him shall the wicked Shimar slay, and sever his head from his body with a dagger from behind. They shall pierce through the throat of my infant child 'Alí Asghar with a sharp arrow. They shall behead 'Alí Akbar with their cruel sword. O poor sorrowful Zainab, they shall also cut off the hands of 'Abbás my standard-bearer. My Kásim shall be maliciously put to death by them, and heaven shall change his mirth into mourning. In all this I recommend to thee, dear sister, submission and resignation, for God indeed loveth the patient and humble.

Zainab.—Ah! dear brother, may the soul of me, the afflicted, be a sacrifice for thee! do not call such a place Karbalá, but a place of slaughter for the family of God's Prophet! Why should the tree of Kásim's stature be felled to the ground with the axe of injustice? Why should 'Alí Akbar, the youth, roll in his own blood? For what crime on his part ought the two hands of 'Abbás to be cut off? What has the infant Asghar done that his poor throat should be pierced through with a malicious arrow?

Husain.—The helpless people of the Prophet of God have no rock of salvation to fly to for a refuge except

Husain. They have no advocate with God on the Day of Judgment except Husain. The way of salvation is shut up against them on account of their manifold sins; and, except Husain, none can make a proper atonement or propitiation for transgression. Who could save the people of God from the wrath to come, seeing the empire of Faith has no other king but Husain?

Zainab.—How many troubles did my grandfather suffer for the sake of his elect people! How many pains did my father endure for the sake of the same! My poor mother was hurt and injured by a cursed wretch, which caused me thereupon to rend my garments. Behold my elder brother Hasan, how he gave his life for the salvation of this people! how he tasted mortal poison at last! Thou also, O light of mine eyes, art going to deliver thy precious soul to death, by the cruel instrumentality of the wicked Yazíd for the sake of this same people!

Husain.—How blessed the moment when I shall joyfully see the dawn of the day of my murder appearing in the eastern horizon! Oh! how blessed the morn, O poor sister, when I shall behold myself surrounded on all sides by the army of Yazíd in the plain of Karbalá! For a long time I have been anxiously waiting for that day; aye, for months, for years, yea, for a great space of time!

Zainab.—I, the sorrowful one, have also consented to see Karbalá, and to be in bonds of affliction and trials for the sake of the sinners of our people. I agree that after thy death my lodging at night shall be the ruinous places in Syria, and that I shall walk bare-footed and bare-headed in the streets of Damascus by day! Since all our sufferings tend to the happiness of our sinful people, I submit to ride, with uncovered head, on the back of a she-camel!

Husain.—Know, O my sorrowful sister, that I am greatly distressed to-day on account of my sad disappointments! Dear sister, after the decease of my brother Hasan it is

14 *

very hard, even a shame, that I should live. Try, kind sister, to alleviate my pains somehow, for I am every minute at war with my ill-luck.

Zainab.—If thou intendest, dear brother, to have thy sorrows mitigated, to have thy bud-like heart open, walk out for some minutes to the holy sepulchre of the Prophet, and complain to him of the cruelties of the people, and of the maltreatment of these thine enemies.

Husain (addressing the sepulchre).—Peace, O sorrowful grandfather of Husain! O brightness of his bleeding eyes! Peace, thou Moses* of the Sinai of faith! Peace, O curer of every spiritual malady! O beloved of the glorious Lord! thou in form the express image of His person! O thou to whom every secret is revealed, thou precious pearl of the sea of God's nearness, I have immeasurable grief in my heart. Order a cure for it, thou sorrow-recognising physician.

A Voice from the sepulchre.—O thou who art immersed in troubles, thou stranger in thine own country, thou general of the field of Karbalá, thou pilgrim to God, and the light of God, if thou wishest to be delivered from these bonds endeavour to get thee soon to Karbalá.

Husain.—Oh! what good tidings! this is the very object of my heart! this is what thy Husain wisheth. The precious gem of the intercession for sinners is worthy to be purchased with the blood of thy Husain, dear grandfather! Life is a trifling thing to be offered up for one's beloved; soul and body have no great value in this market.

The Prophet (from the sepulchre).—Thou light of mine eyes! the time approacheth that thou shalt go to Karbalá. The time of thy drinking the honey of martyrdom is close at hand. A little more, and thou shalt pitch thy

---

* "God said unto him: 'O Moses, I have chosen thee above all men, by honouring thee with my commissions, and by my speaking unto thee," &c. &c.—Sale's "Koran," chap. vii. p. 132, ed. 1734.

tents in the plain of tribulation; thou shalt listen to the mournful voice of those parched with thirst; and thou shalt clothe Akbar, the young cypress* of the Prophet's garden, with a shrouding dress, and offer him to the most beloved as a token of affection. When the dagger of Shimar† shall reach thy throat, oh, take care not to forget to pray for thy poor grandfather's sinful people.

Husain.—Oh! how can I, at such a time as that, forget thy people, since I am going to offer myself voluntarily for their sakes? Yea, however great may be the severity of the trial, I will undergo all most readily if I can but win the great object of intercession for transgressors. Seeing it is the will of the friend that I should obey his voice, I shall most willingly offer my very life to please him.

The Prophet.—Since thou hast wholly prepared thy heart for the undertaking, without any other motive but to do God's holy will; since thou hast taken away the heavy burden of grief that I had on my heart on account of mankind, namely, the great concern I have for their salvation, go in peace! May God help thee and assist thee, O light of mine eyes! I know thou hast been longing in thy heart for this office for many years.

Husain (returning).—God be praised! I succeeded in my object. The news of Karbalá has removed all sorrow from my mind. I have found behind this veil what my heart has sought after for years. Now I am made free. I have washed my hands of life. I have girded myself to do the will of God.

A Messenger from Kúfah,‡ entering Madínah.—O ye daily visitors of the enlightened sepulchre of the Prophet! O ye attendants at the threshold of the just one! be pleased to direct me to that palace, the porchway of which is swept

---

* See note, p. 10. † See note, p. 43.
‡ See note, p. 9.

daily with the wings of Gabriel. I have come from Kúfah, intending to have the honour of kissing Husain's feet, and have brought him letters from Muslim, his cousin.

The People of Madínah.—Know thou, O blessed-faced messenger, that yonder house belongeth to Husain, the illustrious offspring of the Prophet.

The Messenger (to Husain).—Peace be on thee, thou burning candle before the face of the Prophet, thou great founder of the temple of Islám, and cynosure of faith! I have just arrived from Kúfah, thou advocate of sinners, to kiss the dust of this heaven-like threshold. I have a letter from poor Muslim addressed to the dust of thy holy feet, O most excellent king of all creatures, and several others written by the chiefs of Arabs in that country to thy holiness, O Imám of the age!

Husain.—O newly-arrived messenger of the destitute ones! on thee be peace! Come near, for I smell the scent of separation from thee. Thy very countenance testifies to vagrancy and houselessness, and the blackness of thy hair points out gloominess and dejection. Give me the letter of my exiled cousin; let me see how he complains of his misfortunes. Deliver to me also the writings of the irreligious inhabitants of Kúfah, severally and respectively, O good messenger.

The Messenger (delivering the letters).—O royal personage, to whose enlightened mind every secret is manifest! know first of all, this letter is from Habíb the son of Muzabar; this other is from Shís the son of Raba', the unlucky wretch; this unhappy letter is from Shimar the accursed, from the address of which one can smell the scent of blood; this writing, again, is from the impious Ibn Sa'd;* and this one from Barkar the son of Hasín. O intercessor at the Last Day! the remaining letters are from thy sincere

---

* Ibn Sa'd or 'Umar was the leader of the attack on Husain at Karbalá.

friends, who are all anxiously waiting for thy auspicious arrival at Kúfah.

Husain.—O God, thou art well aware that I have no other alternative but that of going to Karbalá in a most miserable manner. Tell me, O messenger, in particular, how fares Muslim amongst the inhabitants of Kúfah.

The Messenger.—May I be a sacrifice for thee, O chief! when Muslim came to Kúfah, the people of the city made the dust of his feet a crown for their head, so glad were they to receive him. He entered the great Mosque and sat on the pulpit to declare to the people his credentials, and all the inhabitants of the town extended to him the hand of loyalty. Now they are humbly entreating thy heaven-resembling majesty to honour them with thine august presence and direct the matter.

Husain.—Alas! thou didst make me, O heaven, to wander away from my home and country! thou didst at last remove me as a nightingale from the flower-garden! I fear, O cup-bearer of the age, thou wilt cause me to taste the same drink, at length, which thou didst previously pour down my brother Hasan's throat.

The Messenger.—O solar orb of the sphere of the Imámat! O sky of liberality and sea of generosity! why art thou disinclined towards the people of Kúfah? why dost thou suspect their sincere assurances of allegiance? The expanse of the city is, throughout, full of beautiful tulips; her lilies are scarred for thine absence! Have the goodness to honour the place with thy gracious presence, and to remain joyously in that abode of delight.

Husain.—O 'Alí Akbar, thou light of my heart and eyes! go and call me the fugitives and wanderers. Say, "Husain, the king of faith, orders you to assemble all in the Mosque, for there have come letters of much importance from Muslim, and he intends to have them read on the top of the pulpit, that all you his friends may know the contents of the same."

'Alí Akbar.—O ye assembly of friends and helpers, be it known unto you that there have come letters from Muslim to my father. Gather ye all from all quarters to the Mosque, according to the order of the chief of religion, the king of the two worlds, to hear there the important contents of these letters when read on the top of the pulpit.

Husain (to 'Abbás, his brother).—Get thee, dear brother, on the top of this pulpit, and explain to the assembly the import of Muslim's letter. Declare to the multitude of hearers the whole of what he states about himself.

'Abbás (in the pulpit, reading the letter).—"A humble letter from Muslim to the king of all nations, the moon of 'Irák-'Arabí, the monarch of 'Irák-Ajamí, namely, Husain." After the ceremonies of sincere service, and the conclusion of heart-felt prayers for success in respect to the Imám, he goes on, saying, "O solar orb of the sphere of faith, although the country of Kúfah is a tulip-field, yet without the rose of thy face all are but thorns in my eyes. The blow of thy separation has rendered me disabled, and the fire of thine absence has set my weary soul in flames. Come quickly to Kúfah, for all the people of the country earnestly desire to see thee, O most excellent Imám! Have the condescension, O sphere of generosity, to move hitherward, as soon as possible, that thou mayest afford direction in the paths of virtue to a people who are cheerfully expecting thy blessed arrival."

Husain (to 'Abbás).—O thou by whose sword houses of enmity have turned into ruins, thou whose awfulness has made heaven's back to tremble, read out also the letters written to me by the perfidious citizens of Kúfah, the obstinate hewers of the tender plants of the garden of "Yaman."*

---

* *i.e.* The family of Muhammad.

'*Abbás.*—The Arab chiefs most humbly petition the dust of thy sacred feet, O prince of genuine genealogy, saying, "The land of Karbalá from end to end is a beautiful rose-garden; the carpet of tulips and lilies is manifest and spread everywhere. The Euphrates is as restless as quicksilver, anxious to meet thee, and the land of Karbalá has worn out its eyes in looking out for thy coming. Come, come, all of us require an Imám; both high and low are, with their souls, desirous of receiving thee. If thou wilt refuse to come to Kúfah, we shall make bitter complaints of thee to Muhammad the Prophet of God."

Husain (ascending the pulpit).—I fly for refuge to God from Satan the reprobate. In the name of God, the gracious, the merciful:—Oh, my lovers at home; ye holy pilgrims of the way of faith; my sorrow-sharing, trouble-accompanied friends, to-day I am going to leave the country of Hijáz for 'Irák, or Mesopotamia, to be a guide or director in religious affairs to the inhabitants of Kúfah. Since we cannot hope to return from this journey of ours, if any of you, therefore, at any time have been offended by Husain's conduct toward's him, I beg him, seeing it is a time of everlasting separation, to pardon the faults of this poor exile!

The Inhabitants of Madínah.—May all the inhabitants of Madínah be a ransom for thy soul! Come, let us revolve around thee, O high priest of all mankind! Tell us how to act after thy lamented departure; and what else can we do but rend the garments of our patience?

Husain (returning home, and addressing Zainab).—O thou who art concealed behind the veil of modesty! thou sounding bell of the caravan of the plain of Karbalá! come, for the time of desolation has commenced; make, at once, preparations for this dreadful journey. The period has arrived, dear Zainab, that thou shouldst leave home for ever, to dwell in the solitary wilds of Karbalá.

Zainab.—Alas! the promised time of the Apostle of God has come! the period of Husain's flight to Karbalá draws near! Alas! woe to me! I am going to wander away from Madínah! I am going to be a captive in the solitary desert! Oh! dear brother, make no mention of travelling before me, for my melancholy heart gets terribly disquieted by this word.

Husain.—Poor sister, what can Husain do, seeing he is under a great responsibility? I am, dear sister, obliged to go away from Madínah, otherwise how would I leave the holy monument of God's chosen Prophet? But I cannot help it now! go I must. There is a mystery not yet disclosed in regard to this journey. Take with thee, sister, funeral garments* and aromatic spices, since such things are the chief provisions for this road.

Zainab.—Oh! name not funeral garments before this sad woman; make no mention of travelling or separation from home. Utter not the name of shrouds, or I will dress myself in them! Make not this afflicted woman devoid of endurance and patience. In the presence of a nightingale whose rose-garden has been visited by withering days, make no mention of the autumn season, nor name any meadow.

Husain.—Wail not, O honey-lipped sister; go and call me my brother 'Abbás. Fetch me also the coat of mail belonging to my father 'Alí, and the standard of Muhammad the universal Prophet, which things alone are left us as memorials in this world. For to-day I intend to give to 'Abbás, with my own hand, the office of a standard-bearer. Fetch me also weapons of war, and put them on 'Alí Akbar my son, the brightness of mine eyes!

Zainab.—Gather yourselves together, all ye multitudes of men, and congratulate 'Abbás on his new appointment, for to-day the uncle of Sukainah† is about to receive the

---

* See note, p. 27. † A daughter of Husain.

standard-bearer's* office from Husain the King of Madínah. To-day my 'Abbás is the commander of the army of Islám.

Husain (to 'Abbás).—Dear brother, light of the eye of the noblest of men, thou blossom of the meadow of 'Alí the chosen of God! O 'Abbás, hold this standard from me, and be thou my helper in the time of adversity; be thou the standard-bearer of my army in this present enterprise.

'Abbás.—May I be a ransom for thee! I am obliged to thee for the great favour conferred on me; most willingly will I serve thee at all times. Think not 'Abbás is a faithless servant, or that he will ever leave thee alone in this journey. I do not consider myself thy brother, but the dust of thy feet; a slave of thine, having the ring of slavery in his ears.

Husain.—Come to me, thou light of thy father's eyes; fasten to thy waist the sword of Haidar† the warrior; place the shield between thy shoulders, dear 'Alí Akbar, and put on all the armour of war, thou brightness of my tearful eyes!

'Alí Akbar.—I am the least servant of thy gate, O eternal king! May I be offered to the dust of thy feet, thou beloved of Muhammad! I wear the armour of war according to thine imperial command. May Akbar be a sacrifice for thee!

Husain (to Kásim, his nephew).—Come to me my poor disappointed Kásim; come, for thy sudden separation shall make my smoke ascend; come, let me put on thee the armour of thy excellent father, for I well remember the command of my highly-beloved brother.

Kásim.—I am ever thankful to thee for the favours bestowed on me; I continually rejoice in thy loving kindness. Till the end of time I shall subscribe my name as thy slave. By the dust of thy feet do I swear that I con-

---

* The office of the standard-bearer was highly prized at the time of Muhammad and his successors.

† See note, p. 39.

sider myself a slave of thine bought with money; the collar of servitude I always wear about my neck.

Husain.—Go thou, dear Sukainah, to thy matchless sister Fátimah the younger; tell her thy father has resolved on a journey, and that I wish to see her before I leave. Bring that poor suffering child here to me that I may see her pretty face once more.

Sukainah (addressing Fátimah).—Come with me, dear ailing, feverish sister, for thy father has made preparations to go to Karbalá; all the relations are busy about starting; it is not time, my dear, to sit still. Come, sister, it being the last hour, lose no opportunity of seeing thy father and receiving his well-wishing adieu.

Fátimah.—Oh, speak not a word as to journeying, lest I should travel away from the world, lest I perish owing to this painful news! Hold, sister, the arm of this afflicted one, that I may pass somehow to my new travelling sun, and seeing once more the luminous face of my father, may be inspired with hope, and may enlighten my tearful eyes with the light of his countenance. I am certain I shall carry with me to the grave the desire of seeing him again; then let me have a full sight of him in this last moment.

Sukainah.—Look upon us, O spheres! we are companionless; we two nightingales belong to one and the same rose-garden! Both of us are bound with chains of separation, and our hearts are sorrowful owing to heaven's cruelty.

Fátimah the Younger (addressing Husain).—O father! why dost thou not inquire after the state of thy poor sufferers? why dost thou not ask about the disturbed mind of thy miserable prisoners? what has happened that thou hast put me out of mind altogether, that thou never inquirest concerning the soul-burning pain of thy distressed children? Thou takest all thy family with thee in this journey except me; thou makest no inquiry after, thou dost not care for, those seized with fever! Why shouldst thou bind me fast with chains of separation, without ever asking the patient what she mentally suffers?

Husain.—O thou who hast waned into a crescent, owing to the effects of continually suffering from fever, thou that hast become as slender as a thread, thou art fatigued with illness, thou art enfeebled by fever; no strength, no spirit, is left thee, poor thing! To take thee with us on such a journey is otherwise than proper; remain thou quietly and cheerfully at home.

Fátimah.—Oh! thou hast set my feverish body in flames, dear father, with this thy saying. Why dost thou bind me with the chains of separation? Consider me as one of the maidens of thy family, if I cannot have the honour of being called thy daughter.

The Imám.—Thou poor, feverish, patient child, who sufferest grievously from the absence and separation of thy dear father! Lament not, thou prisoner of sorrow, the evening of thy longing desire shall ere long break forth into morning. As soon as I arrive at the plain of Karbalá I will send thy brother Akbar to fetch thee there to myself. Be not sorry any more, thou light of my tearful eyes!

Fátimah.—Dear father, if I die at home of grief, who will wrap this destitute creature in winding-sheets? who will mourn and lament for me? or rend his garments to signify sorrow? I know, dear father, I shall die, with tearful eyes, as a stranger in mine own country.

Husain.—Though in thy desolation thou expectest help from me alone, yet remember what I say: God's tender mercy is greater than that of any loving father's. Thou canst not appreciate the high value of affliction in the sight of God. Be sure, dear child, the sigh of the desolate has a wonderful effect. Go thou and wish all thy loving relations and friends a happy journey, for this is the time of our departure, this is the hour of starting.

Fátimah (addressing the family).—Dear ones, you must at last leave me, as the light has departed from mine eyes! You travel on, and my lamentation will follow after! I beseech you severally to take particular care, in this your journey, of my dear sympathising soul, that is, my father.

I beg you all never to neglect your kind duties to Husain.

Husain.—Come, 'Abbás, dear brother, thou equal of my soul! get thee on horseback like a prince royal. Have the things for our way to Kúfah quite ready, and prepare necessaries for the road for the family. Set a golden litter for Zainab, and place Kulsúm on a camel, O solar orb of the height of certainty! Let the caravan of the destitute ones all mount and set out at once for Kúfah. Start, all of you, tearful as you are, on the first opportunity to the graveyard of Bakía',* outside of Madínah.

'Abbás.—Be it known unto you, ye relations, friends, companions, and camel-drivers, Husain, the Imám of the time, has ordered you to lade your camels. And ye family, or household of Muhammad, ride out all of you to Bakía'.

Fátimah.—O camel-driver, do not bind up thy litters to-day; suffer me not to have a heavy weight on my mind!

Sukainah.—Come, sister, let me wish thee adieu! Heaven seems to be maliciously striving with us!

Fátimah.—Come, dear sister, it is the day of separation; let me kiss thine eyes, I may not see thee again!

Sukainah.—Come, sister, let me kiss thy hands and feet, and wish thee farewell.

Fátimah.—God be with thee, Sukainah, dear sister; you are gone, and Madínah is ruined!

Zainab and Kulsúm.—If we were unkind, no matter, we are now gone; if we were a heavy burden to you, we are no longer present. Remain ye in your own houses; we, being homeless, must go from here.

The People of Madínah.—Without you it will not be pleasant at all; without you the candle of faith cannot have its usual brightness. You are going away, and how

---

* See note, p. 169.

difficult it is for us sorrowful creatures to live without you!

Zainab and Kulsúm.—Dear ones, pardon the offence Zainab and Kulsúm may have given you during their stay here. Be kind enough to overlook all their faults. O relations and friends, if we have at any time wronged you or injured you, we humbly beg your pardon.

The People of Madínah.—You were our best friends, but, alas! you are going! You were our soul and spirit, but, alas! you are leaving us! God forbid you should have done us any wrong; you were kinder to us than our true mothers, but, alas! you have departed!

SCENE XIII.

WITHDRAWAL OF HUSAIN FROM THE ROAD TO KÚFAH.

HURRYING on to the treacherous city of Kúfah, Husain "with his little troop had arrived and encamped within three stages of Kadesiah. And a person of the name of Khur ben Yezzeid, secretly attached to the family of Ally, having been directed by Omar Saud to level the wells and places of refreshment in the desert, came rather unexpectedly on the encampment of the Imaum, whom, when he found that he was thus far on his way to Kufah, he earnestly entreated to return without delay, for that his agents had been put to death, and that Omar, the son of Saud, with four thousand men, was just at hand to intercept him. 'Alas!' said Husseyne, 'encumbered with all this family, how can I return?' 'Up,' replied his friendly monitor, 'quit the road and retire to one side.' Husseyne accordingly decamped, and quitting the direct road, proceeded on one side to a place called Kerbela, where he again pitched his tents." —Price's "Chronological Retrospect of Mahommedan History," vol. i. p. 397, ed. 1811.

Husain (encamping in the vicinity of Kúfah).—Fate, in this journey, will release us from the confinement of this world; Destiny's hand will pass us soon from humility to exaltation. The unstable spheres made me wander away from the divine sanctuary, and are now impelling me with strong impulse to the sacred shrine of Karbalá. I see heaven during this journey is about to deprive Zainab of patience, and Umm Lailah* of endurance, by bereaving me of my son.

Zainab.—I know well this journey is freighted with misfortunes, but what the spheres have ultimately in view I cannot tell. From the tinkling of the caravan bells one can well infer that the journey is a dangerous one.

Husain.—Aye, dear sister, this journey comprises numerous troubles; it involves painful sorrows for brothers, distracting grievances for sons! The bank of that river must embrace the elegant stature of thy noble 'Abbás, deprived of his hands, as a palm tree of branches.

'Alí Akbar.—O friends, the ramparts of the city of Kúfah are quite manifest to the view; I can see the very branches of her palm plantation from here. Give notice, O Zephyr, to the inhabitants of the city of the arrival of roses at the rose-garden; whisper in their ears that the sweet-tongued parrot is come.

Husain.—The aspect which thou viewest cannot be a rose-garden, O nightingale. If it be a garden at all it must be one filled with thorns. The long, slender things which thou seest with thine eyes cannot be palm trees, dear one, they are spears and lances borne by the people of Kúfah.

'Alí Akbar.—Father, it is certainly the beginning of our vernal season! Nay, I was mistaken, it is the autumnal time of our verdant meadow, to be sure. It is the hour to strew souls in the path of the beloved; to-day is the first dawn of a happy epoch.

Husain.—This, my child, is the advance guard of Karbalá, the beginning of temptation, the first trial. It is the time of utter desolation for the country of Madínah; the period of mourning and crying for my dear child Sukainah.

Sukainah.—Arise, dear aunt, heaven has plucked me up

---

* Wife of Husain.

by the roots! from the vault of the spheres a stone has been cruelly hurled on the bottle of my life. My body, dear aunt, is trembling and quivering like a weeping willow. May I be offered for thee! I am terribly afraid of that advancing army.

Zainab.—Why hast thou untied the knot of thy curls, dear niece? why art thou so soon alarmed, darling? There is no occasion thy body should tremble as a weeping willow; lean not so sadly on the side of the litter, poor child!

Sukainah.—Nay, dear aunt, it is a time for groaning and a proper place for trembling. Dear aunt, Sukainah has become a nestless nightingale. Heaven's project is to render me fatherless. The army or troop which I see is no more than a pretence.

Zainab.—My nightingale, dear brother, has again commenced her lamentation! O Solomon, show forth thy indulging favour to a poor lame ant.* Thy child's face is turned pale, her curling hair is dishevelled, her mirror† is buried in rust, no colour is left in her face!

Husain.—Thou shalt sigh and groan much hereafter, O Sukainah! Thou shalt have plenty of stories to relate, oppressed child. My beautiful lustrous pearl, my priceless gem, thou shalt suffer grievous thirst on the banks of a limpid river; remember that!

Húr, happening to come to the same spot, says to his band:—I see yonder some tents and pavilions; on the other side thereof I perceive a body of troops. I am sure it is the camp of Husain, the light of Zahrah's‡ eye; for behold, how beams of transcendent light dart from their faces toward heaven!

---

* "And an ant, seeing the hosts approaching, said, 'O ants, enter ye into your habitations, lest Solomon and his army tread you under foot, and perceive it not."—Sale's "Korán," chap. xxvii. p. 310, ed. 1734.

† Mirrors in the East used formerly to be made of metal.

‡ See note, p. 22.

Husain.—O cypress* of the orchard of 'Alí, thou brave hero, 'Abbás, my dear brother, turn the reins of thy horse to yonder crowd and see whether they be friends or enemies.

'Abbás.—O ye noisy, malicious, hypocritical army, on whose slaughter have you and your general with one accord set out? What is the name of your commander? What are his schemes of war or peace? Tell me, are ye of the genuine Arabs of the interior parts, or are ye of the province of 'Irák only?

Húr.—O young man, we are soldiers of 'Ubaid† the son of Ziyád, sent by him to fight the battle of faith. Whose are those troops standing there on one side of the tents, having beautifully set themselves in array like the eyelashes of sacred gazelles?

'Abbás.—That army belongs to the heir-apparent of the cup-bearer of the tank of Al Kauzar,‡ that army appertains to the light of the eye of the dignity of God's Prophet. The commander or general of that army is Husain the son of 'Alí, whose own eldest son is 'Alí Akbar the brave.

Húr.—O sun-faced, exalted, glorious young man! since that camp and the troops there belong to Husain, I have a great many reasons to be joyful. I was seeking him in heaven; but behold, he is before me on earth! I will now destroy his men and make captives of his family.

---

* See note, p. 10.

† "In the perplexity into which he was in some measure thrown by this intelligence, Yezzeid, after some deliberation, determined that this was a difficulty from which the talents and inflexible vigour of Obaidullah, the son of Zeiaud, were alone competent to relieve him. To him, therefore, he immediately transmitted letters, authorising him to assume the entire government of Irák and Kúfah, to which place he directed him to proceed without delay, delegating the government of Bassorah to some person in whom he could confide under his own authority."—Price's "Chronological Retrospect of Mahommedan History," vol. i. p. 392, ed. 1811.

‡ See note, p. 96.

'Abbás.—O commander of the army of the wicked, thou boastest too much, and without reason, of manliness and bravery. Would to God I had permission from his majesty Husain, the King of Hijáz, I would just show thee the folly of thy assertions.

Húr.—Reason says, " Connive at shame and seek also no honour ; " but Love says, " Why hast thou held thy tongue from speaking ? " Unsheath the glittering sword, and put the world in confusion ; slay the horse and his rider one after the other, and make streams of blood flow.

'Abbás.—I am standard-bearer* of the army of Husain the king over land and sea. Nay, I am a slave born in the house of the family of God's Prophet. Be good enough to tell me the number of thy army, and please give me full information about the same.

Húr.—Who art thou, good-tempered young man, that inquirest about the number of the army of 'Ubaid the son of Ziyád ? Why art thou come out against us to prevent our march ? Tell me, thou heaven-throned one, to whom art thou tied by affinity or consanguinity. Thou wonderfully resemblest 'Alí as regards thy complexion. Tell me, art thou related to the king of Karbalá or not?

'Abbás.—I am he whose name is 'Abbás, from the terror of whose sword heaven's back is bent into a bow ! I am he whose father is 'Alí, the friend of God, who could overthrow lions in the field of courage ! If I draw out my sword from its sheath, lions' hearts shall melt into water from fear. Seeing thou hast learned now what my name is, be so kind as to let me know what thine is in truth.

Húr.—I am called Húr. None throughout Arabia can equal me in war. I am one who with my hair-splitting sword can rend the heart and breast down to the waist. If I draw out my flint-splitting sword, heaven and earth shall withdraw themselves through fear. With the dust of

---

* See note *, p. 219.

the hoofs of my gold-stirruped horse I can darken the bright face of the shining sun. I am not boasting, O just and pious man; if thou canst not believe me, come and see.

Abbás.—Tell me, O young man of noble disposition, where art thou going with such a great army? and whence comest thou? What has made thee thus covered with dust?

Húr.—I have come out from Kúfah, I and all my retinue, by order of 'Ubaid the son of Ziyád, to prevent Husain from approaching nearer to that city; to create commotion and uproar in the world; to drench the hair of 'Alí Akbar with his own blood, that the heart of his affectionate mother may burn with grief. Go thou now quickly to the Imám of all men, and inform him of 'Ubaid's intention.

Abbás (addressing Husain).—O sovereign of the country of Bat-há,* the malicious and mischievous army over against us belongs to Yazíd? The commander of the army is Húr, who has received orders to fight with us, O most exalted being.

Husain.—Thou crooked-conducted spheres, how long wilt thou tyrannise over us, and behave unjustly and cruelly towards the family of God's Prophet? I do not mind being murdered, but I fear thou wilt make the daughter of Zahrah a bare-headed captive amongst the inhabitants of Kúfah. Go thou, O 'Abbás, call to me the brave Húr, that I may know what are the intrigues of heaven against me.

Abbás.—O Húr, thou chief of the army of 'Ubaid, Husain, the light of the Prophet's eye, has summoned thee to his presence.

Húr.—O ye multitude of the army, dismount all of you,

---

* See note *, p. 182.

both small and great, and let us go to that caravan and refresh ourselves a little and quench our excessive thirst. O commander of the caravan of faith, we are extremely thirsty! O candle of the way of every leader, we are much parched! We are oppressed by thirst in this vale of affliction and trial; and to thy bounty and liberality, O cloud of mercy, we are looking.

Husain.—Dear 'Alí Akbar, give them water to drink; thou gem of excellent purity, refresh them. O heaven, be thou turned into drops of moisture; O clouds of mercy, pour down rain on sinners!

Húr.—Behold the greatness of benevolence and goodness! Husain the son of 'Alí gives water to his enemy in this vale of fear and trial. See, I on my part drew out my sword against him, while he gives me to drink. Can a person be unmindful of him who mournfully weeps for him?

The Imám.—O happy young man, may the name of thy parents get famous by thy means! You must have pushed on very fast to have become so thirsty! Tell me, however, what thy name is, O fortunate young man.

Húr.—O thou the marks of whose greatness are manifest to all, the shadow of whose palm revives the rose-garden of souls, I am, O chief of the highest position, thy servant Húr. This army—O just and liberal sovereign, may I be offered for thee!—belongs to the son of Ziyád. He has sent them under my command against Husain the king of the good. We have been pressing here and there in search of him, if perchance we might catch him.

Husain.—O noble Húr, thou commander of the army of infidelity, what are my faults or crimes? and what have I done against Yazíd to be thus pursued by him. Dost thou know, O leader of the army, who I am? Hast thou read the praises of my grandfather in the glorious Kur'án? Am I not Husain the son of Zahrah? Didst thou not see how Muhammad sucked my throat? Be now kind enough to decide justly, whether it be proper to pass daggers on the kissing-place of the chosen Prophet.

Húr.—O thou to whom the heavens bow down in adoration! thou new rose of the meadows of the emperor of men and jinns,* I know that thou art Husain, and that thy grandfather is the Prophet of God; but it cannot be helped, for 'Ubaid the son of Ziyád has sent with me a great army, such that if they draw their swords no soul from amongst men and jinns would be left alive! If thou wilt not submit willingly to Yazíd, thou shalt surely be killed by the edge of the blood-dropping sword.

Husain.—O Húr, thou commander of this oppressing troop, thou well-known among the tribes of Persia, if the Syrian armies should cover the face of earth like a deluge, and if the troops of 'Ubaid set their standard on the planet Saturn, one individual from the holy family of Baní Háshim† lifting up his arm with the famous sword called Jú'l fakár,‡ no soul, except the Almighty God alone, should escape the edge of his bent-backed sabre! But it cannot be helped now, for the scribe of fate, destiny, has from eternity written down martyrdom against my name. But I warn thee, as a friend, not to partake in this bloodshed, nor give up Paradise and visit the regions of the lost!

Húr.—I tell thee plainly I cannot deviate from what I am commanded. I must open the door of war and enmity on thy face. I will shed so much blood with the edge of my sword, O king, that the land of Karbalá shall appear a field of anemones or tulips.

The Imám.—O hero of the age, blush before the Lord, and have regard for the honourable face of my grandfather the Prophet. Allow me, then, to go towards Europe, or

---

* See note, p. 24.   † See note *, p. 200.
‡ See note †, p. 65.

let me turn to China, or Cochin-china, Mongolia, or Scythia.

Húr.—O son of the best of the apostles, I am ordered by 'Ubaid the son of Ziyád to show thee nothing but opposition, and to hem thee in on all sides. Unless thou, O poor vagrant exile, submit to Yazíd, the wicked grandson of Sufiyán, I shall not let thee move towards Kúfah, nor allow thee to return to thy country.

The Imám.—Be silent, thou impudent one, and put an end to thy words; have a regard for my majestic grandfather, the Messenger of the living God. O my helping companions, mount your beasts this very hour, and lade your camels with alacrity, that we may go back to our native country Bat-há, and live in the vicinity of the sacred sepulchre of God's Prophet, the glory of all mankind.

Húr (holding the rein of Husain's horse).—I will not let you move one step from here. Come on, O my numerous troops, and arrest the Imám of the time. Surround him on all sides that he shall not be able to move, lest he escape the trapping-place. How can I let thee go hence until I make streams of blood flow!

Husain.—What dost thou intend to do, thou foolish Húr? Why dost thou not tread the path of peace? Thy impudence exceeds all bounds. May thy mother sit in mourning for thee! Be abashed by the face of my grandfather, O Húr; have respect to Fátimah my mother.

Húr.—O thou progeny of the great king of the age, if any other person had thus made mention of my mother's name, I would have answered him in the same improper manner. Nay, I would have returned a most reproachful answer to him. But out of respect to thee and thy mother, the best among women[*], it is hard for me to say the least thing, O thou model of true direction.[†]

---

[*] See note ‡, p. 42. [†] See note, p. 72.

Husain.—If thou knowest me to be the son of Fátimah, Muhammad's daughter, why dost though treat me in this unjust and improper manner? What have I done to you, O ill-natured inhabitants of Kúfah, that you have girded up your loins to slay me, a poor exile?

Húr.—May my hands perish, O king of the age, if I draw out the sword maliciously against thy honourable face! I have not passed in this journey on any stone or clod of earth, but have heard from it good news of my entering Paradise. I wonder what is decreed by God concerning me. I am greatly perplexed in my affairs, O matchless moon, and cannot lift up my head through shame.

Husain.—O thou who art intoxicated sadly with the wine of sorrow, if thou wouldst listen to the advice I give thee, withdraw the hand of cruelty from us; disturb not the mind of this sacred one overwhelmed with grief, but return to thy place quickly, and let me alone bear the burden of my own troubles.

Húr.—O thou the dust of whose feet is a crown of honour to my head, thou royal benefactor of men and jinns, I will never turn aside from thy holy orders, though the name of life be no longer applied to my existence. Return thou also to thy tent quietly; let us see what will turn out hereafter.

'Alí Akbar cries out for prayer.—O noble Húr, since it is the time of prayer, thou mayest go to thy camp for devotion. Turn thy face to the court of the great Creator. I shall see what will happen to me.

Húr.—O champion of the field of battle, thou glory of all mankind, seeing thou hast been entitled the most eloquent among Arabs,* it is very proper thou shouldst take the lead in this solemn act, and both the armies will imitate thee as followers.

---

* See Eastwick's translation of the "Anvár-i-Suhailí," p. 1, note 6, ed. 1854.

The Imám (praying and addressing 'Abbás).—O brother, thou standard-bearer of the faithful army, thou similitude of my chosen father Haidar* the valiant, pitch a tent for me outside of the camp, far from the pavilion, in some proper place, that I may conclude the argument against these idolaters, and leave them no excuse.

'Abbás.—The place is ready, most excellent king; it is on one side, far from friends, helpers, and the wicked enemy.

Husain (addressing Húr and his party).—O ye people of Kúfah and Shám,† O ye tyrannical, bloody nation! all of you, both small and great, wrote letters to me, saying, "Come to Kúfah and manage the government thereof;" but now that I have arrived, you have began to plot against me with your tricks and stratagems, and to play the chess of treachery and perfidy with us. Is this all your fidelity? Thanks for that!

Húr.—May I be a ransom for thee, thou offspring of the cup-bearer of Kauzar! I swear by the spirit of God's Messenger that I know nothing at all about the writing of the inhabitants of Kúfah the faithless nation. But hear me, thou poor exile! turn the reins of the camels to the country of Hijáz at once; give up Kúfah, for there is no fidelity amongst its inhabitants, and thou art not able to make friends with them. By our Lord, I am burning with anguish at thy condition; yea, the very marrow of my bones is consumed with this fire. I do not see I can do thee any other good than this, to retire to a distance from thy army under the pretence that thou hast families with thee, and it is not proper that we should encamp close to one another. When night comes, thou mayst unbeknown to this inimical party go to any place or country thou likest best. God be with thee.‡

---

* See note, p. 39. † Syria.
‡ See Mrs. Meer Hassan Ali's "Mussulmauns of India," vol. i. p. 19, ed. 1833.

Husain.—I am much pleased with thee, thou young man; may thy spirits ever revive! Thou hast given me the best advice. I thank thee. Go in peace; thou hast made the heart of the Prophet of God to rejoice; thou hast both well done and said; God reward thee! Although none can tell what the pen of fate has written for or against him, still we shall leave this place about midnight, according to thy kind advice; peradventure we may be delivered from the mischief intended against us. O ye assembly of my companions, brothers, friends, and lovers, bind up the litters on camels and go before us to the place which my grandfather has pointed out for you. Depart quickly, this very night, dark though it be, with tearful eyes, back to Madínah.

SCENE XIV.

THE MARTYRDOM OF HUR.

"THE next who accosted him, though in very different terms, was Khúr, or Khyr ben Yezzeid, of the tribe of Temeim, the chief by whom he was first apprized of the approach of his enemies, and by whose advice he withdrew from the high road. This person now respectfully saluting Hûsseyne by the name of 'Son of the Messenger of God,' announced that he was come to combat in his defence, and to sacrifice his life at his feet. 'Mayst thou taste the blessings of martyrdom,' said Hûsseyne, 'while I congratulate thee on the endless joys of Paradise, which will be thy reward, brave and generous as thou art, and as thy name imports,' alluding to the benevolent influence felt through nature from the presence of the sun, the latter being in Persian Khour and Khyr and Khúrshaid."—Price's "Chronological Retrospect of Mahommedan History," vol. i. p. 402, ed. 1811.

Husain.—Thou deceitful sphere, how long wilt thou oppress us? How long wilt thou injure, ill-treat, and tyrannise over the holy family of the elect of God? It may be a light thing to see Kásim my nephew, 'Abbás my brother, and 'Alí Akbar my son slain before my eyes. I fear thou wilt make my dear helpless family captive slaves for the army of the enemy. It may be a trifle, if the wicked Sinán put my head on the top of his spear,

I fear lest thou make my poor 'Abdín* destitute and houseless at the same time.

Sukainah (addressing Zainab).—O blessed aunt, may I be a ransom for thee! vehemence of fever has made me sleepless and averse to my food. See, aunt, how long I am burning with fever's heat! I wonder why to-night we do not arrive at the halting-place! Ask father's camel-driver, please, the secret of this matter; why this our journey has become tedious and long?

Zainab.—Dear Sukainah, weep not; may thy aunt be a sacrifice for thee! May I be a ransom for thee and thy tearful eyes! Wail not, dear niece, nor smite so oft on thy breast and head! I will inquire of father's cameldriver about the road. Come to me, thou good cameldriver, for I intend to inquire somewhat of thee.

The Camel-Driver.—What is thy order, thou well esteemed lady? explain it to thy humble servant the cameldriver.

Zainab.—Tell me if the halting-place is far or near? Oh, the world is always dark to me! Sukainah has fever, and she is sadly groaning; for God's sake hasten to reach the station!

The Camel-Driver.—Alas! what shall I say, thou afflicted lady? What is this that has happened to-night unto us? I am certain we have lost our way; and his saintship, Husain, to be sure, has strayed too.

Zainab.—Where is Husain, the light of the eye of God's Messenger? What has become of the lord of the martyrs, the asylum of poor me? Where is the chief of religion, his lordship Imám Husain? Where is the brightness of the eye of the sovereign lord of both worlds? How is it that the neighing of his winged horse is not heard? How is it his sunlike majestic countenance is not to be seen?

The Camel-Driver.—May I be offered unto thee, thou sister of the king of both worlds, thou who art named

---

* See note †, p. 96.

Zainab! The brightness of the eye of God's Messenger is not visible; wherever I look there is no trace of him to be seen.

Zainab.—How is it that thou art continuing thy march, and do not linger a minute to see what has become of him? My brother Husain must be in this wilderness, though the star of my fortune is hidden from view.

Sukainah.—Whither is the shadow of my dear father removed from my head? Why does he not kindly come to me to-night? Has he met with symptoms of death in Sukainah? Has he found me on the point of death, and so given me up for lost? O my dear friends, for God's sake kindly take me to my father.

Zainab.—Weeping Sukainah, may I be offered for thee! why wailest and sighest thou so much? Declare unto thy dear aunt Zainab what makes thee a playing flute in this dead of the night?

Sukainah.—O aunt, what dost thou ask of poor wretched me? May the dust of sorrow be on my head! Dost thou not know my dear father is lost in this wilderness? Oh! I am quite certain I have become fatherless, a captive vagrant in the city of Kúfah. God is my witness, dear aunt, if my father will not come to see me in a minute more, I can scarcely live without him, and I shall carry with me to the grave the sorrow of his separation.

Zainab.—Have patience, dear Sukainah, for a moment; let me inquire in this dark night after thy father. My dear Sukainah, may I be offered for thee! Weep not, O joy of my heart, beat not so much on thy head and breast.

Sukainah.—Oh, speak not, speak not, I have no more patience! I shall carry with me to the grave the desire to see my father. What is the good of my living after he is gone? The tree of the fatherless ones will never bear fruit.

Zainab.—O heavens! what shall I do to make Sukainah quiet? How can I look her in the face any more? Hear me, O good camel-driver, make thy camels kneel in this dark night, and let me come down from the litter and search after my dear Husain with weeping.

Sukainah.—Dear aunt, I, the oppressed creature, will also accompany thee in searching after my dear father. Let me see what cruel heaven has done to my darling parent, and what has happened to him. May the dust of sorrow be on my head.

The Camel-Driver (to Zainab).—O Venus of the station of certainty, sit like a moon in thy litter. It will not continue so for ever. Husain may be found after all.

Zainab.—O camel-driver, my heart is bleeding through grief; untie the litter and put it down. I want to know what has become of the lord of the oppressed ones.

The Camel-Driver.—O daughter of the prince of Arabia, thou princess of high pedigree, wail not in this midnight; peradventure Husain may be found out.

Zainab.—Remain quiet, O camel-driver; cut the reins of the camels, let them rest awhile, and see what has become of the leader of the caravan, the lord of the oppressed.

The Camel-Driver.—O afflicted lady, thou who art unable to do anything, thou who never findest rest in the world, sit still a minute; peradventure Husain will appear.

Zainab.—O dear brother, may I be offered for thee! Where art thou? Lift up thy voice; may Zainab be a sacrifice for thee! O son of the elect, 'Alí, where art thou? Why art thou separated from thy poor family?

Sukainah (fainting).—Where art thou, O my affectionate father, may I be a ransom for thee? lift up thy voice, may I be made a sacrifice for its sweetness! Come, come quickly, otherwise Sukainah will die through grief, and carry thy scar on her breast to the grave.

Zainab.—O God, what shall I, the sad, sorrowful creature, do? Where shall I look for my brother in this dark night? Ah! alas! Sukainah has fainted from pain, her extreme affection for her father has sadly upset her.

'Abbás.—I do not know what has happened to thee, sister,

to make thee so sad and impatient. Why art thou shedding tears from thine eyes? Why does blood run down thy cheeks?

Zainab.—May I be offered for thee, O brightness of the eye of the noblest of mankind, dear brother 'Abbás, what shall I say? Earth be on my head! Husain, the beloved of 'Alí, my dear brother, is lost. Though as the sun he is hidden from our sight in this dark night, certainly he must be somewhere in this wilderness.

'Abbás.—Where art thou, dear brother? may I be a ransom for thee! Where art thou? may all the family be offered a sacrifice for thee! Come, Zainab, thy poor sister is restless for thee! Come, dear Sukainah is anxiously expecting thee!

'Alí Akbar.—Thou flower of the rose garden of Haidar* the warrior, where art thou? May 'Alí Akbar be offered a sacrifice for thee, where art thou? Come, come, may 'Alí Akbar be a ransom for thee! Nay, may a thousand persons like me be a sacrifice for the dust of thy feet!

Kásim.—O flower of the rose-garden of Lady Zahrah,† where art thou? May Kásim be offered in this very spot a ransom for thy soul! Come, dear uncle, (may my life be strewed in thy path!) my cry can no longer reach thy ear, dear uncle.

Husain (suddenly appearing).—O great God, how can this be right that Husain should be separated from the holy family of God's Prophet? Where are my Kásim, 'Abbás, and 'Alí Akbar? What has become of oppressed Sukainah? and where is little 'Alí Asghar?

'Abbás.—May I be offered for thee! tell me where hast thou been? why wast thou hid like light from our sight?

Husain.—Come to me, come, my sympathising brother! Why dost thou shed pearls from thy world-seeing eyes?

---

* See note, p. 39.   † See note, p. 22.

I had gone to Najaf* to visit the tomb of my father 'Alí and bid him my last adieu with tearful eyes.

'Abbás.—Come, let us be going, for all the family are lamenting for thee. Sukainah, Kulsúm, and Zainab are scarred with grief for thee. Come, Zainab is burned with fire owing to thy absence, and Sukainah is grievously tormented by fever to-night, for thy sake.

Husain.—Come to me, Zainab, thou who art nourished by grief, for blood runs from my eyes on account of separation from thee.

Zainab.—May Zainab be offered for thee, where wast thou? Why didst thou leave thy poor family and go away?

Husain.—Practice patience, dearly beloved sister; let God's will be done as regards me. Please tell me why my daughter Sukainah is lying there on the ground in such distress.

Zainab.—What shall I say, dear brother? Poor Sukainah has beaten so much on her head and breast since thy absence, and has been so extremely excited as to have fallen in a sudden swoon. Through excessive weeping, crying, wailing, and groaning, she has fallen on the ground and fainted.

The Imám (standing over Sukainah's head).—Come, sorrowful Sukainah, thou beloved of the father, let me embrace thee like my dear soul in my bosom. Come, darling, sit a while in my lap, let thy disturbed heart be a little pacified.

Sukainah.—May I be offered for thy soul, father, where

---

* Najaf, four miles from Kúfah, is the supposed burying-place of the Khalif 'Alí, whose tomb and mosque fills "an ample space in the middle of the city. It is a handsome structure, encircled by a high wall, within which it is death for an infidel to pass, unless in disguise, and under the protection of the Imám, who must be secretly bribed with a large sum."
—Kinneir's "Persia," p. 283, ed. 1813.

wast thou? Why didst thou leave us alone in this dark night? As soon as thou hast departed from us we lost our refuge, we became shelterless, and by reason of the thick blackness of the night we mistook our way altogether. All the time we have been in a fearfully disturbed state, we could not have one minute's peace in the litters.

Husain.—Ah! I do not know what my poor child will do? or who will console her grieved, oppressed mind, when the inhabitants of Kúfah treacherously and cruelly make me a martyr in the land of Karbalá.

Sukainah.—O my sorrowful father, may I be a ransom for thee! what makes thee so bitterly grieved at heart? I am now quite certain that I am about to be fatherless, that the revolution of the heavens is going ruthlessly to render me a wanderer.

Husain (addressing the family).—Enough wailing and shedding of tears down your cheeks; better mount your camels and proceed. There will come a time for moaning, sighing, and wailing. Now rather let us journey on until the evil days arrive.

'Abbás.—Come, O camel-driver, fix the litters on thy beasts and lead on; but as the stage is near, thou mayest proceed as slowly as thou likest.

Husain.—O 'Alí Akbar, be thou and Kásim about Zainab's camel, and explain to her the matter concerning Karbalá and the manner of its occurrence.

'Abbás.—Oh, 'Alí Akbar shall fall on one side rolling in blood, and Kásim on another side; the scar of this sorrow shall consume me and my progeny with unquenchable fire.

Husain (speaking to his horse).—Why dost thou not go, O poor dumb beast? Art thou exhausted under the burden of trust? Art thou acquainted, O winged horse,[*] of what

---

[*] The charger of 'Alí was called "Maymun, or, according to others, Zu'l Jenah (the winged)." (Burton's "El Medinah and Meccah," vol. ii. p. 207, ed. 1857.) Here the same term is applied to the steed of Husain.

shall happen to us in Karbalá? If not, what has become of thy galloping and trotting? thou must certainly mean something.

Abbás (addressing Husain).—O thou who as regards miracles art like Christ, and as concerns signs and wonders resemblest Moses; O thou who in dignity and honour art equal to Muhammad; may I be offered for thee, why groanest thou like one seized with fever? O glorious as Solomon, handsome as Joseph, and brave as 'Alí the elect, why makest thou thy horse to run here and there like lightning? If thou hast any plan or scheme in view, may it please thy highness to declare it to this thy home-born slave.

Husain.—The view of this landscape has rendered me very dull and sad, and I do not know why my steed has lost his usual spirits and become, as it were, lame. Get me another horse; let me ride on, for my sorrow and distraction of mind are from this landscape only. (*Riding another horse.*) Bring me another horse, for assuredly this does not go too; there must be some mystery in this bewitching ground. O lion-like 'Abbás, thou valiant prince, thou shield and refuge of my army, and my confidential friend, go and call me the camel-driver that I may question him about this dismal plain and its peculiarities.

'Abbás (addressing the camel-driver).—O honest camel-driver! the grandson of God's chosen and glorious Prophet calls thee to his presence.

The Camel-Driver (bowing to Husain).—What is thy object in calling me, thou high priest of men and jinns?* Order, thy servant is ready to obey.

Husain.—Tell me, O good man, what sort of plain is this? It is a wonderfully melancholy land, a sorrow-producing ground.

---

* See note, p. 24.

The Camel-Driver).—May I be a ransom for thee! this plain is called Karbalá.

Husain.—If the name of this land be truly Karbalá, then my lot in it will be affliction and trial. O similitude of the Prophet, my dear 'Alí Akbar, make proclamation for halting.

'Alí Akbar.—The king of the thirsty ones* has ordered you to unload your beasts in this place.

The Imám.—Come, O majestic 'Abbás, my worthy-mannered brother, call unto me Zahír, the happy child of this place.

'Abbás.—O good-principled Zahír, the model of the pious wishes to see thee.

Zahír and other Chiefs, bringing some lambs.—Peace be unto thee, thou king of the empire of faith, thou offspring of the chosen of God, and rose-bush of the meadows of truth! May Zahír and his party be a sacrifice for thee! O ye chiefs, slay your lambs as offerings to Husain, the priest of the universe.

The Chiefs laying down their sheep for slaughter, Husain says:—Withhold your hands, all of you, O ye Arabs; add not new troubles to my sorrowful heart. What is the reason, O Zahír, that each of you intend to slay a lamb? Explain to me the mystery of this, O Zahír.

Zahír.—May I be a ransom for thee, O thou enlightener of heaven and earth, thou fresh plant of the orchard of her ladyship Zahrah! They intend to shed the blood of these animals at the dust of thy sacred feet to avert misfortunes and calamities and accidents.

Husain.—O 'Abbás, thou good-natured brother, go, number these animals, and see how many they are.

'Abbás.—May I be a sacrifice for thy soul, O flower of the rose-garden of God's presence! altogether they amount to seventy-two animals.

---

* See note, p. 14.

Husain (addressing the Arab chiefs).—Take away these cords from the animals. I myself am ready to abandon my life. I am willing that 'Abbás, the champion of God's faith, should lose his hand. Take away the cords from the throat of these poor animals. I will consent to expose the throat of Asghar to the flying arrow of trial. None has ever made such an acceptable sacrifice in the world. I will stretch my throat before the dagger for the sake of the beloved truth.

Ibn Sa'd,* with his troops, arriving at the same place.— I address myself unto thee, thou fine-looking Húr. Why didst thou not make war with the offspring of the Prophet? It is incumbent on us to fight with Husain the son of 'Alí. It requires no consideration at all; commence fighting.

Húr.—Come, thou 'Umar son of Sa'd, hearken to my advice; do not be led astray by Yazíd's cursed wealth. Listen unto me; do not fight with the light of Zahrah's eyes for the sake of perishable riches.

Ibn Sa'd.—Know for a certainty that I will make war with Husain. I must fight with the family of God's Prophet. I cannot but obey the command of Yazíd my king. I must conform to his sovereign will at the risk of my life.

Shimar (arriving).—Tell me, O Ibn Sa'd the brave, what hast thou done to Husain, the model of true direction? I am the chief of 'Irák, I am the mighty champion of the age, Shimar the skilled in battle. Thou scoundrel and fool! how long wilt thou abstain from fighting with Husain, the ornament of the royal seat? If thou fearest him, or hast a dread of his pompous camp; if thou reverencest his moon-like† countenance to such an extent, leave the command of the wicked army to myself, that I may give the colour of pomegranate blossoms to hills and valleys with the blood of Husain, that I may not leave one of the Háshimites alive in the world.

---

* See note *, p. 214. † See note, p. 7.

Ibn Sa'd.—Woe to thee, thou tyrannical, impudent Shimar, how dost thou dare to draw thy sword against the grandson of the chosen Prophet. Blush for the favours thou hast received from the leader of the age, and reverence the face of Fátimah* the virgin, his mother.

Shimar.—O son of Sa'd, I am not at all ashamed before God's Prophet, and I scoff at what 'Alí the elect has done for me. I sneer at all favours bestowed on me by Husain's mother, and I will lead his sisters into captivity in a most unjust and cruel manner.

Ibn Sa'd.—O Shimar, thou art terribly excited to anger; thou hast turned me also from the way of God by thy cursed conversation. Well, at what time must we begin to fight with Husain? When wilt thou set out to contend with the king of the two worlds?

Shimar.—To-day I am going to shake to its foundation the Divine throne, to-day I will draw out the hand of cruelty from the pocket of consideration. We must make an attack on this highly exalted king, we must carry Husain's sisters to Syria as captives.

Húr (speaking to himself).—O gracious Lord, I am sunk deep in the bottomless sea of perturbation. I am on a journey with two roads before me. Hell and Paradise are open to my view, and I am preplexed between the two, not knowing which path to choose—that which leads to rivers of delight, or that which is full of pricking stings.

Musáb (addressing his brother Húr).—O thou who possessest the power of two hundred lions in thy fist, what has terrified thee so that thou hast put thy finger in thy mouth wondering? I see thy cypress-like† stature trembling as a weeping willow; what has made thee repent and hang down thy head in this manner?

Húr.—O brother, the trembling that has seized me is not through the fear of men valiant in battle, but rather

---

* See note, p. 57. † See note, p. 10.

of God, the Avenger of blood. I feel ashamed before Ahmad* the elect of the Lord. Being astonished and thoughtful, I have put my finger between my teeth. My duty is to go to Husain, the most illustrious king, and fall on the ground before him, asking his pardon, but I feel ashamed. Well, brother, what wilt thou do when I am gone from thee? If thou wilt be so kind as to accompany me, I shall be much obliged to thee.

Húr's Brother.—I will not say to thee what I will do, it would look like plotting: I shall act as God from eternity has decreed for me. I would willingly follow thee to the infernal regions, much more to Paradise. I may be young in age, but I think I am not so in understanding.

Húr.—O fresh plant of my garden, my most dearly beloved son, tie my hands fast with this noose, and put a yoke on my neck together with my boots, and close my eyes with a handkerchief, and then lead me to Husain (for I am so much ashamed before him), that I may fall on the ground in his presence and ask his pardon.

The Son of Húr.—With all my heart. I will do just as thou hast commanded me, I am obliged to obey thy orders, dear father.

Húr.—O Husain, thou son of God's lion, thou pearl of the sea of generosity, forgive me. I beg thy pardon, thou king, chief, and ruler of Hijáz and Bat-há.† O Husain, thou sovereign of the empire of faith, forgive a humble suppliant.

Husain.—Welcome! welcome! thou handsome young Húr. May God, the great Creator, be pleased with thee in the day of gathering. Take away thy boots from thy neck, young man, thy sins are forgiven thee by our Lord. You are all of you welcome, my newly arrived guests. You have made the bountiful Creator pleased with you.

Húr.—I most humbly beg thee, O crowned king, to

---

* See note *, p. 37.   † See note, p. 182.

permit me to give my life for thee. Having been the first person to have troubled thee, I intend to be the first also in offering my life for thee. Be pleased to permit me, O highly exalted prince of faith, to engage in this holy war for thee.

The Imám.—As thou hast the wish to combat with the wicked, and personally assist the King of Karbalá, put on, O Húr, thy last garment, the funeral shroud, for thou art to-day journeying to my holy grandfather, the Prophet.

Húr (addressing the enemy).—I am the champion of the field of battle, I am Húr, a man of great intelligence and understanding. I am a servant to Husain, the thirsty-lipped prince. I have letters patent, sealed with Husain's signature, that I am saved in both worlds. Oh, what a glorious title to me, if I be called in the day of account "Húr the martyr!"*

Ibn Sa'd.—O ye people of Kúfah and Shám,† Húr, the fortunate, has played the ungrateful in deserting his post. Take ye the essence of his life with the edge of your sword, and make his helpless family lament his death.

The Brother of Húr (to Husain).—May I be a ransom for thee, thou offspring of the glorious Prophet! I am, O unique Imám, Musáb, the brother of Húr. Give me permission to fight the battle of faith and be slain; for I cannot see the murderer of my brother alive.

Husain.—Put on thy shrouding garments, O disappointed youth, and run with a cheerful mind toward the garden of Paradise.

The Brother of Húr.—O ye profligate inhabitants of Kúfah, I am Musáb the brave, the renowned. I will sacrifice my humble soul on behalf of Husain, as my brother did. I will follow your lines just now without minding at all the greatness of your number.

---

* Húr-i-Shahíd, or "Húr the martyr," is the appellation by which he has been handed down to posterity.

† Syria.

Ibn Sa'd.—Vaunt not so much, O young man, for this very minute thou shalt roll in thy own blood.

Húr's Brother (falling on the enemy).—O possessor of Zú'l fakár,* it is the time of help! O 'Alí, the parent of seven and four,† it is the time of help!

The Son of Húr (to Husain).—May my head be offered for thee, O king of the sons of Adam, whose army are angels, whose breath is like that of Christ in its effect, and whose coming is after the manner of Elias, let thy majesty know that I am the son of the renowned Húr. May the shadow of thy favour never diminish from my head! permit me, please, to be offered a sacrifice for thee; for I am thy home-born slave, and so bound to obey thy orders.

Husain.—Thou alone hast remained to remind me of Húr. Oh, mayest thou ever prosper in thy undertaking! Go and fight with this treacherous party, but put on first funeral garments, thou famous youth.

The Son of Húr (going to battle).—Thank God I am delivered from the snares of this world. I am set at liberty by the king of time and place. Thanks be to God, I have obtained that which I was seeking with the utmost desire; I am so happy!

---

* See note, p. 65.

† That is the eleven Imáms who, according to the Shí'ah tradition, succeeded 'Alí.

SCENE XV.

THE MARTYRDOM OF ABIS AND SHAUZAB IN DEFENCE OF HUSAIN.

THE object of this Scene is apparently to show that even the attractions of this world are powerless to turn aside from their intention those devout Muslims who seek martyrdom in the defence of their religion. 'Abís was offered by Ibn Sa'd honours and riches if he would desert the Lord of Karbalá. The reply to this tempting offer was significant. "O thou infidel! Yazíd is the master of a crown, while Husain, the king of the martyrs, is the possessor of Paradise and Heaven. Yazíd can bestow territory, but the king of the martyrs directs to faith and religion; as a man of the world, judge fairly, is this advantageous, or that?" Scarcely less magnanimous was the conduct of Shauzab, the slave of 'Abís, who, when the latter offered him the choice of associating himself with his master in his perilous undertaking, at once begged to be allowed to take part in the enterprise, "though a slender gnat is too insignificant a prey for a phœnix." Both 'Abís and Shauzab were slain fighting in defence of Husain.

'Umar, the son of Sa'd (challenging* Husain).—Is there any warrior, O pearl of the junction of seas? Is there any combatant, thou posterity of the great Prophet? Is

---

* It was a custom amongst the Arabs to begin the contest with one or more single combats between the leaders or persons of distinction.

there any brave soldier, O thou for the birth of whom the Holy Spirit announced good tidings from the Creator? Is there any one prepared for war, O thou whose pearly throat the Messenger of God caressed and kissed? Is there any champion, O thou for whose amusement the Prophet miraculously brought several musk deer? Is there any valiant man, O thou to whom the Seal* of the Prophets thousands of times with great affliction said, "May I be made a ransom for thee"? If thou dost not come to the field thyself, send then some of thy companions to undertake the contest. Either a full submission to Yazíd,† or a severe battle; choose which thou likest. Be it war, or peace, let our request be granted us.

Husain.—Out upon thy tyranny, thou revolutions of time! Fie to thee and thy fidelity, thou faithless spheres! How can I, the new rose of the meadows of the illustrious Prophet's flower-garden, the esteemed child of 'Alí the lion of the great Maker of the universe, surrender to Yazíd, though my head be severed from the body by the edge of a glittering sword? I am willing to be killed for the sake of God's people, that I may intercede for all in the great plain of the last account. It is hard for me that Zainab should be led into captivity; but easier than to surrender to an adulterous‡ generation.

Zainab.—O benevolent Judge and Defender, O ineffable Maker of all things, shall I complain of the spheres, or of the violence of time? Atbá, the wicked and cursed infidel, broke the gem-like tooth§ of thy chosen Prophet with the throw of a stone! The irreligious son of Muljam,‖ at the time of prostration, cleft, with his glittering sword, the pate of 'Alí, the defender of Thy cause; and now the people of Damascus and Kúfah¶ put their horses

---

* See note †, p. 40.   † See note, p. 17.
‡ An allusion to the profligacy of the wife of Abú Sufiyán.
§ See note, p. 129.   ‖ See Introduction, Scene viii.
¶ See note, p. 9.

maliciously to full speed against Husain in the field of battle!

Sukainah.—O glorious Omnipotence, Thou art my witness! Thou art my Avenger for numberless outrages. I hourly suffer: although I cry out that I thirst, none of this malicious party ever pities my miserable condition! I am but a weak and little child: how can my feeble body, slender as a piece of straw, be able to bear the mountain-like weight of the burden of thirst! O dear aunt, the anguish of thirst is well-nigh consuming my spirit; tell me, what is the crime I have committed in this world?

Zainab.—O new rose of the meadow of my little-armied king, my tears and sighs have passed beyond the limits of heaven and earth! To-day thy father, my royal brother, has no helper and no shelter; indeed, his own lips are parched with thirst! The accursed inhabitants of Kúfah have maliciously shut up the Euphrates against my mighty and glorious king Husain! Thou hast committed no crime dear Sukainah, but there is a failure of water, a scarcity of drink; my own dry lips are a witness of what I have asserted.

Sukainah.—O dear aunt, do not make such excuses for me, I want nothing but water. I shall never yield to these thy sayings; let my king whose garments are rose-coloured be the judge. How can the emperor of faith bear in his life-time to see me have such tearful eyes? A physician cures every disease with a certain medicine; let him endeavour to get water for me, that is the best treatment. Mention the state of me, a poor ant,* to the Solomon of Karbalá; he will in common honesty and generosity advise me what to do.

Zainab.—O gracious Creator, send me death! Oh that my eyes would become blind! Dear niece, no longer put me to shame. Soul of thy aunt, get thee to Kulsúm, my

---

* See note *, p. 226.

sister; she will think for some water for thee instead of me.

Sukainah (to Kulsúm).—Kind aunt, look mercifully upon this miserable creature! Behold with compassion this feeble, broken-hearted, spiritless child. I ask thee, dear aunt, for one drop of water only. Oh, pity the flood of tears running down my cheeks! I beg thee to make no excuses at all, but consider how I humble myself to obtain but a drop of fresh water.

Kulsúm.—O coronated father, 'Alí, look upon thy destitute family! Hear the cry, sigh, and lamentation of these children. Sukainah is humbly asking me for water. Oh, pity poor miserable me, who am well-nigh consumed with shame! Beasts and birds get their supplies of water, whilst thy family are tormented with thirst. Oh, look at the injustice and cruelty of the Marwánian * family! Dear niece, may the soul of thy poor aunt be offered for thee! See how I shed torrents of tears for water; suffer not thy aunt to be ashamed more than this. The people of Kúfah have not allowed us even water to drink.

Sukainah.—O dear aunt, I have no patience; I cannot remain quiet, I am altogether undone. I long for death, but it does not come to me; my wish to die exceeds all bounds. Is there not one godly man in all this army to have compassion on my tearful eyes? Carry my humble petition kindly in an imploring manner to my noble, brave uncle 'Abbás.

Kulsúm.—O lion-like, dragon-hunting 'Abbás! O successor of the sovereign, the possessor of Duldul,† O power of the army of God's servants, the thread of my patience and endurance is snapped in twain. Sukainah is grasping the skirt of my garments for water. Dear brother, thou art the sower of humanity and zeal, by whom all my

---

* See p. 155.   † See note, p. 152.

affairs receive their proper decision. Help me, O thou shelterer of strangers in this land of exile, for resolution and fortitude have abandoned me in this case.

Sukainah (to 'Abbás).—May my afflicted soul be a ransom for thine! May my galled body be a sacrifice for thy zeal! If thou wilt assist me, a wounded-hearted creature, to-day, my lord will reward thee in return to-morrow.

'Abbás (to Kulsúm).—O my afflicted, grieved, troubled sister, thou in every adversity the solace of my fretful heart, I am much ashamed before Sukainah at my inability to get her water. Oh, dissolve not my poor frame for want of a drop of liquid, thou offspring of the king of the two worlds! O lord of thirsty-lipped souls, I have lost all patience owing to Sukainah's never-ceasing importunity. She is continually moaning and groaning for water to drink, and by her sad noise has turned my spring to autumn. Give me permission to go and fetch her some water to wet her throat, for water-carrying is the duty appointed to me.

Husain (addressing 'Abbás).—Dear brother, look upon Husain, who is already distressed with grief! Behold him as a ship in the whirlpool of destruction. I know the sea of thy zeal is in its full tide and rage, yet have pity also on me who am drowned in the abyss of Karbalá. O my dear brother, if thou, God forbid, be killed, the inhabitants of Kúfah will be encouraged to strike me; think of that. As the glorious Lord liveth, I cannot allow thee to go. Oh, look upon my destitute state, for God's sake!

'Abbás.—Behold thy little girl Sukainah, O unfortunate one! Look at the throats of thy thirsty children, my lord! The fruitful cypress * of the Háshimite † garden is withering away from drought, and I am melting away through sorrow, as thou well see'st! Death thousands of

---

* See note, p. 10.   See note ‡, p. 231.

times is better to me than the life I am living. Behold innumerable cruelties done in Karbalá! Give me permission to fight, and suffer me not any longer to be put to shame. Look upon me, wretched creature that I am.

Husain.—Oh, how can I bear to see one like thee die, and roll in his own blood in the centre of the field! Never mind that Sukainah should perish from thirst. It is wrong to esteem a locust above an eagle. May a thousand such as Sukainah be a ransom for a single hair of thine!

'Abbás.—Oh, may I be a sacrifice for thee! To roll a thousand times in one's own blood is better than to behold children suffering thus with dried lips! It is hard to see Sukainah crying in the palace tent for water while the cruel inhabitants of Kúfah at the same time use reproachful language towards us. Oh, be kind enough to permit me to be offered for thee! It is customary for friends to be sacrificed for their beloved ones!

Husain.—O most dearly beloved, it is difficult, not easy, to risk one's life. Yet to give up the soul is easier than to part with the beloved 'Abbás! To behold the elegant body of thine rolling in dust is an overpowering sight. The intention of this people is to have me killed without sustaining any damage themselves, and if thou give thy life for me, that will not in any way facilitate my escape from slaughter. Have patience, dear brother, for patience is the key of relief; it is hard to plunge oneself to the bottom of the sea.

'Abbás.—To give up one's life is not difficult when at the feet of thee, the beloved of the soul! If thou be absent from the pillow, to give up the ghost is arduous. It is easier to be drowned thirsty-lipped in one's own blood than to hear the groans and sighs of destitute women and children for water. Thou friend of God, to return from thy presence alive and unsacrificed is indeed hard. (*The enemy begin to challenge as before.*)

'Abís, the son of Shíb.—Sovereign-love came and con-

quered the empire of my heart. Abraham-like it repaired, or rather built anew, the ruinous temple. Reason says, "Speak not on the subject, be silent awhile." Love proclaims, "Nay, rather lay hold to the sword." The reproaches of Shimar,* and the sad complaints of the martyred king of Karbalá, have pierced my breast and penetrated into my heart. "How can I remain quiet," says love, "when I observe so much injustice? when I see the fox vaunting in the presence of the lion?" Reason urges, "Yazíd's fortune is in its meridian, and time has pulled down the house of faith."

Shauzab, his slave.—O terrible art thou as a lion; thy words have made great impression on my mind. Every malady has a remedy; thou must manage that. I see the hair of thy body standing forth from thy cuirass out of zeal; be pleased to declare the cause to this thy humble slave. If the eagle of thy resolution has begun to soar on high, inform me what has happened. Thou must impart to me thy secret plans plainly, as to a trustworthy servant.

'Abís.—Oh, do not ask about my condition, for this pain is without remedy; neither interfere with my affairs, for it is a perplexing case. The vessel of my patience is wrecked in the ocean of Karbalá, and reason, the pilot, cannot but be drowned in this deluge. O Shauzab! love, the unmanageable steed, has snatched the reins from my hand; he is carrying me off heedless of what may happen. If I disclose my mental pains, that will not bring a cure from any quarter; otherwise, to speak my mind to thee were an easy thing.

Shauzab.—Reveal to me thy secret, thy difficulty may thereby be facilitated. If I am not a physician, still every pain has a remedy. If thou hast anything to say on the subject of dispute between reason and love, speak on,

---

* See note ‡, p. 43.

that I may confirm the matter, as to whether the truth be on this side or on that.

'*Abís.*—O good and faithful slave, I have here a journey before me; though thou art my slave, thou mayest have thy choice either to accompany me or stay behind, as thou pleasest, for it is without doubt a dangerous undertaking. At every step, instead of sweet pleasures, there will be severe and innumerable hardships. Tell me whether thou wilt oppose my scheme, or, on the contrary, wilt affectionately and faithfully follow me in this hazardous enterprise?

Shauzab.—May my head be offered for thee, thou forecasting master! Explain to thy humble slave what thy project is. What control and power can slaves have over this or that when a master undertakes a journey to some particular place? If it be a delightful thing, I will cheerfully enjoy it with thee; if it be a perilous matter, or an affair of hazard, I will not refuse to accept anything offered to me by thee. Who am I that I should oppose thy schemes, or disobey thy orders? Please to tell me, then, what thy plans are?

'*Abís.*—O faithful slave, I intend to set out at once for a journey to Paradise. That is what I seriously have at heart. The few drops of blood I possess I intend to sprinkle at the dust of Husain's feet, he being the king of jinns * and men. Behold him standing there with dried lips and humid eyes. Sukainah is asking for water, while 'Abbás the majestic, and Husain the thirsty-lipped king, are melting away with entreaties.

Shauzab.—Thanks, that by the grace of the Omnipotent Judge I am overshadowed by the wings of the phœnix of happiness, that I am going to shed my own blood at the stirrup of Husain, though a slender gnat is too insignificant a prey for a phœnix. Oh, how happy if, in spite of the

---

* See note, p. 24.

blackness, I could be raised to life on the Resurrection Day with a white, shining face! I am much obliged to thee for this thy inestimable favour, master; may the Lord and His Prophet be pleased with thee as thou hast gratified me!

'Abís.—God bless thee, thou faithful slave! May the illustrious Prophet and 'Alí, the cup-bearer of the tank Al Kauzar,* defend thee. Come, let us go together to the thirsty-souled Husain and ask his permission to go to war. Let us have the happiness of kissing the feet of his royal highness, and as soon as he gives us the opportunity we will fall on the line of the enemy. We shall fight, then, till we become martyred, since that is the eternal felicity which is going before us as our guide.

Shauzab.—I, poor creature that I am, am obedient to thy order, and will follow thee whithersoever thou goest. I have girded up my loins faithfully ready for death. Walk before, I am coming behind thee. May the great Judge be thy helper and defender!

'Abís.—May I be a ransom for thee, thou guide of all men, thou beloved of the Prophet and elect of God! since thou art superior to Solomon in point of dignity, grant, then, the request of this ant by way of benevolence. I have in my hand a humble present, valueless as the leg of a locust. May it please thy majesty to condescend to receive it. Oh that thou wouldst be gracious enough not to refuse me! it is usual with kings to be favourable and indulgent to their attending slaves.

Husain (addressing 'Abís).—O hero of the army of Islám, O phœnix of the age, thou lion of the forest of contest, thou growling tiger, thou refuge of my army, my worthy 'Abís, who art a very ocean of zeal in the field of battle, what is thy wish that thou humblest thyself in such a manner with dried lips and weeping eyes? Tell me thy

---

* See note, p. 96.

request, that I may grant it just now in the very form thou desirest me to do.

'Abís.—O thou who art of blessed disposition, my petition at the dust of thy feet is to grant instantly to these two oppressed creatures permission to fight the battle of faith, that I, together with this ill-starred black slave, may fall suddenly on the line of the enemy, be it as it may; that from the centre to the wing, from the right to the left, we may make an utter destruction of this unprincipled nation; that we may fight so as to become either martyrs, or defeat, to thy glory, the army of the wicked son of Ziyád.

Husain.—A thousand curses from God be on 'Ubaid the son of Ziyád,* for the unprincipled mean fellow always sows seeds of discord and malice! In Husain's lifetime it can never happen that he should permit thee to go to fight the battle of faith, for I have many hopes grounded on thee, and the meadows of my heart flourish through thy reputation. Thou art in the sight of Husain as dear as 'Akbar and 'Abbás, yea, more precious than all friends and loves, O thou youth of happy disposition.

'Abís.—Oh, I am no more than a door-keeping dog in the street of thy affection and faith! Who am I that I should enter that noble mind of thine? What a wide difference there is between 'Abbás and Akbar and myself! Thy favours are much above my merit or desert. Oh, be the dust of thy foot the crown of my head! I will not cease holding thy skirt until thou grant me permission to tread the path mentioned.

The Imám.—Oh, do not groan any more, thou burnest my heart with grief! Instead of thee, I shall send to the field my son Akbar, the hopeless youth, the similitude of my grandfather, the new rose of my flower-garden, the

---

* See note *, p. 177.

brilliant light of my eyes. Abandon this request of thine let me give up my 'Alí Akbar, the blooming youth.

'Abís.—Permit me, O Imám of men and jinns.

Shauzab.—Permit thy slave, for the sake of thy grandfather the Prophet.

'Abís.—Permit me, thou chief of the thirsty-lipped.

Shauzab.—Permit me, for the sake of God Almighty.

'Abís.—Permit 'Abís, for the sake of the great Creator.

Shauzab.—Permit Shauzab, for the sake of the cup-bearer of Al Kauzar.

'Abís.—Give me permission, I am the least of thy slaves.

Shauzab.—Give me permission, I am thy money-bought slave.

'Abís.—Give me permission, I am the attending slave of thy court.

Shauzab.—Give permission, I am a black slave of thine.

'Abís.—Permit 'Abís, for the Omnipotent Judge's sake.

Shauzab.—Permit Shauzab, for the sake of the Prophet's dignity.

'Abís.—Give permission to Shauzab, for the sake of the seven and four.*

'Abís.—Permit 'Abís, thou praised by men.

Shauzab.—Permit Shauzab, for the sake of 'Abbás.

'Abís.—Give me permission, for the sake of Akbar the unhappy.

Shauzab.—Give me permission, for the sake of Kásim thy son-in-law.

'Abís.—Permit me to offer my soul a sacrifice for thee.

Shauzab.—Permit me to be offered a ransom for thy soul.

'Abís.—Oh! give me permission, I am much in need of this thy favour.

---

* See note, p. 2.

Shauzab.—Oh! give me permission, I am most obedient to thy orders.

'Abís.—Oh! give me permission; I am weary of my life.

Shauzab.—Oh! give me permission, for the flood of tears I am shedding from my eyes.

The Imám.—Sigh not, nor lament, O brave 'Abís, thou warrior in the ranks of battle. Thy tears have passed the centre of the earth, and thy sighs the sun and moon. My heart is much grieved for thee, thou art very young, very young; thou art a well-wisher to us, a well-wisher in deed and in truth.

'Abís.—I am the servant of the court of thy majesty, O asylum of the world. I feel a blush on my cheeks like a beggar in the palace of an emperor. When my body shall be cut in a hundred pieces with the sword of the enemy, and I am in a miserable condition; when my head shall roll on all sides, like a ball, at the hoof of thy horse, and thou seest my mutilated corpse fall in the dust of the road, then I shall deserve praise. Thou showest immense favour toward me, but I am sorry to say I do not deserve it in the least, and I am so ashamed of myself that I cannot even lift up my head.

Husain.—Thou art my friend, O 'Abís, and none likes that his friend should be troubled. Thou art a faithful man, and it is inconsistent with benevolence and justice to send a faithful man to slaughter intentionally. Do not ask of me permission to fight, nor complain if I do not grant it at all; and knock not at the door of a house whereinto thou mayest not have admittance. What a physician prescribes is the thing which it is advisable to follow, for to every malady experience has assigned a particular treatment.

'Abís.—Thou art in knowledge the Plato of the age; here is to-day an incurable case set before thee to be treated generously. Seeing thy bounty is universal and thy disposition in the highest sense liberal, it is not far from possible

if a fault be overlooked by thee. It will deserve the point of an arrow should my eye seek any other collyrium* but the dust of thy gate. The head that is not worthy of the dust of thy feet, is fit only to be knocked about with spears and lances of the enemy. Oh! how improper for a most magnificent king to push off ungenerously a poor beggar from the gate of his palace!

Husain.—O 'Abbás, thou general and defender of my army, seeing 'Abís, my help and support, has resolved to set out on this fatal journey, do thou get him funeral garments to put on, for he seeks our good always and everywhere. And thou, O Akbar, get a shrouding dress for this slave Shauzab, who is going to avenge me on the enemy.

'Abbás (bringing the sheet).—O amphitheatre of wonders and miracles, thou object of God's favour, it is the time of help, step forward to assist us, lay thy hand on the hilt of the glittering sword. See the helpers of Husain one by one putting on their funeral garments and going to battle. May I be a sacrifice for thy destitute state! O king of the age, take the winding-sheet from the hand of thy bereaved servant.

'Alí Akbar (bringing a funeral garment).—Alas for thy revolutions, thou crooked travelling sphere! Fie for thy malignity, O thou indigo-coloured vault! From thy malevolence the king of the empire of religion is surrounded in Karbalá by the tyrannical, villainous inhabitants of Kúfah. All his companions have been cruelly slain; he is standing there singly, pitifully ill-treated by the enemy. Take the shroud from me, thou sovereign of the age, through separation from whom I am heaving flame-scattering sighs from the heart.

'Abís (putting on the funeral garment).—How pleasant it is to see thy bright moon-like face! or to gather a rose from the fresh flower-garden of thy countenance! How can I desire to have the honour of kissing thy feet, I who

---

* See note, p. 135.

am constantly in the habit of venerating the very dust thereof? How blessed it is to lose the head by thy orders! to be slain by thy command is to enjoy eternal life. Well, it is my last adieu, thou heaven-like personage, for I have no mind to return from this journey.

Shauzab.—After God, His Messenger, and Haidar,* the defender of God's cause, it is one of my incumbent duties to serve thee, O Husain. God be thy helper, and may thy glorious grandfather, together with thy father, befriend thee! the time has come that we should endeavour to die the death of God's martyrs.

Husain.—God be pleased with you, ye two friends of Husain, who willingly give your lives for him. May the Messenger of God, my venerable grandfather, the great sovereign of the worlds, be your refuge and helper in the field of battle.

'Abís.—O ye assembly of infidels, ye chiefs of Kúfah and Syria, both small and great, be it known unto you that I am he to whose manliness the sword always gives a decisive testimony, in the day of battle, by the grace of Haidar the warrior. My name, ye obstinate nation, is 'Abís the son of Shíb, a slave of the slaves of Ahmad† the elect. I intend to give my head on behalf of Husain, the chief of the thirsty-lipped ones; you may send a champion,‡ if you please, from the wicked party to contest with me, that I may show to-day my manliness and bravery, and that you may see the assault of the lion, and the flight of jackals.

Shauzab.—O ye impudent and unbelieving assembly, I am the slave of this lion-hunting dragon. I speak plainly to those who know me not, I am Shauzab the slave of Haidar the champion. He who has the desire of death in his heart, let him come forward to the field of battle from the unbelieving army, that manliness and skilfulness in war may be manifested to all, that we may at the hour of

---

* See note, p. 39. † See note *, p. 37.
‡ See note, p. 250.

contest weigh the drop and the ocean simultaneously and find out the difference.

'Umar the son of Sa'd.—O ye soldiers of Kúfah and Shám,* and ye chiefs who have the mark of unbelief, put your horse of malignity to full speed in the battle-field. Knock 'Abís and his slave down in a moment and make both of them roll in their own blood, for they have vaunted too much before me, and beyond the limits of my capacity. Thou, O drummer, beat thy drum for battle, in a manner that the heavens may tremble and shrivel up through dread thereof.

'Abís (asking help from 'Alí).—O commander of the commanders of Arabia, thou judge of judges in pedigree and origin, thou lord of the sword, and lion of God, thou who art named "the hand of God," and art entitled Haidar, be thou my helper in this crisis, for from thee alone I seek assistance in time of trouble and need.

Shauzab (falling in the field).—O my blood-drinking tiger, save me! O my lion-like master, I am undone! I have fallen into a whirlpool of blood like a fish! O my skilful lord, take me under thy protection!

'Abís.—O Shauzab, my blood-drinking hero, thou my defender in all afflictions and trials, I cannot find my way thither to save thee and give thee life, notwithstanding my eager endeavours.

Shauzab.—O 'Abís, thou brave champion, thou commander of an army, thou renowned lion-hearted warrior, seek help from 'Alí Akbar the youth, the similitude of Muhammad the king of men and jinns, He will come to the field to help thee and cheer thy sorrowful heart.

'Abís.—O Shauzab, thou faithful of the age, thou who art skilful in war, the famous hero! the wicked party has intercepted my way, at the centre and the wing, on the

---

* Syria.

right and on the left. There is no chance for me to make my whale-like steed get out of this whirlpool of blood, and ask help from the youth Akbar at such time.

Shauzab.—O lion-hearted hero, thou chief in the assembly, ask assistance from 'Abbás the army-conqueror. If 'Abbás come to the battle-field, he will leave no enemy on the surface of the earth. He can snatch me out of this field of battle, and, carrying me as a bird in his claws, put me in the camp.

'Abís.—Know thou, O my faithful slave, my helper in this crisis, that if I could possibly get me where 'Abbás is, every difficulty would soon be over; but the adverse army have all drawn swords and javelins in their hands, and rush on me from every side, so I can scarcely get a chance of coming to thee, unless I make a full end of them first.

Shauzab.—Oh! May I be a ransom for thee! I am in a very bad condition. I am killed, slain with the sword of the enemy. My body is turned into paste by the clashing hoofs of horses, my garments are little better than a coat of mail, for so numerous are the holes; try, however, thou faithful master, and carry me out by some means from the midst of this army to our own camp.

'Abís.—By God's help I shall deliver thee: spite of my own helplessness I may give thee life. Come on my back, thou noble slave, a man such as whom the eye of the spheres has not seen. If thou have any commands to issue, inform me, that I may execute them in the best way possible.

Shauzab.—Oh! what shall I say? I scarce know how to speak. Thou canst not live more than a minute after me. Thou wilt instantly be made a martyr like myself; what is, then, the good of making requests, thou hopeless one? Be kind enough to close my eyes, and stretch my hands and feet towards the Kiblah,* the cynosure of faith.

---

* See note, p. 168.

'Abís.—Come, let me close thine eyes most affectionately. Blessed art thou, O brightness of the skies, who hast given thy soul in defence of ¡Husain. (*Hearing the beat of the drum he rides his horse, challenging the enemy*). Who will rush forth to fight with me, thou son of the wicked Sa'd? Who will come forward, O thou that feelest no shame or remorse? O impudent reprobate wretch, if thou hast any skill, come forth and contend with me.

The Son of Sa'd (addressing his troops).—O ye renowned chiefs of Kúfah and Shám, methinks you never care for reputation and honour at all. 'Abís the son of Shíb is standing all alone there challenging you to go and fight with him if you dare; let one brave soldier among you run to the field, and, slaying him with the edge of the sharp sword, put an end to his bragging.

Shimar (to Ibn Sa'd).—Thou cursed, profligate, impious wretch! we have been to battle with him more than a thousand each attack; but he cut through the centre, the wing, the right, and the left, now assaulting like a lion on this, now on that side, and at last we were put to flight by him in a most shameful and despicable manner, all wounded, mutilated, broken-hearted. How can we go one by one to fight with such a person? cease at once from such nonsensical sayings of thine.

Ibn Sa'd.—Thou wicked Shimar, I am now in great distress; hasten to my relief without any delay. 'Abís the son of Shíb has laid with his sword the burden of disgrace and shame on the shoulders of me and thee and all. He is no more than a single man, while I and thou have a hundred thousand troops at our command, and yet not one of us dares to move on his horse to the field of battle to struggle with him.

Shimar.—Thou villain, 'Abís the brave is a hero. Tell me, how can a jackal attack a lion? Go to him, like a fox, with cunning tricks and subtle stratagems, and try to entrap him, and, having succeeded in thy design, turn aside then from him.

Ibn Sa'd (to 'Abís).—O son of Shíb, though thou art a brave man, a valiant hero of thy age, think well of that which may be good for thee. Thou art but a solitary man, whilst our army consists of hundreds of thousands of souls; thou canst not but, sooner or later, fall a martyr to their cruel swords. It is a pity this cypress-like* stature of thine should fall on the ground, and this delicate body be cut into pieces with the points of spears. Dost thou seek honour and riches? come then to me. I will most willingly make thee commander of the army, and Yazíd the unfortunate will certainly give thee certain districts, and invest thee with the title and authority of governor-general of 'Irák. But Husain has no estate, no property, no money, and his service is not worth a fig. Do not then, for nothing, lose thy precious life, together with the enjoyment of the pleasures of this world.

'Abís.—O thou infidel! Yazíd is the master of a crown, while Husain, the king of the martyrs, is the possessor of Paradise and heaven. Yazíd can bestow territory, but the king of the martyrs directs to faith and religion. As a man of the world, judge fairly; is this advantageous, or that?

Ibn Sa'd.—If thou truly seekst the righteousness that belongs to the next world, and hast made up thy mind to drink the cup of martyrdom, why dost thou not throw off, then, thy coat of mail, thy helmet, thy cuirass, thy arrow and quiver, and thine other brilliant armour, and come forward with a single naked, glittering sword to fight? A sword is quite enough for thee to put a world at defiance, if thou speakest the truth.

'Abís (throwing off his armour).—A head that is appointed for offering requires no helmet, indeed; the waist of one ready for martyrdom wants no dagger, to be sure. In the service of God I can protect my body with my own hands; I am going to offer my head on behalf of the Lord's servant. I require no shield then. By the favour of my beloved, I can receive the arrow of the enemy with

exultation in my soul; what is, then, the good of my bearing arrows and quivers with myself, and what are all these gold decorations! Let my breast be a butt to be shot at, let no cuirass shield it at all, as I expose my body to the darts of fate. I must wear no coat of mail at all. In battles for faith a winding-sheet is the only thing needful, as I am ready to give up my soul. What need have I of these gold and silver garments? What are hands and feet, since I shall soon be without them? I throw off, then, boots from my feet as I did the helmet from the head. A sword alone is sufficient for me when anybody comes to attack me. By our Lord, I am a solitary man, but can rush upon a whole army.

Ibn Sa'd (to his army).—O troops of valiant men, lose not this opportunity for a minute. The brave 'Abís has come naked to battle; surround him on all sides with the intent of killing him, make him fall like a stately cypress-tree on the ground. Thou, O drummer, beat out the drum of battle joyously and cheerfully, for the revolution of the spheres is now certainly in our favour.

'Abís falls fighting.—O God, be thou my witness that I have given up my life and the world for the sake of Husain! Though my head be an unworthy sacrifice, still I do offer it most willingly in the cause of the Imám of the age. Let the cause of Husain, who voluntarily sacrifices himself for the salvation of his people, be supported through thy humble offering.

Shimar (to Ibn Sa'd).—Good news, O chief of the wicked party! 'Abís is fallen down from the back of his swift horse. His body is cut to pieces with daggers and swords; his hands are, too, unable to save him now that he is undone. The star of fortune has effected the business according to thy heart's desire, for 'Abís has neither hands to fight nor feet to fly.

Ibn Sa'd.—Once more, O ye troops, be ready; and ye Khaulí, and Shimar, and other chiefs of this malignant army, with the view of pleasing the great king of Shám and Kúfah, the son of Abú Sufiyán, the potent sovereign, and in order to scatter salt over the wounded liver of Husain, by the announcement of the death of the bloodthirsty lion, 'Abís the son of Shíb, be ready to stone the body of the great champion of Husain; and thou, O drummer, beat on thy drum, the supporters of the defiant chief are slain, the enemy of our master is destroyed. (*They stone the body of 'Abís.*)

'Abís (expiring).—O Lord, be thou my witness that I die happy, having given up my life for the Imám of the age. O God, receive the offering of Thy poor humble servant, who lays down his life that he may inherit an eternal reward. Verily, there is no God but God, and Muhammad is His Prophet.

SCENE XVI.

A NIGHT ASSAULT ON HUSAIN'S CAMP.

"OBAIDULLAH despatched a person to demand of Omar Saud, if he had employed him merely to converse with Husseyne; if he attacked him without further delay, it was very well, if not, he should find no difficulty in sending one who would be less scrupulous in the execution of his orders. By this message it might have been expected that all further procrastination would have been put an end to; and the son of Saud, mounting his horse, accordingly disposed his troops for the attack; but he felt himself impelled once more to address the devoted Husseyne aloud in these words: 'Every effort in my power has been exerted to avoid the opprobrium, or imputation, of having dipped my hands in thy blood! I find that those exertions are in vain.' 'Yet,' said Husseyne, 'give me the respite of this day; suffer me to remain unmolested only till to-morrow.' And in this, from whatever motive, Omar again indulged him. In the meantime, provoked by these repeated delays, Obaidullah Zeiaud sent for Shemir or Shamer Ziljousheny; and having told him that the son of Saud seemed disposed to prevaricate with him, and that his heart appeared to be with Husseyne, he directed him to proceed immediately and deprive that chieftain of his command. 'Whether he has commenced hostilities, or whether not,' said he, 'his command and his appointment are thine; go and bring me either Husseyne, or his head.' About the hour of prayer, at three in the afternoon of the day on which Imaum Husseyne had contrived to obtain a further delay of hostilities, this person arrived in the camp of Omar, and declared that it should not continue an hour longer. On which Omar again led his troops to the presence of the unhappy prince, and announced that Obaidullah had sent another person to command against him. Husseyne urged, notwithstanding, that as the day was far advanced, and night approaching, the truce might still be allowed to continue to the following morning; and as he was supported in this by the intreaties of the adverse troops, Shemir thought fit to comply."—Price's "Chronological Retrospect of Mahommedan History," vol. i. p. 398, ed. 1811.

Husain.—Alas thy tyranny! thou mean-minded sphere. How long shall I heave sighs against thy hand? How long wilt thou continue thy malice against us? Why art thou not subverted for this thy malignity? By thy revolutions the habitation of religion is brought to desolation. Fie on thee and on thy doings towards the children of men!

'Abbás.—O heaven, to what extent wilt thou be satiated with malice and ill-will! How long must we suffer from the malevolent enemy, and from the son of Ziyád?* By the revolutions of time I have been expatriated from Madínah, my native town; what is the cause of your antipathy, O ye skies? are ye naturally disposed to cruelty?

'Alí Akbar.—O Lord, have compassion on the sad state of poor Akbar's heart! How can I see the offspring of God's Messenger so sorrowful? By the treacherous call of this wicked people, and by the tyranny of the spheres, I was forced to leave the monument of the Prophet.

Kásim.—O Lord, I am the poor orphan of Hasan, even I, Kásim. From the violence of time I am brought low and made contemptible. Thou, O orbitless sphere, didst maliciously pour the poison of thy malignity down my noble father's holy throat, and thy turn has come to injure my dear uncle Husain. Rest in thy place, O heaven, for a minute.

The Imám.—O time, let me complain of thy oppression; let me inform the world of the fire concealed in my heart.

---

* See note *, p. 177.

To-morrow is the day when the Háshim's * youths are all to be slain with the edge of the sword; and how can I behold it!?

Zainab.—O heaven, how can I see Husain's face without making the hearts of men and jinns bleed by reason of my sighs and groans! O 'Alí, thou King of Najaf,† behold the helpless state of thy dear child, and how the fire of my heart is consumed for him. To-morrow shall the elegant cypress of Fátimah's garden fall on the ground, and my eyes shall pour down tears for him.

Sukainah.—O Lord God, look upon poor wretched me! The heavy burden of my father's approaching end weighs hard on my heart. I can willingly bear any pain or grief, but to be a fatherless child, this is what I cannot possibly endure.

The Imám.—Alas for thy oppression, O malignant sphere! Behold how the parched-souled Husain suffers affliction and misery! Only to-night I have a little time to rest, to morrow my throat will be cut with the edge of the enemy's sword. It is not, however, grievous that I and all my companions should be slain, since the thing is done for the salvation of the people of my grandfather the Prophet.

Zainab.—O dear brother, thou poor exile in the city of trials, what aileth thee to-night that thou sighest so heavily from the bottom of thy heart? I am distracted by thy soul-consuming groans. I am shedding tears on account of thy miserable state, O royal personage. What has happened to thee that thou art so restless to-night—that thou dost moan so involuntarily?

The Imám.—Come to me, O poor afflicted sister, thou who hast withered from the blast of injustice and cruelty. Come, for my soul has reached the tip of my lips by

---

* *i.e.* Husain and his family.
† See note, p. 241.

reason of destitution, knowing that this is the last evening of my life. Come, let me satisfactorily behold thy dear face, as I have but this one night to live.

Zainab.—O fate, let me bitterly complain of thy oppression. To whom shall I turn, and to whom else should I complain? In whom shall I cheer my drooping heart after thou causest 'Abbás, my brave brother, to be a martyr? I fear thou wilt make Husain's body headless by thy malice. Let me, then, weep over the destitute state of his surviving son, the lord of God's worshippers. O death, be pleased to come quickly and visit me, that the bird of my soul may be set at liberty from this cage-like prison, the body.

The Imám.—O nightingale of the meadow of trial and affliction, thou poor wretched Zainab, go, for the sake of my wounded, sorrow-stricken heart, to thy own bed and rest. Thou hast but one night left to thee; after that this world shall flee from thee.

Zainab.—O brother, even now the tranquillity of this world is removed far from me, my bed of rest has been already taken away by the cruel tyrannical spheres. How can I go to sleep again from this time forth? Heaven's cruelty has removed sleep from my eyes.

The Imám.—Thy speakest the truth, sister, thy rest is altogether cut off. On the appearance of infidelity the trappings of religion are of necessity put aside. Go thou to thy tent and remain quiet awhile, although rest in this world is far removed from thee.

Zainab.—Fate is very hasty for the slaughter of the innocent. My heart is palpitating within me as a half-slain bird. Oh, bid sleep not to come to-night to my eyes; the island wherein they reside has been inundated by a deluge!

Kulsúm.—O Lord God, how grieved am I in the land of Karbalá! My heart bleeds for the outrageous acts of the treacherous spheres. I fear lest I become destitute and helpless, not having either brothers, nephews, or helpers.

The Imám.—Thou my poor miserable sister, cry not, and let not thine eyes shed tears of blood. Go and rest thyself a little, and forget awhile thy overwhelming grief.

Kulsúm.—O sleep, enter not my wet eyes to-night, for my eye-lids are suffused with tears. Let not sleep overtake me at all, for I have, forsooth, a bed spread over with embers.

Sukainah.—O Lord, I do not know what is the cause of this confused noise to-night in this camp. From the cry and lamentation of those whose lot is sorrow, there is a fire kindled in my very innermost soul. To-night my dwelling-place shines with the light of a sunny day from the candle-like face of my good father giving light thereunto.

The Imám.—Dear Sukainah, wail not to-night nor lament. Let not my soul be set on fire owing to thy great sorrow. I do not know what thou wilt do to-morrow when thou art fatherless. My eyes, forsooth, must even now drop blood for thee. Dear child, to-morrow thou shalt be fatherless; have thy last sleep, then, in the lap of thy dear father this evening.

Sukainah.—Dear father, may I be a sacrifice for thee! make me sleep in thy kind lap. As I am unable to bear the burden of separation from thee, favour me graciously ever with thy presence. Let me always behold thy moon-like* face. Oh, may my sad soul be a sacrifice for thee!

Husain.—Sleep in thy father's lap, my withering flower. Sleep on, O newly-grown rose of my pleasure-garden. Thou shalt weep abundantly on thy journey to Kúfah and Damascus; lay thy head now quietly on the flaming bosom of thy father. Alas this pretty face, when the accursed Shimar shall buffet it! Alas this shining moon!

Sukainah.—To-night, while my head is placed in my father's dear lap, I would not care if I were to be thrown in the fire like, as it were, aloe-wood.

Husain (to 'Alí Akbar).—My dear 'Alí Akbar, thou

---

* See note, p. 7.

cypress tree * of the garden of thy father, thou first-fruit of thy father's meadow, how can I behold thy beautiful eyes dull for want of sleep! Be at rest in thy bed, thou shining moon of the father.

'Ali Akbar.—O heaven, to-night I must pour down blood from my eyes instead of tears, on account of thy cruelty. Thou hast maliciously put fire to the stock of my life to-night. I fear lest the flame of my sighs should burn up the whole of my constitution if I now heave but one groan from the bottom of the heart. I will, conformably to the command of my father, go to repose in my place, though the star of my fortune will never shut its eyes to-night until daybreak.

Husain (to Kásim).—O Kásim, thou cypress of the rose-garden of Hasan's heart and soul, may the soul of me, thy afflicted and miserable uncle, be a sacrifice for thy handsome face! go and sleep quietly in thy resting-place a short time, for the king of the age is moaning sadly for thy misfortunes.

Kásim.—Enter to-night, O dear father, by the door of my habitation, for my eyes are full of tears. Where art thou, O father, thou whose liver became a hundred pieces from poison? Pass by my bed to-night for a minute. How can I go to my place to rest, since sleep is far from entering my eyes?

The Imám.—O Zainab, my poor afflicted sister, thou destitute, helpless, and unfortunate creature, thou mother of my nurseless children, thou in all pains and grievances my best physician, I have to-night one single request to make to thee, which I hope thou wilt be kind enough to hear attentively.

Zainab.—May the sorrow-allotted soul of Zainab be a sacrifice for thee! May all thy pains come to the soul of Zainab the comfortless! What is that single request of

---

* See note, p. 10.

thine, O friend? relate it without reserve to this thy home-born slave.

Husain.—My heart, dear Zainab, is burning for Sukainah. I have lost patience and endurance on her account. If a hair be lost from her ringlets it will put me in pain and anxiety indescribable.

Zainab.—How long wilt thou make thyself sad, dear brother, for the sake of Sukainah? She is ever dear to me, she is the flower and the ornament of my lap; trouble not thyself about her, she is, and will ever be, the light of my eyes. Come now, dear brother, take thy rest, for thy lamentations have rendered me beside myself.

Husain.—May I be a ransom for thy soul, thou light of Zahrah's * eye! Sleep has fled from me altogether, I am so sorry for my poor orphans. My eyes are streaming with tears for their destitute condition. Come, sister, let us take a walk in the camp of the holy family; let us see the elegant statures of our dear helper and friends, and delight ourselves, if possible, with the sight of our brethren's rosy cheeks.

Zainab.—O mother, O Fátimah, come out a minute from thy grave to witness in the plain of Karbalá the very day of resurrection; and thou, O my father, the elect, come to the help of thy Zainab's heart, and behold in what manner she is distressed.

Husain (at the head of 'Abbás' bed).—Alas! shall this elegant body of 'Abbás be hewn into pieces to-morrow by the violent deed of the enemy? Oh, what a pity these hands shall be cut off from the body, in the plain of Karbalá, with the sword of the antagonist in a most cruel way!

Zainab.—Unfortunate brother, may the soul of Zainab be offered for thee! cease thy groanings, and shed not pearly tears from thy eyes, for, by our Lord, I cannot bear to see thee in this state, it is unendurable for me to find thee in such a condition.

---

* See note, p. 22.

Husain (at the bed of 'Alí Akbar).—O 'Alí Akbar, thou light of my eyes, thou art in a sound sleep now, disregarding that to-morrow, dear one, thou must become a martyr. O flower of my garden, the palm tree of thy stature shall be struck down from the saddle to the ground with the axe of injustice.

Zainab.—May thy sister be a sacrifice for thy bleeding heart! pour not so many tears from thine eyes. If a thorn, God forbid, should pierce thy foot, it would be as if my breast or wounded body were to receive two hundred cuts at once. Groan not so much, for thy lamentation entirely overthrows the foundation of my fortitude and patience.

Husain (standing at Kásim's bed).—O thou first-fruit of Husain's garden, thou nightingale of the rose-garden of pain and tribulation, thou are gently sleeping in thy bed of rest, careless about trouble and anguish of heart. Alas this symmetrical body of thine! Alas these thy rosy cheeks!

Zainab.—Dear brother, may I be a sacrifice for thee! May Zainab's life avert thy misfortunes! Mourn not so much, thou brightness of the east and west. O Husain, may I be offered as a ransom for thy elegant stature!

Husain (coming to Sukainah's bed).—Sukainah, thou nightingale of my garden, my unblown rose, my peace of mind, sleep well to-night, for to-morrow thou shalt not be able to rest, thy heart will burn with longing desire to see thy father's face; he will for ever be absent from thee.

Zainab.—The morning is near, the moon has disappeared and gone to bed, dear brother, deprive not thyself of sleep. My most beloved one, shed no more blood from thine eyes, take a little rest, for I am anxious respecting thee.

Shimar* (consulting Ibn Sa'd.)—Listen unto me a minute, thou son of Sa'd, as thou art the commander of this army and their general. It is night now, the world is wrapped

---

* See note, p. 43.

up in clothes of darkness; the sun, the source of light, is hidden from view, and Ahríman, the prince of darkness, is at work. March with the army towards Husain's encampment, and have a night assault upon the army of the lord of the two worlds.

Ibn Sa'd (to Shimar).—O Shimar, I have never met with one more wicked than thyself, nor heard of any throughout the world as merciless as thou art. Thou hast closed thine eyes and art seated in thy saddle. O cursed one, the Prophet of God is the noble grandfather of this personage, and his mother is Zahrah the Prophet's daughter; do not, then, contemptuously slight him; return to thy rest at this midnight; do not attempt to disturb the sleep of Husain the son of 'Alí.

Shimar.—O son of Sa'd, it is the order of Yazíd that Husain should be killed by daggers, swords, and spears; and now I have got the best opportunity for so doing; do not, therefore, point out to me his noble descent or ancestry. The kingdom of Rái * is the charming reward for putting him to death. What do I care if, for example, the celestial globe be inverted?

Ibn Sa'd.—O Shimar, this night invasion (listen to me) is not a trifling matter. Thou hast roaring lions in ambuscade against thee. See not thou out there is 'Abbás the brave, the heaven-elected king? his hand is the hand of 'Alí, and his sword like Zú'l fakár.† First, thou must put down 'Abbás before thou show any hostility against Husain; with such a foe as 'Abbás thou canst prevail by tricks and stratagems, and nothing else.

Shimar.—O son of Sa'd, the mother of the famous

---

* " Among others he (Obaidullah Zeiaud) sent for Omar the son of Saud, to whom he proposed the government of Rái, if he would undertake to seize the person of Husseyne."—Price's "Chronological Retrospect of Mahommedan History," vol. i. p. 396, ed. 1811.

† See note *, p. 65.

'Abbás is closely related to my mother; I will try first to draw him to our side if possible in a friendly way, that I know best how to plan. If I do not succeed, or he will not hearken to me, then I shall immediately throw the palm of his stature down to the ground by way of violence. I will treat Husain in this heart of the night with such malicious violence as to create commotion and tumult in the indigo-coloured heaven itself.

Ibn Sa'd.—Set out quickly then on this expedition, O Shimar, but be circumspect concerning thyself. Beware of the lions of the tribe of Háshim,* for they have flame-effusing swords in their hands.

Shimar (departing).—The wicked Shimar does not fear anyone in the universe, he can throw confusion and noise in the two worlds. If Shimar but draw out his sword from the sheath, the spheres, from dread, will tremble like quicksilver. Where art thou, O 'Abbás son of God's Lion? Come out of thy tent for a while; be pleased to set thy feet in this field for a time, O thou who art the first-fruit of the garden of true direction. Kindly walk out of thy tent in this midnight, as it were the sun, to light us with thy presence.

'Abbás (awaking from his sleep).—Who was he that called me from behind the partition? that made such a noise at this hour? Who was he that so disrespectfully screamed out to me from behind the curtain? All the family are now in bed and fast asleep; being tired by the fatigues of the road, they are hushed to rest. What makes thee raise thy voice so rudely, making me restless and upset?

Shimar.—May I be a ransom for thee, thou heaven-elected king, thou lion of the forest of manliness and humanity! 'Abbás, come near; it was I that called thee.

---

* See note *, p. 200.

To-night I could not rest through excess of sorrow and grief. I am thy humble servant, Shimar the warrior, who in the day of battle and at the time of war am the most expert in the use of the dagger.

'Abbás.—What made thee call me at such an improper time? and why didst thou approach the tent, O black-faced rogue? Art thou regardless of the sharp edge of my sabre? Or what has made thee hasten to thine own destruction? If thou hast come for war, let me, then, lift up my sword and cut off even the very name of unbelief from the plain of Karbalá.

Shimar.—Know, O 'Abbás, that we have received orders from Yazíd to cut the body of Husain into a thousand pieces with scymetars and spears. There are hundreds of soldiers who have drawn out their swords and daggers with great malignity, all ready to come and fight thee. I am as certain as certain can be, that thou canst not escape with thy life, but must drink the poison of death at the hands of our army; but as I have some cordial affection for thee, being at the same time related somehow to thy mother, humanity and the tie of relationship have compelled me to call on thee at such a time to inform thee of the danger before thee. Hearken unto me, thou poor heart-wounded creature, and come over at once to our camp without the least fear or hesitation. If thou follow my advice, I shall in time ask Yazíd to appoint thee commander of his majesty's victorious army; that is all.

'Abbás.—God make thy tongue dumb, thou infidel, for thy speech has set my soul on fire! Hast thou no fear of God thy Creator? nor carest thou for the holy spirit of His Prophet? Thou cunningly spreadest the snare of thy enticement before me, wickedly persuading me to sell my religion for this world, to leave a holy brother like Husain, in order to rub my head on the threshold of Yazíd the impure. Brotherhood is not like the attachment of a bird to its nest, which, wherever it goes by day, will at night

surely return to nestle there. Fraternity is not a tree to blossom yearly and produce dear brothers. A brother is not like a companion with whom one associates for awhile, and, if gone, one may easily get another to fill up his place. A brother is not a physician for the cure of diseases, that if he does not do it well thou mayest change him for another better than the former. O cursed one, I do not think I am worthy to be called a brother of Husain; enough if I am considered even as an attendant at his holy threshold. I swear, by the spirit of the Prophet, I shall never depart from him, though I be cut by the dagger into a thousand pieces.

Shimar.—O moon of Bani Háshim, thou lion-like prince, I told thee to abandon Husain's service because he is alone and therefore unable to succeed. I know that if thou refuse to hear me thou shalt most cruelly be put to death, and that Husain shall be cut to pieces after thee with this dagger; then shall we lead his family away as captives, and I myself will set fire to the tent of that chief.

'Abbás.—Dost thou frighten me with battle, thou cursed wretch? 'Abbás dost not lose heart, thou knowest well. I have risked my head and hand, earnestly desiring martyrdom. Oh that this honour could be granted me even now!

Shimar.—O thou handsome youth, as a friend I have given thee the best advice I could. Let the rest be between you and the sharp daggers of this wicked people. It appears thou must be killed with the edge of the sword. O ye multitude, acquit yourselves like men, and sound the drum for war.

'Abbás (about to fight).—O honourable and powerful Lion of God, thou piercing arrow or meteoric dart in the hand of the Almighty, help me soon by stretching forth thy divine palm. I am clinging to thy skirt for help, O 'Alí!

'Alí Akbar (awaking).—What commotion is there in the

desert of Karbalá? O Lord, what can have happened in this vale of trials? Methinks the malicious troops are going to surprise us; they seem to have gathered together, intending to take our life.

'Abbás *(coming back, falls on the enemy)*.—O theatre of wonders, thou best of defenders, my sovereign father, 'Alí the elect, the time of help is come. March forth to our assistance, and lay hold of the hilt of thy Zú'l fakar.

'Alí Akbar *(joining him)*.—Be not dismayed, dear uncle, by the unbelieving army; 'Alí Akbar is coming to thy help. I shall make an utter destruction of the infidels by thy favour, leaving them neither troops nor generals.

Kásim *(following 'Alí Akbar)*.—My noble cousin, be not sorry, I am coming; I have already drawn out my sword against the enemy.

Sukainah *(awaking)*.—Oh! what is this howling noise, good Musulmans, that I hear throughout the camp? Is the Day of Resurrection at hand, that there are such tumults and confusions all around? *(Goes to Zainab.)* Melancholy aunt, awake! awake! the enemy is come upon us, awake! awake! There is the wicked Shimar with his party; they intend to destroy our lives. Oh, what a time is come! Awake! aunt, awake!

Zainab.—O my sweet-songed nightingale, why dost thou thus moan at midnight? Thou singing-bird of my orchard, what is it that makes thee groan? What is the reason thou art in a distracted state with dishevelled hair? Why dost thou tremble so sadly, poor thing?

Sukainah.—Come out, O aunt; behold what turbulence and confusion! hear the roaring sound of the drum of Husain's enemy! The plain of Karbalá is become a cane-field of spears. It is filled all over with troops.

Zainab.—Oh, again Zainab is in a distressed state! good luck is turned aside from her for ever! O Zainab, make the garland of sorrow a crown for thy head! Congratulate thyself on thy captivity, poor thing! O brother, arise from thy sweet sleep! behold the miserable condition of thy sister Zainab. O thou asylum of the destitute, awake a minute from the sleep of rest, may thy sister die for thee!

Husain (awaking).—Why dost thou pour forth sad notes like nightingales? I hope there is no bad news. Why art thou in a distracted condition? I trust things are all going right.

Zainab.—O solace of my dark hours, the enemy is come upon me; thou comfort of my disturbed soul, behold the enemy attacking us! What thou hearest is the sound of the drum of war from the enemy. I fear my head-dress will get blackened by thy sudden death.

Sukainah (to Husain).—O revered father, I am thy poor Sukainah, hold me kindly awhile in thy bosom. I am so afraid of the confused noise of the enemy, my heart is quite melted, and I am shivering like a willow tree.

The Imám.—Fear not, dear Sukainah, nor be disturbed in thy mind, thy father is standing by thee; there is no occasion to lose thy heart. Cry not, darling child; who dares so much as to look at the camp while I am alive? (*The drums beat.*)

Zainab.—Dear brother, the uproarous noise is becoming more and more; surely the enemy is invading us on all sides. My fortitude and patience have left me. Oh! order some remedy for the sad case of Zainab.

Husain.—Worthy sister, go thou to Abbás my brother, the noblest of all mankind, the successor of 'Alí the elect, and rousing him gently from his sleep, say, Husain is calling thee to his presence.

Zainab (at the bed of 'Abbás).—Lift up thy head, brother, from thy pillow, and behold my miserable condition, O thou lion-hearted hero! The spheres to-night are overwhelming me with sorrow; it is my turn to be wakeful, seeing my fortune has sunk in sleep. O dear brother, the light of my eyes, earth be on my head! 'Abbas is not in his bed.

Husain.—Shed not blood from thine eyes, dear sister; go now to my son Akbar, and waking him gently from his sleep, bring him to his unprosperous father.

Zainab (at 'Alí Akbar's bed).—Where art thou, O 'Alí Akbar, thou similitude of the intercessor of the Day of Judgment, may thy afflicted aunt be offered for thee! Oh, the weight of grief has bent 'Alí Akbar's stature into a bow! Dear brother, Akbar is not to be found in his bed.

Husain.—Wail not, dear sister, may I be a ransom for thee! beat not thy breast and head, but have patience, nor groan so much, thou child of Zahrah; go and fetch me Kásim my nephew.

Zainab (at Kásim's bed).—O nightingale of Hasan's garden, awake! awake! O singing-bird of the assembly, awake! awake! Behold the tent empty, without Abbás and 'Alí Akbar. Thy poor uncle has summoned thee; awake this moment! O Lord God, what a night I am passing! I am exhausted by so many soul-diminishing groans. Alas! Kásim is also not in his bed. There is no power or strength but in God.

Husain.—O poor Kulsúm, my sorrowful sister, thou who art wounded in heart by heaven's injury and violence, lament not so much, but arise quickly from thy place, and bring for me my Zú'l janáh* or winged horse.

Kulsúm (bringing the horse).—How often must my eye reach the heavens at this hour of midnight? I do not know for what I have fallen in this snare of affliction. O mean, tyrannizing spheres, how long must I undergo affliction through your cruelty?

Husain (riding).—Such a luminous work could not proceed from this mean people alone. It is certainly heaven's decree and cannot be reversed. Out upon thy foul deal-

---

* See note, p. 242.

ings, O perverse heavens! Yet I must not let the idea of martyrdom go from my head.

'Alí Akbar (*returning from the field*).—Father, what is the reason thou hast set the cluster of Pleiades on the moon? why dost thou shed tears on thy cheeks? Why art thou mounted on the horse, girded with thy sword-belt? Is thy heart, dear father, inclined to the dust, its original substance? Return, now, 'Alí Akbar has not yet died.

Kásim (*returning*).—Dear uncle, may I be a ransom for thee! Why art thou seated in the saddle in such a sad manner, and with tearful eyes?

'Abbás (*coming back*).—Why art thou on horseback, O king of the righteous? thou lookest sad, and thy eyes shed pearls of tears. 'Abbás, thy humble servant, is still alive, and the strength of his arm and his world-consuming sword have not failed him.

Husain.—Seeing there was a tumult of war in the plain of Karbalá, and the noise of the commotion reached the skirt and border of the Pleiades, and you were not in the camp, I rode in order to protect the family from the assault of the wicked unbelievers.

'Abbás.—Yes, dear brother, the troops of Kúfah and Shám* had come with the intention of surprising us at this time. I, together with Kásim and Akbar, rode out to guard the camp from the infidel soldiers.

Husain.—O brother, the cruel spheres seem to seek to supplant me to-night! and therefore will not cease from doing mischief at such a time as this. I certainly know that I cannot escape death in this plain of trials, but as I intend to pass the night in devotion, by our Lord it is better that thou shouldst kindly go just now to Ibn Sa'd, and ask him to respite me to-night, it being a period of sorrow for me.

'Abbás (*addressing the enemy*).—Say ye to Ibn Sa'd, who

---

* Syria.

does not recognise a God, 'Abbás, the servant of Husain, wants to speak to him.

'Umar the son of Sa'd.—What hast thou to say, thou moon of Baní Háshim? I am ready to do for thee anything thou art pleased to order.

'Abbás.—O cruel, cursed tyrant, art thou not ashamed before Ahmad* the elect of God? It is night, all the wild beasts of the desert are now at rest, and thou, impudent creature that thou art, dost not cease troubling Husain. Art thou unacquainted with the glorious position of the Imám of the age? Dost thou not see him to be the offspring of Ahmad the elect of God? My brother, however, intends to pass his time to-night in devotion to God, and so he asks respite from thee, thou treacherous dog.

'Umar the son of Sa'd.—With all my heart, I will instantly do as thou hast said, and chase away from my mind the thought of fighting to-night with Husain. Let it be reported to Shimar, that the army of Kúfah and Shám must return from the field of battle.

'Abbás (to Husain).—O brother, I have done as thou didst order me; proceed without the least anxiety to the thing which thou hast in view.

---

* See note *, p. 37.

SCENE XVII.

DEATH OF ALI AKBAR.

On the plain of Karbalá Husain's "eldest son Ally Akbar, conceiving that as such he might aspire to the distinction of being the first of his family to lay down his life in defence of his parent, presented himself to the weapons of the enemy, and having announced aloud his name and descent, intrepidly rushed among them. In ten different assaults, in which, animated by the presence of his father, he forced himself into the thickest of the enemy, he sacrificed to his vengeance, at each assault, either two or three of those who stood opposed to him; but being at last almost suffocated with heat and thirst, he implored his father's pity, by complaining bitterly of the sufferings which he was compelled to undergo. In this state, after assuring him that if he could relieve him at the price of his own existence, it would be a willing sacrifice, his father arose, and introducing his own tongue within the parched lips of his favourite child, thus endeavoured to alleviate his sufferings by the only means of which his enemies had not yet been able to deprive him. The gallant youth then rushed for the last time into the conflict; and being wounded from behind by one of the enemy, whose name was Kerrah son of Saud, he fell, and was immediately surrounded and cut to pieces by these execrable betrayers of the family of their Prophet. This was a spectacle which entirely overwhelmed the feelings of Hûsseyne; for the first time in his life he gave utterance to a transport of grief, which he no longer attempted to suppress."—Price's "Chronological Retrospect of Mahommedan History," vol. i. p. 404, ed. 1811.

Husain.—O heaven, thou hast undermined the foundation of my hope, by unjust means! My unhappy mind has not for a minute been gladdened by thee. Thou hast determined to make my Akbar a martyr to-day. O God, who art aware of my state, have compassion on me! What shall I do, if I do not complain, mourn, and bewail, seeing ever and anon a new grief arises, as it were, to congratulate me?

Zainab.—O death, the time has come! hasten to save me, and deliver me from the sad occurrence of Karbalá! How long and how often must I see the unexpected death of my dear friends? O Lord, in what an unlucky hour must I have been born!

Husain.—Zainab, thou grieved sister, O afflicted sorrow-stricken girl, thou luminous daughter of virtue and piety, thou brilliant star of the heaven of chastity, the time of my departure has drawn near; listen, dear sister, to what I enjoin thee.

Zainab.—O poor, sore-hearted, thirsty one,* O helpless, destitute leader, thou support of my spirit and the strength of my soul, burn thou not my heart with this thy saying.

Husain.—O sister, it is so predestined, they shall sever my head from the body. The sea of my trouble is without a coast, and I see no remedy besides resignation to the will of God. When I leave this perishable world, thou must try to resign thyself with patience as far as thou canst. Take care, O worthy sister, not to curse any infidel!

Zainab.—Oh, thy sorrow continually makes me shed tears! O brother, do not call me thy sister, but thy slave. I am neither strong to fight with fate, nor swift to run away from destiny. I know patience is the only remedy in this case, but what shall I do? I am not the possessor thereof.

Husain.—O my worthy sister, when Husain thy brother is killed, give great attention to my orphan girl Sukainah.

---

* See note, p. 14.

Yea, be kind and indulgent to all my fatherless daughters, have a maternal regard for them all in a manner thou knowest best. Take care, especially, that none ever ill-treats Sukainah, the joy of my heart, or strikes her on the face.

Zainab.—O thou who art the fundamental part of the divine scripture, do not any more distress Zainab with thy impressive discourse. May that day never come when thy sister shall see thy daughters fatherless! O good-natured brother, tell me if thou hast any other request.

Husain.—The desolate fortress of my heart is again invaded by grief. I feel I must leave this world soon for the next. O afflicted sister, as this is almost the last hour of my life, I earnestly desire to see once again the dear face of 'Alí Akbar. Go, and call to me the similitude of the Seal* of the Prophets, saying "Husain is anxiously desirous to see the face of the Prophet of God."

Zainab.—Alas! woe be unto me! grief is again going to plunge my head-dress in blood! calamity intends to wrap my head with a sanguinary veil! O 'Alí Akbar, thy father Husain waits to see thee! Methinks we must visit one another only in the Day of Resurrection.

'Alí Akbar (to Husain).—Good morning to thee, O thou on whose bright face the Súrah "By the sun" † is but a brief comment. Good morning, O thou of whose hair the Súrah "By the night" is but an explication. If there is any service to be performed, tell it forth; 'Alí Akbar, like a slave bought with money, is standing at the door.

Husain.—O parrot of the banquet of eloquence, thou art welcome! O nightingale of the rose-garden of mercy, thou art welcome! Having a great desire to see the face of God's Prophet, I sent therefore after thee, that I might

---

* See note ‡, p. 40.
† Sale's "Koran," ch. xci. p. 492, and ch. xcii. p. 493, ed. 1734.

behold thy moon-like* countenance. When the rose has vanished, the perfume must be sought out in the rose-water; so now that the Prophet is no more to be seen, I ought to smell his scent from thy odour; come then.

'Alí Akbar.—May I be a ransom for thee, O thou full-moon of the heaven of glory! May I be a sacrifice for thy stature and visage, O chosen of the highest! The effect of the autumnal blast of malice is but to increase our joy; it is time we should freely give our life for the sake of the thirsty-lipped king.† O sire, I greatly wish to stroll about in the garden of delight. I have, in a word, made up my mind to go to Paradise.

Husain.—O moon of the heaven of bashfulness, thou similitude of the elected one of God, thou champion of the army of the plain of Karbalá; thou hast burnt my poor heart with thy expression, not thinking that thou art the only produce left in the field for me. Nay, it is not proper at all, child, that thou shouldst leave thy father a destitute exile in this country, a friendless prisoner.

'Alí Akbar.—O father, I have heard that when Ismá'íl‡ was about to be offered, God sent him a ram as a ransom. Am I inferior to a lamb or a ram in that respect? let me then,

---

* See note, p. 7. † See note, p. 14.

‡ "It is the most received opinion among the Mohammedans that the son whom *Abraham* offered was Ismael, and not *Isaac, Ismael* being his only son at that time; for the promise of *Isaac's* birth is mentioned lower as subsequent in time to this transaction. . . . Some suppose that this victim was a ram, and, if we may believe a common tradition, the very same which *Abel* sacrificed, having been brought to *Abraham* out of Paradise. Others fancy it was a wild goat, which came down from Mount Thabír, near Mecca: for the Mohammedans lay the scene of this transaction in the valley of Mina; as a proof of which they tell us that the horns of the victim were hung up on the spout of the Caaba, where they remained till they were burnt, together with that building, in the days of Abda'llah Ebn Zobeir; though others assure us that they had been before taken down by Mohammed himself, to remove all occasion of idolatry."—Sale's "Koran," ch. xxxvii. p. 369, ed. 1734.

dear father, be offered as a ransom for thee. Besides, if thou intendest to invite thy real friend at the table of thy love and obedience, it is but most proper that thou shouldst offer thy first-born to him as a sacrifice first of all.

Husain.—Mourn not so much, my poor ensnared nightingale, go to thy tent without scarring my afflicted soul. Thou hast not yet sat with the bride on the throne of matrimonial happiness, nor hast thou dyed thy hand and feet with wedding colours.*

'Alí Akbar.—Hinder me not, father, from this dangerous intention, for I am made of earth, and unto earth I must return. My marriage will take place, dear father, in the pleasant chamber of the grave! By our Lord, O father, it is necessary I should die to-day.

Husain.—O light of my eye, thy father has willingly yielded to thy being slain. I resign myself to fate, let God's will be done. Since thou meanest to burn up my already distracted heart, go thou and bid adieu to my weeping family.

'Alí Akbar.—Thanks be to God that the tree of my hope has borne fruit, that the tears of my earnest wish have produced desirable pearls! O family of Husain, the time of Akbar has arrived; the prospect of visiting one another again shall be realised only in the Day of Judgment. O well-behaved Zainab, my comfortless aunt, the morn of my joy is passing away.

Zainab.—O light of the two eyes of the Prophet! alas my 'Alí Akbar! Alas 'Alí Akbar, the brightness of the eye of the virgin† Fátimah! What does thy sad moaning signify? It is not time for thee to say farewell. Who will help thy poor father? Oh, do not cast earth on my head!‡

'Alí Akbar.—O well-conducted aunt, thy Akbar is going,

---

* See note ‡, p. 118.   † See note, p. 57.

‡ A sign of grief.

is going! Cast earth on thy head and lament; thy Akbar is departing, departing! Yea, he is about to vanish with dried lips and tearful eyes, groaning from the depth of his heart; he will pass away like a morning breeze.

Zainab.—Look, dear nephew, at the multitude of the perfidious people, and do not go. Consider the miserable state of this thy poor aunt, and stay away. Behold thy entangled father, thy broken-hearted aunt, and thy destitute sister, and do not attempt to start.

'Alí Akbar.—O aunt, patience and forbearance have left my soul, and I must go. My heart also has abandoned its fixed abode. I must therefore depart. Meadows look like places for mourning in my sight; and here, too, blood gushes out from my eye. I cannot therefore hold back.

Zainab (addressing Husain).—O sphere of glory, humanity, and dignity; O chief of the caravan of the destitute ones, thou manifest Imám! 'Alí Akbar is bidding adieu to thy family and household. Is it true that thou hast permitted him to undertake this journey?

Husain.—O what shall I say to thee, worthy-conducted Zainab? Ask me not concerning 'Alí Akbar's story any more. Yes, it is by my permission that he sets out for the journey. He has tearful eyes owing to his father's destitute state. I have given up my son 'Alí Akbar for the people of my grandfather the Prophet.

Zainab.—O dear brother, 'Alí Akbar is quite young, it is not right that his spring should be turned into autumn. Oh, do not add sorrow to my sorrow! Come, let me fall before thee with supplication. How can I yield assent that such a beautiful form and elegant stature should roll in blood by the edge of the enemies' sword.

Husain.—Yes, dear sister, 'Alí Akbar is young, he has not yet enjoyed the pleasures of this life; but I sacrifice him for the sake of the beloved, since I want to prove my devotion for my friends. Intercession for sinners, dear sister, is the great price of his blood. Yes, 'Alí Akbar is a ransom for many nations.

Zainab.—O Umm Lailah, put out thy head from the tent for a moment. Dost thou not know that 'Alí Akbar is going on a journey? Thy Joseph has resolved to set out from this Canaan-like world, while his father is looking after him with eyes full of tears. There is a son hastening towards the Egypt of martyrdom, whilst the father is left behind in the Canaan of faith, thirsty for water.

Umm Lailah.—O 'Alí Akbar, my youth, wilt thou after all go away? Why dost thou not cast a glance at thy poor old mother? Look at the pretty face of thy youngest brother Asghar; or return, that I myself may behold thy handsome countenance.

'Alí Akbar.—Yes, sorrowful mother, 'Alí Akbar is going away on some journey; it appears thou art not aware of fate and destiny. Here is a father saying farewell to his son, and here is a son becoming a ransom to-day for his father.

Umm Lailah.—O nightingale of the moon, thou hast cast a flaming fire in my heart. I have no other remedy but wet eyes. How is it thou passest before my face like a morning breeze? hast thou forgotten the troubles I underwent while nursing thee?

'Alí Akbar.—Oh! thou dost burn my soul and heart, thy saying has made such an impression on me, thy sad groans have set my poor heart on fire. Let 'Alí Akbar be a sacrifice to-day for Husain. Imagine thou didst not bear a son at all in the world.

Husain.—O Umm Lailah, let the house of thy heart be ruined by grief, let thy dwelling-place be henceforth in a corner of the habitation of sorrow. Light up the candle of zeal in the lantern of love; although thou art a woman, show forth here a manly resolution, that is to say, make a sacrifice of self by assenting that 'Alí Akbar should die, and by this voluntary submission of thine perplex and distract the wise of the earth.

'Alí Akbar.—O father, may I be a ransom for thee!

there is no opportunity left for discussion. The time of uniting together in friendship is clean gone, it being now the hour of separation. Come, please settle what weapons of war I must wear on my body. I want to go to battle, be kind to dismiss me soon.

Husain.—O my good-starred sister, thou who art in every sorrow and pain my comforter, bring weapons of war for Akbar, namely, those left behind by my father Haidar * and my grandfather Muhammad. Fetch me the head-piece of my coronated grandfather, together with my noble father's sword; bring also the shield of Hamzah † the Prophet's uncle, that I may adjust all on 'Alí Akbar's body.

Zainab.—O Lord, what shall Zainab, the poor, helpless, luckless Zainab, do? Where is the heaven-throned King, Muhammad the chief of chiefs? Does he see how Husain looks at 'Alí Akbar his son, with tearful eyes? Take, O dear one of Zahrah,‡ the holy turban of the chosen Prophet.

Husain (to 'Alí Akbar).—Come to me, my son, thou light of the eye of Zahrah, take the turban of the Messenger of God, and put it on thy head; fasten too the

---

* See note, p. 39.

† Hamzah was uncle of the Prophet Muhammad, and one of the most renowned warriors of his time. He was slain at the battle of Ohod, A.D. 625, under the following circumstances:—"The Lion of God, Hamzah-bin-Abdul-Mutalib, slew many and carried all before him in the battle. The cursed Hind promised Váshy, a Habeshah slave belonging to Jabeer-bin-Mutám, any reward he chose if he would kill either Muhammad, or Aly, or Hamzah. He declined engaging the first two, but posted himself in ambush for Hamzah, who, advancing over a spot that had been undermined by a torrent, his horse sunk, and he fell to the ground; upon which Váshy hurled a spear at him with such force as to transfix him. Váshy, or Hind, then cut out his liver, which the cursed woman gnawed in fiendish joy."—Merrick's "Life of Mohammed," chap. xiv. p. 253, ed. 1850.

‡ See note, p. 22.

sword of 'Alí to thy belt; wear also this coat of mail belonging to Ja'far* my uncle. Come, dear Zainab, as 'Alí Akbar has resolved to part with us for ever, do thou kindly dress him with a shroud† instead of wedding garments.

Zainab.—Oh, would that my eyes had become blind! How can I dress such a lovely youth in a shroud? Mayest thou be destroyed, O heaven! Consent not any more that a woman should see the death of her beloved son. Come, darling nephew, let me dress thee with funeral garments. Alas! would to God the eyes of thy aunt were deprived of vision ere they had witnessed such a sight!

'Alí Akbar.—Oh, how earnestly do I desire to go and be killed! I long to bend my throat to the edge of the sword. O king of religion, permit me to go and fight the battle of faith. Being a bird, I am eagerly desirous to repair to the meadows.

Husain.—My dear son, be not hasty, thou shalt be cruelly killed. Have patience, that thy sorrowful sister Sukainah may see thee once again. Come out of thy tent, O Sukainah; thy brother 'Alí Akbar is going to battle.

Sukainah.—O my brother 'Alí Akbar, tell thy sister where thou art going.

Alí Akbar.—Alas! what a great calamity! Sukainah is

---

* Ja'far, the brother of 'Alí, was killed in A.D. 629, fighting in defence of the Prophet. "Having his right hand cut off, he raised the banner in his left hand, which likewise losing, he sustained the standard by pressing it to his bosom with folded and bleeding arms, till at length he fell a martyr."—Merrick's "Life of Mohammed," chap. xvi. p. 283, ed. 1850. "To console the afflicted relatives of his kinsman Jauffer, he represented that, in Paradise, in exchange for the arms which he had lost, he had been furnished with a pair of wings, resplendent with the blushing glories of the ruby, and with which he was become the inseparable companion of the archangel Gabriel, in his volitions through the regions of eternal bliss. Hence in the catalogue of martyrs he has been denominated Jauffer Teyaur, the winged Jauffer."—Price's "Chronological Retrospect of Mahommedan History," vol. i. p. 5, ed. 1811.

† See note, p. 27.

coming to me. Ah me! the moon of Madínah has appeared in view.

Sukainah.—Why hast thou thrown a winding-sheet around thy neck? put it rather about my shoulders, dear brother.

'Alí Akbar.—It is not a winding-sheet, sister, it is a nuptial garment; it is rather a time for joy than for disappointment or sorrow.

Sukainah.—If thou really goest to war with the infidels, then assign me alive to the earth before thou departest.

'Alí Akbar.—Oh! hinder me not. Look at our father, a solitary exile.

Sukainah.—How wouldst thou approve that I, being brought up in luxury, should become a captive slave in Kúfah or Damascus.

'Alí Akbar.—How wouldst thou urge that the royal ascender of the heavenly ladder should hinder me from his society or his service?

Sukainah.—Do' not consent that the impious Shimar [*] should maliciously buffet me on the face.

'Alí Akbar.—O Sukainah, cease thy lamentation and cries.

Sukainah.—Ah, brother, thou knowest not the state of my heart!

'Alí Akbar.—I go, sister, to bring water for thee.

Sukainah.—I will run bare-headed after thee.

'Alí Akbar.—Didst thou not ask for water, beloved sister?

Sukainah.—Come, brother, cut my throat; I had rather.

'Alí Akbar.—Oh! there is not much strength in my body.

Sukainah.—Oh! Husain is destitute of all help or aid.

'Alí Akbar.—O father, deliver me, for God's sake!

Sukainah.—Nay, father, pity me, Alí Akbar is too young.

---

[*] See note, p. 43.

'Ali Akbar.—I adjure thee, by the Kur'án, to send her back.

Sukainah.—I adjure thee, by the soul of Asghar, to make him change his mind.

'Ali Akbar.—Go to thy tent, girl! do not beat so on thy breast.

Sukainah.—Come, brother, let us go back to Madínah.

'Ali Akbar.—I have no inclination to go to my country.

Sukainah.—Fátimah, thy youngest sister, awaits thee.

'Ali Akbar.—I, being a sacrifice, must proceed towards the altar, and being a traveller on the way of faith, must repair to my destiny. We may see one another on the Day of Resurrection. I therefore bid adieu to all the family, and say, God keep you!

Husain (addressing 'Ali Akbar).—May thy father be a ransom for thee, O my most beloved son! Thou art the Egyptian moon to me, and I am the Canaanitish old man.* Come here; there is one desire or request which very much weighs on my mind: let it be granted me unhesitatingly.

'Ali Akbar.—O thou who art so situated as to be only at the distance of two bows' lengths from the Deity, thou whose heart is tempered by the holy elements of the heavenly region, tell me what is the thing which is so much desired by thee. May my soul be a sacrifice for this heart of thine!

Husain.—My desire is to kiss thy throat tenderly. Oh, may Husain be a sacrifice for thy sweet talk!

'Ali Akbar.—How long, dear father, wilt thou let me have dominion over the kingdom of the body? How long must I blush at being too much fondled by thee? No father has ever dealt with his son so tenderly or indulgently as thou dost.

Husain.—Dost thou know, my son, why I love thee so much? why I treat thee with affection above the rest of

---

* An allusion to the story of Joseph and Jacob.

my thirsty-lipped dear sons? If I ever pour out my soul for thee, my dear, it will be next to nothing compared to what I ought to do, because I know I am offering thee a sacrifice for the sins of mankind.

'*Alí Akbar.*—Dear father, I am now going to the plain of war and field of battle to offer my soul a ransom for thee with tear-shedding eyes. We may see one another on the Day of Judgment. Behold how the land of Karbalá is turned into a poppy-field through the blood of our companions shed there!

Husain.—Yes, child, the desire of seeing each other will only be gratified on that day. Since thou art going to Paradise, the garden of delight, I wish thee joy and peace.

'*Alí Akbar.*—Dear father, at all times my kind friend, be pleased to say the summons for prayer as soon as I set my face towards the field of battle.

Husain.—O God, thou knowest I have none besides Akbar. Into Thy hand, O Lord, do I commit him. Darling son, may I be a sacrifice for thy faithfulness! I will summon for prayer after thou art gone.

'*Alí Akbar (addressing the enemy).*—O ye hewers of the palm trees of the Háshimite* plantation, ye subverters of the foundation of every Háshimite structure, come to the field and combat with heroic young men; try the strength of the hand of the Háshimite youths.

'*Umar-i-Sa'd.**—Who art thou? and what dost thou want, O noble youth? thou, by the shining of whose face the sun is blushed and eclipsed. Thou hast a striking resemblance to the Prophet of God. Methinks, O young man, thou art 'Alí Akbar, the son of Husain.

'*Alí Akbar.*—Yes, accursed villain, I am Alí Akbar. Yes, thou infidel wretch, I am the similitude of Muhammad.

---

* See note *, p. 200.   † See note, p. 214.

I am a guide in the way of love. I am the glory of the family of Abraham, the friend of God. I am the likeness of the rose-cheeked Prophet. I am, in short, of the seed of Husain. I am none other than 'Alí Akbar.

'*Umar (addressing the army*).—O brave army of Kúfah,* 'Alí Akbar is come to battle; rush on all sides against him most maliciously; cast him down from the saddle, and make Umm Lailah, his mother, mourn for his death!

'*Alí Akbar (attacking their line*).—O my illustrious grandfather, come to my assistance. O owner of the Zú'l fakár,† come and help me! 'Alí Akbar is left alone in Karbalá in the field of battle; hasten and deliver him.

Umm Lailah.—O Musulmans, my son has not returned my sweet-tongued king has not come back! Oh, my sad thoughts have distracted my mind! I am turned mad, for I have lost my son.

Zainab (to 'Alí Akbar's mother).—O Umm Lailah, why goest thou from thy tent towards the wilderness, like Majnún?‡ Be at ease, and sigh not, neither cry. Akbar will soon be back from the field.

'*Alí Akbar's Mother*.—O sorrowful Zainab, is it an easy thing to see a son dying in the prime of life? Being a tree of lamentation, I must not be without fruit. Oh, may the Lord never deprive me of the society of 'Alí Akbar!

Zainab (to Umm Lailah).—Come, dear sister, into the tent for a moment, and beat not so much on thy head and breast; for thy noble child will ere long be back, thy desperate hope will soon return to thee.

'*Alí Akbar (returning from the field and addressing Husain*).—O father, father, I thirst!

Husain.—Come, let me place the ring§ of the glorious

---

* See note, p. 9. † See note †, p. 65.

‡ The loves of Majnún and Lailá form the subject of a well-known Persian poem by Nazámí.

§ See note, p. 81.

Prophet in thy mouth, O meadow-dresser of the plain of hope!

'Alí Akbar (to Sukainah).—Come, Sukainah, let me see thee once more; let me again behold thy face, for I must part with thee for ever!

Sukainah (to 'Alí Akbar).—May I be a ransom for thee and thy soul, now about to perish! Strange that the afflictions of time have not made thee forget Sukainah. If thou hast anything to be done for thee, or any service that can be performed by me, tell it to thy sister.

'Alí Akbar.—Dear Sukainah, when thou arrivest at Madínah, give my love to my beloved sister. Inform her that her dear brother, the beloved of her heart, died in the plain of Karbalá, and that her Joseph was devoured by wolves; and give her this coat of mine, telling the miserable creature that my body has fallen here in the desert of Karbalá. Apprize her how well her brother prospered in his undertaking, for he has fallen here on the ground, with his body cut into pieces; death did not allow her brother Akbar to return to Madínah and see the dear face of his sister, and fetch her thence to Karbalá to her father. Tell her I am very sorry for the failure.

Sukainah.—Oh, may Sukainah be a ransom for this thy shirt, and a sacrifice for the manner of thy speaking! Thy shirt is quite stained with the blood of thy head. Oh! speak on; how sweetly dost thou utter thy words!

'Alí Akbar (again joining the fray).—We may again see one another on the Day of Resurrection. Good-bye to all the family. (*After fighting until he is exhausted.*) O result of the hopefulness of the lovers, come and save Akbar, who is rolling in his own blood!

Husain (following the voice).—My red-robed Joseph! alas my 'Alí Akbar! Thou art lost in Karbalá, alas my 'Alí Akbar!

'Alí Akbar.—O father, I am dying of thirst; help me! I am worn out from fatigue; father, do thou save me! Pour some drops of water on my dried lips, patience

and endurance have left me; father, do thou deliver me!

The Prophet (bringing water).—Oh, may thy grandfather be a sacrifice for thee! drink water, drink it; may my soul be a ransom for thine! Come, here is water, I have brought it for thee from Paradise. Drink, pretty creature, drink; may Muhammad, the Arabian Prophet, be a ransom for these thy dry lips! drink water, for thirst has altogether exhausted thee, poor thing!

'Alí Akbar.—O my famous ancestor, I am still thirsty, have compasion on my blood-pouring eyes! I am still parched! Grant me generously the other cup of water also, for thirst has exhausted me and deprived me of all strength.

The Prophet.—This is not your share, O light of my two eyes; that cup only was intended for thee. As for this one, it is Husain's; I am bearing it in hand for him, as he is the brightness of my eye, he is my sorrowful, thirsty-lipped guest. He will come to see me a few minutes after thy arrival, even he, the destitute, the expatriated, the parched in soul.

'Alí Akbar (to Husain).—O father, I am dying for the many wounds that I have received; do thou help me! Thou hast lost thy 'Alí Akbar; father, help me! This very moment I am going to embrace the beloved of my heart, death. I shall fall from the saddle down to the ground, fainting; father, help me, help me!

Husain.—Woe be to me! the arrow of fate has at last mortally injured my Akbar! The poor child could not escape the deadly shaft of fate! How happy the hour when thou stoodst, cypress-like,* before thy father, with the hand of self-sufficiency placed ostentatiously on the waist! How blessed the time when thou badest farewell to Zainab thy aunt! Yea, even the moment at which thou didst

---

* See note, p. 10.

set out on this thy journey was a blessed time compared with the present.

'Alí Akbar.—Thou hast come at a good time to me, O majestic being; I am dying from thirst! I am parched to death!

Husain.—O dear child, thou dost die after all, thirsty and in the bloom of youth! As for water, I am, my son, shame-faced before thee, at my inability to procure it.

'Alí Akbar.—Well hast thou had me married at Karbalá, father! fate has at length dyed my hands with my own blood!

Husain.—Oh, what misery I have to bear in heart, until the Day of Judgment! Alas, what overwhelming pain! alas, what great injustice!

'Alí Akbar.—O father, if thou intendest to carry my body to the camp, wait till I give up the ghost! hasten not in the matter.

Husain.—Nay, darling; I must carry thee alive to our camp, that thy poor sister may once again see thee before thou diest.

'Alí Akbar.—I had promised to get water for the children of our family; should they demand the same thing from me, what answer am I to give them?

Husain (addressing Umm Lailah).—O Umm Lailah, the newly married Akbar has returned from his journey! Congratulate him on his marriage-feast, O unhappy Zainab.

Umm Lailah.—Help me, O women, on this the wedding-festival of Akbar. O Sukainah, bring with thee ambergris, aloe-wood, and some rose-water.*

'Alí Akbar.—This is the last thing that I have to speak

---

* It would be beyond the province of a note to describe the wedding festivities in Muhammadan countries; it will suffice to say that there is a vast deal of elaborate form and ceremony, necessitating the use of a variety of compounds well-nigh unknown in Western regions.

to thee, O aunt. There are two things I expect thee to do after I am gone. First, when I die, do not cut thy locks of hair through thy grief for me, nor scratch thy face with thy nails, as some women do. Secondly, rest as quietly and patiently as possible, and set all thy affection on God alone, without giving occasion to Akbar's enemies to rejoice triumphantly. Now I go, with eager desire, to the Prophet of God, testifying, in the meanwhile, to the truth that "there is no God besides the true God."

www.ingramcontent.com/pod-product-compliance
Lightning Source LLC
Chambersburg PA
CBHW021158230426
43667CB00006B/459